The Life and Times of
RAJJU BHAIYA

The Life and Times of RAJJU BHAIYA

(Includes his own recorded audio memoirs)

Translation from the Hindi book
Prof. Rajendra Singh Ki Jeevan Yatra
by Dr. Ratan Sharda

Ratan Sharda

Published by
PRABHAT PAPERBACKS
An imprint of Prabhat Prakashan Pvt. Ltd.
4/19 Asaf Ali Road,
New Delhi-110002 (INDIA)
e-mail: prabhatbooks@gmail.com

ISBN 978-93-5521-326-6
The Life and Times of RAJJU BHAIYA
by Shri Ratan Sharda

Edition
First, 2023

Price
₹ 400.00 (Rupees Four Hundred only)

Printed at
R-Tech Offset Printers, Delhi

Professor Rajendra Singh (Rajju Bhaiya)
(19 January, 1922 — 14 July, 2003)

Sangh Geet (Poem)

Written by respected Rajju Bhaiya
The fourth Sarsanghchaalak of RSS

दसों दिशाओं में जाएँ
Let us go out in all the ten directions

दसों दिशाओं में जाएँ, दल बादल से छा जाएँ,
उमड़-घुमड़कर हर धरती पर नंदनवन सा लहराएँ।
Let us go out in all the ten directions,
and spread like rain filled clouds,
Let us provide rain over every land and make it blossom like a beautiful garden.
यह मत समझो किसी क्षेत्र को खाली रह जाने देंगे,
दानवता की बेल विषैली कहीं नहीं छाने देंगे,
जहाँ कहीं लू झुलसाती, अमृत रिमझिम बरसाएँ।। 1।।
...नंदनवन सा लहराएँ।
Do not think that we shall leave any field bare,
We shall not allow evil forces to spread poison,
We shall sprinkle with nectar;
the fields being scorched with hot winds.
फूल सुकोमल खेती पर हम बिजली नहीं गिराते हैं,
किंतु अडीले बालू टीले वर्षा में ढह जाते हैं,
ध्वंस हमारा काम नहीं, अविरल जीवन बरसाएँ।। 2।।
...नंदनवन सा लहराएँ।

We do not hurl lightening on delicate flowering farms,
But obstructing hillocks and sand dunes get washed away by powerful rains,
We are not here to destroy, we nurture life.

देश-देश के जीवन दर्शन अनुभव कहता पूर्ण नहीं,
आदि सृष्टि से हिंदू धर्म की पूर्ण धर्म उपलब्धि रही,
ज्ञान किरण फिर प्रकटाएँ, शांति व्यवस्था समझाएँ।। 3।।
...नंदनवन सा लहराएँ।

Experience tells us that philosophies of different nations are not complete,
Since the dawn of nature, complete understanding of Dharma has been the accomplishment of Hindus,
Let us again spread rays of knowledge, explain people about peaceful way of life.

मानव जीवन की स्वतंत्रता नष्ट नहीं होने पाए,
यंत्र व्यवस्था हृदयहीन में स्वत्व नहीं खोने पाए,
जीवनस्तर का अर्थ न हम भोग डगर में भरमाएँ।। 4।।
...नंदनवन सा लहराएँ।

Let not the freedom of human life be destroyed,
Let us not lose our Self in the heartless mechanical life,
Let us not confuse our prosperity with consumerist path.
Let us go out in all the ten directions...

Foreword

It is a matter of great happiness that *'Prof. Rajendra Singh ki Jeevan Yatra'* written by Shri Ratan Sharda is reaching the people now in English as 'The Life and Times of Rajju Bhaiya.'

Prof. Rajendra Singh's life journey is 81 years 5 months and 16 days long. His circle of friends and colleagues is present in all the five continents of the world. Putting together incidents collected from many of the memories of those people and events narrated by Prof. Rajendra Singh himself, Mr. Ratan has woven together a biography. The beautiful result is 'The Life and Times of Rajju Bhaiya.' By the standards of a biography, this is not a historic biography because it does not unveil his life in terms of date, month and year. Still readers will be able to experience the height and depth of his life. Readers will be able to understand the glowing life of a true and ever evolving personality. Possibly, therefore, the writer has by his own acceptance, not called it a 'biography,' but a 'journey of life.'

Just as it is not a historic document, in the same vein it is not a hagiography either. Unknowingly or knowingly a biography takes the form of glorification. Adorers make a mount of a molehill for their hero. Many times, they make a God out of an angel of a God. There may have been many such events in the episodes that he collected. The people who sent them would be surely the ones who knew him well and who respected him. In such a situation, it is very difficult to cross check or filter such experiences and a person can get caught in a dilemma. Shri Ratan has played the role of a skilled player of *Kabaddi* who stays firm in his playground. Therefore, this 'life's journey did not turn into a journey of worshippers singing praises.

In short, *'Prof. Rajendra Singh ki Jeevan Yatra'* is able to inspire a common man towards attaining heights in life with honesty, integrity, dedication to the goal and action-oriented strength. When we witness decay in moral values and falling of great persons from grace, then this kind of book becomes the beacon of light.

"I am just a person made of soil,
I cannot do anything, but I can do something
And I will do at least that and do it till I am alive."

This book is an illustration of this small poem.

There are two streams in the life of Prof. Rajendra Singh alias Rajju Bhaiya. 1. Teacher and 2. Sangh kaaryakarta (worker). He became a teacher in Prayag University. Climbing the academic steps, he went on to become the Head of Department of Physics. After teaching for 24 years, he took voluntary retirement at the age of 44 years. From then on, he got involved in the Sangh work with unwavering devotion. His student circle was huge. While doing Sangh work when he travelled in and outside Bharat, he would meet some or the other of his former students. Both of them would be emotionally awash in reliving old memories, forgetting the present for those moments. Even the people who watched such reunions, would feel happy. This can be called the Yamuna stream.

The second stream was the stream of Ganga – that of Sangh work. Confluence of the two happened in Prayag University. Within a year of joining the Sangh, at the age of 21, he was appointed karyavaah (Secretary) of Prayag city. After three years, he was appointed the Secretary of Prayag Division that included 4-5 districts. And after three years, he was appointed the Secretary of Prayag Sambhaag, sub-part of state that comprised of 14 districts. His age at that time was only 27.

At the age of 30 years, he was given the responsibility of the biggest state of Bharat, Uttar Pradesh as its State Secretary. He worked as the State Secretary for six years. Till that time, he remained unmarried as per his own plans. When he was 35-year-old, respected Sarsanghchaalak Shree Guruji officially declared him a prachaarak (full time karyakarta).

This was the confluence of a Professor and a prachaarak. In the entire Bharat, there was only one more such example, that of state prachaarak Babarao Bhide in Maharashtra who was a highly successful lawyer too. He carried this dual responsibility of the State Secretary of UP for eight years. After this, he resigned from the university after discussing the matter with senior office bearers of the Sangh and became free to do the Sangh work full time. From there on the 24 years long life of formal teaching became a part of history. Then, he who had worked with dual responsibility, left teaching and accepted traditional Pracharak life.

During Emergency, responsibility at all India level fell on his shoulders. In that dark uncertain atmosphere, it was not easy to designate a person. Who gave a name to a child born in the jail of Kansa? From the point of view of geography, Rajju Bhaiya's all India travels began in that period. As the atmosphere cleared, he was nominated as Joint General Secretary of the Sangh. After that he was elected as 'Sarkaryavaah'. At that time, his age was 56. This highest responsibility for carrying on the Sangh work was on his able shoulders for 9 years. After that, he handed over the responsibility to H.V. Sheshadri due to failing health and stepped back to work as Joint General Secretary. In that condition, when he was 72-years-old, respected 'Sarsanghchaalak' Balasaheb Deoras appointed him as 'Sarsanghchaalak' when he retired from his post. After holding that post for 6 years, he too retired from his post in March 2000 like his predecessor. Three years and 4 months after retirement, he passed away on 14th July, 2003. This was 82 year long journey of life of Rajju Bhaiya. Journey of an idealist, truthful pure person's life guided by a goal. Last shloka of Vivekananda Kendra's prayer is—

"Jeevane yaavadaadaanam syaat pradaanam tatodhikam
Ityeshaa praarthanaasmaakam bhagwan paripooryataam."

(O' God, I have only one request. I should give more than what I have taken. Please fulfil this prayer.) This was the agony of that pure 'aatman'; nobility of that personality.

Let us take a short look at his life. He lived a very simple, straightforward life. When a visitor mentioned about "your greatness," he would promptly reply, "O, brother, I am an ordinary worker made to take on a big responsibility." There was honesty in this response. He travelled in higher class in trains only when the organisation insisted on it. When there was no insistence during Emergency, he always travelled by third class. When he was a Reader, he paid out of his own pocket even when he travelled for Sangh work. Please remember that this kind of behaviour is not an exception in the Sangh.

During his time as a Reader, he used to go out to enjoy nature for nearly a week with his 2-3 close friends. At that time this group used to make its own arrangements and did not depend on the Sangh. In this way, Rajju Bhaiya had visited many spots of natural beauty from Ooty, Kodaikanal to Darjeeling. Actually, his innate nature was that of a wandering monk. It was his nature to go out to people, meet them and converse with them. Conversation was not just hollow chit chat. It used to be profitable and knowledgeable for both the sides.

There is an adjective used by Valmiki for Ram – '*poorvabhashi.*' To understand this word, it would be easier to look at easy simplicity of Rajju Bhaiya. Upon meeting someone, salutation and initiating a dialogue would be from Rajju Bhaiya's side and that too with a warm smiling posture. This is what is called *'poorvabhashi.'* Management experts tell us that the top-ranking people should keep a respectable distance from people from lower ranks. Finally, the result is that respect is lost and distance stays. Dr. Hedgewar's style was totally opposite to this idea. In this approach, there is internal and external openness and natural brotherhood. Talented Rajju Bhaiya, coming at a later stage of life in the Sangh, imbibed this style. No one felt any tension while meeting him or conversing with him. Along with *poorvabhashi,* he was also *priyamvad* i.e. one who speaks sweetly, in a likeable manner.

'Aparigrah' (non-possession) is supposed to be a holy quality. Practical implementation of this quality can be seen in Rajju Bhaiya's life. He analysed what was very necessary, necessary and unnecessary. To strive for first two is desirable and not a demerit. But, desire for the third is not only a demerit but also leads to decadence. This was his attitude. His direction and insistence were that these standards should be followed in personal and organisational life.

Before he became *Sarkaryavaah,* Rajju Bhaiya would be present in almost all top-level meetings too in half pants of the Sangh uniform. He was one of the singers of Sangh Geets (songs) in those meetings. Second was Man. Sudarshan and third was Man. Ashok Singhal. All the three would sing from memory without any paper. During those days, it was not something special, it was a habit in the organisation.

Rajju Bhaiya's role in all the meetings used to be inspirational and motivational. It was not his style to make remarks or interrupt someone. Like a teacher, he would present topics point wise. Therefore, it was very easy to remember and make notes. This also made life of the translator easy in non-Hindi speaking states. All the participants would come out of his meetings with smiling faces. Rajju Bhaiya was a organiser from every angle – soft spoken, affectionate and forgiving.

Whether it was a Sangh get-together or a public meeting, Rajju Bhaiya spoke like a teacher. He would not make dramatically gesture like popular political leaders. There were no highs and lows in his lecture but a sense of continuity prevailed. Speed of speaking too was even. Some people have such a speed that it is even faster than the audience's ability to grasp. Rajju Bhaiya did not belong to that category. His style was that of Hanuman as described by Valmiki, that is –

'avistaram, asandighdam, avilambitam, avyayam,' meaning not too long, without confusion, neither slow nor rapid. If the earlier speaker had spoken more than the allotted time, he would edit his speech in the interest of time management so that the programme ended in time. He had a rare quality of editing his speech even as he spoke. Truly speaking, such speakers are called *'vaagmi'.* (*Vaagmita* is the quality of presenting a measured, highly meaningful speech). Rajju Bhaiya was a *vaagmi.*

Rajju Bhaiya began the tradition of presenting and reading out *Sarkaryavaah's* report in printed format in the Akhil Bharatiya Pratinidhi Sabha. I have been present in many of the earlier Pratinidhi Sabhas when respected Bhaiyaji Dani, Eknathji Ranade, Balasaheb Deoras and Madhavrao Mulyeji were Sarkaryavaahs. Their submission of the report used to be guidance in the light of evaluation of information. They used to speak with right notes from their sharp memory. But, Rajju Bhaiya began the practice of presenting printed report. Now, in the present stage of multi-purpose, multi-sectoral multi-faceted growth of Sangh movement we can understand how important it is to provide an all-encompassing printed report. When I asked Rajju Bhaiya about it at that time, he replied, "It has never been my habit to go to a class without preparation and notes. When I carry notes, I feel sure about myself."

Very few people know that present reporting style was begun by Rajju Bhaiya. This means Rajju Bhaiya was not bounded by any existing practice. He was always ready to add anything new that was necessary and beneficial. Truly speaking, this has been the way of working in the Sangh from the beginning. We saw an example yet again from respected Rajju Bhaiya, that is all.

One more learning is about Rajju Bhaiya's death. He had already told his caretakers—"I should be cremated wherever I die. Every piece of land is a part of my Motherland, Bharat. There is no reason to shift my body anywhere." And that is how it happened. He died in Pune and he was cremated in Vaikunth Dhaam of Pune.

My mind goes back further on this subject. That is why, I think, it would be ideal to talk about it here. All the three Sarsanghchaalaks before Rajju Bhaiya had also given specific instructions about their last rites. I recall them here.

First Sarsanghchaalak had instructed that his cremation should not be done in a military style, which meant, it was to be in normal civilian way. It was necessary in the initial phase of the Sangh work in those days. Whether it was right or wrong, Sangh work seemed similar to military style of functioning at that time. It was natural for the well-wishers of the Sangh to think of having the funeral with military honours. Poojaniya Doctor's thought was to keep this social organisation away from this idea, therefore he gave this direction.

Second Sarsanghchaalak was respected Guruji. He had left behind a written instruction that there should be no memorial except that of the founder of the Sangh. There was a meaningful purpose behind it. Smriti Mandir in memory of the founder had been built in 1962 by Dr. Hedgewar Smaarak Samiti chaired by Madhav Sadashiv Golwalkar, that is, Shri Guruji. Guruji could well understand the inner feelings of swayamsevaks. Therefore, he gave the above instructions to save the organisation from a possible problem. What could have been the consequences? Think about it. There would have been another memorial in the same campus where Sangh founder's memorial is standing.

Third Sarsanghchaalak, Man. Balasaheb was a practical person. He had told his personal assistant Shri Shrikant Joshi that his cremation should be done in a public crematorium. He clearly remembered that due to the stand taken by the senior office bearers of the Sangh, cremation of Guruji was done in Reshim Bagh. He was clear that this practice should not become a tradition in Sangh. He must have in his mind that Reshim Bagh should not become a place that would have such landmarks like *'chhatris'* of kings.

The four instructions of the four Sarsanghchaalaks may look different on the surface. But, if we look these instructions carefully, they present the same principle that Sangh does not wish to become another *'sampradaay'* or sect. Sangh has a belief and a way of conducting itself accordingly, that Sangh is an organisation of the society, it is not an organisation in the society. Surprising part is that all the four respected Sarsanghchaalaks gave one important direction, using their spiritless bodies as the medium.

When we think of the personality of Rajju Bhaiya, we recall the words of respected Guruji while he analysed the personality of a kaaryakarta (worker). "Coal and diamond – both come from the root element 'Carbon'. When they burn, they leave behind only ash. But, when a big piece of coal burns, no one goes near it. People watch it from a distance due to unbearable heat. Now, look at diamond. It doesn't burn, it shines brightly. Everybody rushes towards it, holds it in hand, appreciates it and wishes to own it. From the point of view of objectivity, both coal and diamond are same. But, from utility and acceptability coal is coal and diamond is diamond. A kaaryakarta (worker) should be like a diamond. Yes, Rajju Bhaiya was an attractive diamond.

'Jeevan yatra' outlined by Ratan Sharda is the journey of this diamond. It is desirable to go near it and hold it. It will benefit the readers. He will become a co-passenger in this journey. He/she will become a selfless devoted servant of this great nation. Today, there is a huge requirement of this type of servants for the motherland. This book will be able to fulfil this demand to some extent. With this belief,

—Ranga Hari
Kochi

Respected Ranga Hariji,, an intellectual giant,
is former all India head of Intellectual training of RSS.
He is a polyglot with command over 7 languages and
prolific writer in Malayalam, Hindi and English

Preface

This is the only book about Rashtriya Swayamsevak Sangh (RSS) that I wrote in Hindi. It was my heartfelt wish that this inspiring book should also reach English reading audience and I had hoped someone will do the translation. However, it seemed I was destined to study Rajju Bhaiya's life's journey word by word again. It has been a learning period again for me, as I translated this short book on the life of one of the greatest RSS swayamsevaks who rose from the primary ranks and ascended to topmost level of RSS and led the organisation. It has been an inspiring and moving experience indeed. The Hindi book was published in 2014 and I have read it and quoted from it many times. But last few years have been a period of growth for me too as I studied RSS more deeply for my other books and also for my Ph.D. Thus, it was a different person who read his own work again and impact was deep.

Prof. Rajendra Singh more popularly known in India and outside as Rajju Bhaiya, was the fourth Sarsanghchaalak (Chief) of RSS. He was an ideal swayamsevak, therefore, aversion to publicity was embedded in his nature. We do not know much about a person who, as the head of the largest socio-cultural organisation of Bharat, played a critical role at a historic juncture of independent Bharat.

When Keshav Srushti trust invited me to write this book, it was indeed a matter of privilege for me. However, when I began work on it, I had no clue about where to get the information about Rajju Bhaiya and how big the proposed book would be. Initially, I had thought of collecting some experiences and memories from Mumbai and areas around it and collecting information about him from old literature and magazines. Idea was of a small booklet. I was not a full-time writer till about a year back, so it was not possible to travel all over Bharat for the purpose. But it was a blessing of elders that when I went to the documentation centre of Delhi office of RSS, I could get hold of a couple of good pieces of literature from Kashi Vishwa Samvad Kendra. They had published a special issue of their periodical *'Vichar Pravaah'* as a homage to Rajju Bhaiya. Before he rose to the top at national level, Rajju Bhaiya's field of work was Uttar Pradesh, Bihar and also the entire region of East for some time. Therefore, this issue proved very useful for writing about his life.

The biggest golden haul, by the blessings of Parmaatma, from the same documentation centre for me and readers were the audio memoirs he had recorded himself when he was staying in Pune during his last years. This is nothing less than a treasure. I also talked to many people who had first hand, close experiences with Rajju Bhaiya. I collected many incidents when I sent out a request through RSS related publications for information. These recollections touch our hearts and enlighten us about his personality. All these memories and his own records of his life thus got compiled together into this life's journey of Rajju Bhaiya.

Though I had attended some of his meetings and intellectual discourses as a young swayamsevak and kaaryakarta, I have tried to keep control of my urge to put my own views about Rajju Bhaiya in this writing. I have just tried to present his work in different phases of his life based on well referenced information from different sources in a readable and easy flowing manner. I have limited my own writing to connecting and underlining situation of a particular time and socio-political scenario. Thus, this book is a 'word picture' of this great personality that has taken shape based on people's experiences who came in close touch with him in RSS and other areas of social life. I have tried not to make this into a hagiographic account. Therefore, the image about character and personality of Rajju Bhaiya that a reader would form is based on the experiences and memories of hundreds of people who interacted with him.

The audio tapes that I discovered have given a personal touch to the entire narration. These audios of Rajju Bhaiya cover the period of his childhood to the time when Janata Party came to power in 1977. I have worked hard to transliterate his autobiographic memories faithfully and present them as they are, including his style of speaking and language. Of course, in English it will lose some flavour. However, I am sure people who have met him, will experience the fragrance of his affectionate, smiling and dignified personality through them.

I would like to thank Keshav Srushti Trust for giving me this opportunity. I sincerely thank Kashi Vishwa Samvad Kendra, the Delhi and Nagpur documentation centre of RSS who allowed me to use the rare treasures. I am obliged to all the swayamsevaks, kaaryakartas (workers) and prachaaraks who shared their experiences with me and helped me present Rajju Bhaiya's multi-dimensional, multi-faceted personality in this book. I express my gratitude to his well-wishers and workers of Hindu organisations overseas who made special efforts to collect and share old literature about his visits to their countries. I must also mention with respect and affection, Shri Bimal Kedia, Shri Virendra Yagnik and Dr. Avinash Sinha who went through the manuscript of the book and suggested improvements.

I am especially indebted to senior prachaarak and great thinker Shri Ranga Hari. He not only helped me collect experiences and memories of swayamsevaks of Kerala but also read the text making necessary corrections and suggesting improvements. He is an affectionate and kind soul who always encourages new workers, writers and any well-intentioned person who seeks his help. He worked with Rajju Bhaiya for many years at all India level and experienced his personality from close quarters. I consider it my privilege and his blessings that he agreed to write the foreword for this book and huge value to it. He has captured the very essence of Rajju Bhaiya's personality and his work and some key elements of Sangh's working in 2,700 odd words that I might not have done in 80,000 words.

When I wrote this book, I was sure that better writers than me and specialists would be able to write full-fledged biography of a rare gifted person like Rajju Bhaiya. Only that would do justice to his enlightening and inspiring persona and motivate more people to sacrifice their lives for this great nation. I offer my respect and homage to this great son of Bharat with this small offering.

—Ratan Sharda
Mumbai, Bharat
December 2022

Glossary of RSS terms used in this book

Sarsanghchaalak (सरसंघचालक) : Guide and Philosopher of the Sangh.

Sarkaryavaah (सरकार्यवाह) : General Secretary, topmost elected office-bearer.

Sahsarkaryavaah (सहसरकार्यवाह) : Joint General Secretary.

Sanghchaalak (संघचालक) : Guide and guardian of local activities and local volunteers.

Prachaarak (प्रचारक) : A person who dedicates his entire time to the Sangh without earning money and doing marriage and expecting nothing in return.

Vistaarak (विस्तारक) : A full-time worker who dedicates a brief period to the Sangh.

Shakha (शाखा) : Daily assembly or gathering for personality development and building an organaisation.

Mukhya Shikshak (मुख्य शिक्षक) : The one who is responsible for conducting regular shakha activities.

Kaaryavah (कार्यवाह) : Leading person in achieving the goal of a shakha.

Gatnaayak (गटनायक) : Team leader of a small area or a group of swayamsevaks.

Kaaryakarta (कार्यकर्ता) : An activist.

Kaaryakram (कार्यक्रम) : Programme.

Baithak (बैठक) : Meeting for discussing, deliberating and decision-making.

Pravaas (प्रवास) : Visiting and staying in other places as a part of Sangh work.

Bouddhik (बौद्धिक) : Intellectual exercise or an intellectual discourse.

Sangh Shiksha Varg (संघ शिक्षा वर्ग) : Training programme for kaaryakarta scheduled over three years.

Shivir (शिविर) : Camp.

Prabandhak (प्रबंधक) : Manager.

Vividh Kshetra Sangathan (विविध क्षेत्र संघठन) : Other organisations inspired by the ideals of the Sangh, also referred as allied organisations.

NOTE

a. I have translated a few words from RSS terminology in plain English in this book to make for easy reading, but they do not convey the meaning adequately. The most used word is 'worker' for **'kaaryakarta.'** A kaaryakarta is not just a 'worker' as conveyed by its English meaning. Karyakarta is evolution of a **'swayamsevak'** (again inadequately translated as 'volunteer.' A swayamsevak is a self-motivated person who has, on his own volition decided to dedicate himself selflessly to the service of the society and nation. A swayamsevak becomes a Karyakarta when he begins giving more of his time for RSS work, sometimes all his hours except his time for earning for his family. He does all this from his own resources in every sense.

b. I have used phonetic spellings in many places for typical Hindi/Sanskrit words, instead of normal spellings used for Indian names and terms that may look odd to people who know Indian languages. However, this flexibility makes it easier for English speaking people who do not know Indian languages, so please bear with me.

Contents

ANNEXURE

1

Mananiya Rajendra Singh's family and his entry into RSS

Prof. Rajendra Singh was born in Banail village in Bulandshahar district in Uttar Pradesh on 29th January, 1922, to Mrs. Jwala Devi and Kunwar Balveer Singh. This child Kunwar Rajendra Singh was known later in life as 'Rajju Bhaiya' due to his loving and caring nature.

Kunwar Balveer Singh was a highly educated member of his family. He had earned his degree in Engineering from the only engineering college in Roorkee and stood first in the University. He went on to pass IAS exams and was appointed as Engineer in the irrigation department of Uttar Pradesh. He had the honour of being appointed the first Indian Chief Engineer (Irrigation) post Indian independence. He was well known as a dignified, sharp and honest officer. Young Rajendra Singh's personality was highly influenced by the simple life style, frugal living and high ethical values of his father.

Rajendra Singh was the eldest of three sons of Kunwar Balveer Singh. Vijendra Singh and Yateendra Singh were his younger brothers. Vijendra Singh graduated as engineer from the famous Roorkee engineering college, passed UPSC examination and was appointed as an engineer in Central Govt. Yateendra Singh finished his M.Sc. and then joined Rajasthan an IAS officer. His wife was also an IAS officer. Yateendra Singh's elder daughter named Gauri Singh was also an IAS officer in Madhya Pradesh cadre. Now she is working in Dubai. Her spouse is Sanjay Singh an IAS officer in Delhi. Her brother Gaurav Singh became an Engineer. He is the only son in Rajju Bhaiya's next generation. But he is not married. Rajendra Singh had two sisters. The elder sister Susheela was married to General Mahadev Singh. He was the Principal of Military Academy, Masoori. His elder son settled down in Austrelia. Second son is Aaditya Pratap Singh. He retired from Indian Army as Lieutenant General. The second sister was married to Dr. R.B. Singh, who went on to become the Principal of Lucknow Medical College. They have two sons; one Rajnarayan Singh became Professor of Physics in Lucknow University. Second one Dr. Gireesh Singh was a Director of AIIMS, Patna. Both are enjoying their retired life in Lucknow. Rajju Bhaiya's cousin brother named Prem Pal Singh is now living in their parental house in village Banail. He was a Principal of Khurja College. Rajju Bhaiya had strong loving relations with his family and he maintained them till the end. His love and affection were reciprocated in equal measure by his family members and younger nephews and nieces.[1]

Rajju Bhaiya did his initial schooling in the family itself, as his father had a transferable job. A teacher used to travel with the family and was responsible for the education of every child. During some light conversations with his attendant Amarnath, who was his personal assistant deputed by RSS, from February 2002 to April 2003, he told him:

"I passed fifth grade in 1932. When I joined school in grade VI, I did not go to school one day. When my father asked me why I was at home, I told him that somebody had stolen my pencil yesterday, so I haven't gone to school today. My father did not allow me to go to school on hearing this. He said, "If he goes to school, he will also learn such despicable habits there." He then, appointed a teacher to teach me at home. When I wanted to give private exams for grade VIII in Unnao in 1935, my father told me to go and meet the principal. In the meanwhile, my father got transferred again to Roorkee and I had to go to Roorkee within 3 months. I got admitted to grade VIII there with great difficulty. When I was asked to appear for a test to get admitted, I failed in science and got 30 marks in English and 17 marks in Hindi. I got zero in science. Principal refused to admit me. He was my paternal uncle (Chachaji's) friend. My Chacha persuaded the principal by reminding him, "Don't you know whose son this boy is? He is very good in studies; you should understand this." Principal finally relented and admitted me. I was asked to work with the cleverest boy in the class for practicals. It was here that I dissected a frog for the first time. I stood third in the class that year. But I had to return home again after three months and passed out of high school in 1937 from there. I went to Nainital to do my Intermediate and scored distinction in all the three subjects. Chancellor of Allahabad University, Shri Amarnath Jha, used to send congratulatory letters to talented students to join his university. I too received such a letter and felt very good. I showed the letter to my father and came to Prayag for higher studies. There were 9700 students in the University at that time. I stood first in the first year of B.Sc. Examination."[2]

After completing his B.Sc., Rajju Bhaiya did his M.Sc. from Prayag University. He shared another amusing incident from his childhood with Amarnath which shows his strength of character and determination—

"I have not really done heavy exercises at any time, but I do light exercises even at this age. I did exercise heavily for four months in gymnasium once. Our college had many Anglo-Indians. One of the students among them was quite well built. We had a big argument one day in the class about Mahatma Gandhi. He said, "Gandhi is absolutely wrong." I countered him immediately and said, "No, Gandhi is absolutely right." Argument turned ugly and he hit me with two punches. I decided to take revenge for this attack. I asked a friend and began doing special exercise to increase my strength. I used to exercise for minimum two hours every day. When my father saw my condition, he asked me one day, "Don't you want to study?" We had another argument with the hefty Anglo-Indian boy one day. I used this opportunity to punch him hard and felled him."

Rajju Bhaiya's father used to be on tours due to his government job. He also travelled along with his father many times. Therefore, father and mother left a major mark on his personality. Both carried a spiritual aura and positivity, though both had different personalities. Rajju Bhaiya carried their imprint throughout his life. In his own words, he came in close touch with outsiders and people who later affected his personality only after he turned twenty and went to Prayag.[3]

Rajju Bhaiya shared an experience with Amarnath, which according to him, was one of the many experiences that imbibed ethical values from his parents—"I went on Jammu trip with my father. As per railway rules, his helper could travel only in third class and he was travelling in second class. Before Independence, first class was for Europeans only. Train stopped at a station and father was in washroom. I spread out his sleeping mat properly and lied down waiting for his return. When my father came back, I went back to third class bogey. After I left, other neighbouring travelers complained to his father about his 'servant' who lied down on his bed! My father smiled and told them, "Arrey, he is not my servant, but my eldest son. He teaches in University." People who had complained were left highly embarrassed. Despite availability of all comforts of life, I got into habit of travelling in third class since my childhood. Because of this training, I never faced any problem after I became a prachaarak."[4]

Rajju Bhaiya has provided sufficient information about his family in the audio he recorded in his memoirs after his retirement. It is interesting that Rajju Bhaiya got introduced to RSS after Quit India movement of 1942. He had not yet decided about the direction his life would take. But he already had a deep inclination to work for the society, about which we shall learn later. But, family elders were already making preparations for settling down their son as per traditions of those times.

"All parents naturally think about marrying their wards like my own mother and father. So, my mother set up my engagement while I was doing my final year B.Sc. in 1942. My mother had finalized a girl for me without informing me. I was very surprised. I was just 20-year-old at that time. I tried to reason with my mother that I still had to complete my studies and I don't even know what will I do in my life after this; and it was not a good idea to finalize my relationship. My mother then tried to persuade me by saying, "We have only finalized your fiancée, and there is no hurry to get you married. We shall marry you only when you tell us." Then I persuaded my mother that we shall keep this discussion suspended and I will talk to the girl's father myself and reason with him. Girl's father was in army. I met him and told him clearly that I do not wish to get married yet. But, whenever I get married, I will do so as per my parents' wishes. Therefore, it would be better if they married off their daughter anywhere they wished. It would not be good to make her wait for so long. This gentleman became my good friend later in life and he also helped me during my illness."[5]

After Rajju Bhaiya joined Sangh (RSS) many incidents took place – Ban on RSS, imprisonment and the satyagrah followed. These proved to be decisive events that decided for him a firm direction that his life would take. Incidents of this period resulted in shaping his views decisively about his life. In his own words—

"After I was released from jail in 1949, I decided that I will not marry. I told my mother in clear words that with the kind of life I am leading, I may be going in and out of jail routinely. Any girl with whom I may get married, will face lot of hardships. Therefore, I will not marry."[6]

Because of his decision not to get married, his parents couldn't plan wedding of his younger siblings. How could they get married before their elder brother got married? Rajju Bhaiya tells us how he convinced his brothers and sisters—

"My younger brother also kept shirking off his wedding proposal saying, he could marry only after his elder brother got married. I persuaded him with great difficulty by explaining that my life was going to be difficult since I work for Sangh. You must marry to keep parents happy. He finally agreed in 1957-58, at a comparatively advanced age. Then, it was decided that he could marry a widow or a single lady. Coincidentally, my sister was married to Col. Mahadev Singh. Maharani of Ratlam was his good friend. Their daughter Shanti was engaged to Maharaja Karan Singh. But there was misunderstanding between her father Maharaja Sajjan Singh and engagement was called off. She was married to Vijayendra Singh. Princess Shanti was very charming, outgoing, physically fit and easy-going personality. She used to play every type of sport. She went to England to seek medical advice to overcome problem of conceiving due to her age. Unfortunately, she had an accident and was bed ridden for long. Finally, she died due to failure of lever. My brother was 40 by then. He decided that he will not marry again. But I reasoned with him that he had a long life ahead of him, and he could marry a widow. He finally married a widow of an army officer (Major Bhupendra Singh, decorated with Mahavir Chakra). He fulfilled his family obligations and married off her three daughters and saw them well settled in USA after taking care of completion of their graduation as doctors."

"Third brother married the daughter of a forest conservator at the age of 30. He had a daughter. My mother could see the face of her granddaughter and was happy to be a grandmother before she died. She died in 1965 and my brother had a son in 1966. His son is holding a senior post in a private corporation."[7]

Prof. Rajnarayan Singh 'Ruby' reminisces, "Whenever we kids went to Prayag, we would always stay at Maternal Uncle's (Mama) home '26 Park Road'. Mamaji would return home, exhausted after a busy day, but he would always spend sufficient time with kids. He would talk of various things, especially about the glorious ancient history of Bharat. There was no radio or TV at that time. We used to spend our evenings with him over such chats. Mamaji would always enquire a lot about our studies whenever he came home. We used to study in English medium school and Mamaji would insist that we speak in Hindi. Some of us would remain quiet as we could not speak good Hindi. My father then made us appear for Hindi '*Prathama*' exams to help us practice and improve our Hindi and Sanskrit."[8]

He loved kids and played and laughed with them. Padmakar Mishra talks about his humorous tackling of young children. Children from Kadamkuan shakha in Patna were sitting informally with Rajju Bhaiya for introductions. There was a young child who pronounced 'sh' as 'f'. He introduced himself as. "Failendra." Rajju Bhaiya told him lovingly, "No, no. Please do not speak like this. Speak out 'sh' by turning your tongue upward and not closing your lips, and now say 'sh' – 'Shailendra.' Child kept trying distorting his face in the process and was finally able to say, "Sh..Sh... Shailendra." He then told him smilingly, "Yes, keep practicing like this or else you will get into confusion of 'sher' and 'pher'." You can imagine squeals of laughter from among children after this.[9] Thus, with affection he received from his nephews and swayamsevaks, he never missed his family life and he never felt that he did not have his own family.

Ashok Singhal and his family were very close to Rajju Bhaiya's family. Man. Ashok Singhal went on to lead Vishwa Hindu Parishad while Rajju Bhaiya led Rashtriya Swayamsevak Sangh. Rajju Bhaiya talks about close relations between their two families—

"Ashok Singhal's father Shri Mahaveer Singh and my father Balveer Singh studied together and their relations went years back. His was very affectionate family. We were swayamsevaks of the same shakha and studied together since 1942 and grew together. They were seven brothers and a lone sister. His elder brother, Pramod Singhal, was President of Rajasthan unit of

Vishwa Hindu Parishad. One brother was M.P. in Rajya Sabha. The last brother named Peeyush is settled in Mumbai. Ashokji was a great lover of music. He had a booming and beautifully controlled, musical voice. We took part together in many competitions and received many prizes too. May be, he wished to grow in this field. But he went into mining engineering in BHU after inter exams. Being in Kashi he was in close touch with Bhaurao and also being member of a Sangh imbued family, he became a prachaarak. He had a great quality. He could meet anybody without any reservation and talked from the heart. He is able to meet even important people very easily. He is highly respected in his family too."[10] He recalled their association and participation in musical competitions much later in 1982 while talking to Shridhar Damle.[11]

Remembering his friend since teenage who was like an elder brother to him, Ashok Singhalji says, "Rajju Bhaiya's father and my father studied in the same Gurukul and were very close. It is because of him that my brothers and I began going to Sangh shakha. We completed First year OTC (Officers Training Camp, later renamed Sangh Shiksha Varg) together. Rajju Bhaiya was a post graduate in Physics and I was in XI." He then talks about his entry into Sangh thus, "Rajju Bhaiya used to visit our home regularly. But his visits kept dwindling over time. My mother asked him one day, "Rajju, why are you visiting so infrequently now a days?" Rajju Bhaiya, then, told mother that he had got busy with Sangh shakha and then sang Sangh Prarthana. By listening the prayer, my mother was very pleased and insisted that he should also take along Ashok and other brothers to shakha."[12]

Rajju Bhaiya used to take interest in activities of Congress while he was studying. Visiting Anand Bhavan and meeting Congress leaders was part of his routine. Anand Bhavan was home to Nehru family and also centre of Congress activities in Prayag. He was active during 1942 Quit India movement. But this agitation failed due to lack of farsightedness and planning. All the disappointed senior

Congress leaders sat back in their homes. He confirmed this part of his life with Shridhar Damle in 1982 in US during his chat with him. Rajju Bhaiya met many leaders and asked them about their future plans. But nobody had anything to offer. He felt highly disappointed with this lack of direction in a huge organisation like Congress. It was in the last year of his M.Sc. It was during this period that he got introduced to Rashtriya Swayamsevak Sangh (RSS). He met the Vibhag prachaarak of RSS, Bapurao Moghe, through his student from neighbourhood, Shantaram and a compatriot in his class, Shyamnarayan Shrivastav. Bapurao Moghe was just 5-6 years senior to him. This contact turned slowly into close friendship and Rajju Bhaiya became a regular swayamsevak of Bhardwaj Sayam (evening) shakha.[13]

Sangh was a new organisation. From historic perspective one could say it was in its infancy. Shakhas used to have only young boys and young college going students. Workers and prachaaraks were also young. This situation led to a strange situation. There is an interesting episode at the time he gained entry into the Sangh. Rajju Bhaiya describes this funny episode himself—

"Mataji (mother) used to stay with me to guide me and help in my study. Ashok Singhal's mother and my mother happened to be very good friends. They used to keep track of our education. They would also keep an eye on who were our friends. She would always say, "Bring your friends home, we would like to meet them." 1942 Quite India movement had just got over. She found that I had become a part of a new organisation. So, she insisted that I bring a person associated with this organisation so she could see who is the person with whom he spent his time. I brought home Bapurao. He was just 5-6 year older to me and looked like me only. She asked, "Don't you have any senior person in your organisation?" I brought along Bhaurao (Deoras). She was not satisfied as his age was also similar to Bapurao. When Babasaheb Apte came to Prayag once during his tour, I took him home to present him to my mother. His personality with a turban, a cotton muffler, a thick spectacle – all this satisfied her. She said, “Ok, I am happy that there are senior people too in Sangh.” Otherwise, she used to wonder if I was involved in some revolutionary work which involved violence, blowing up something. After that many senior Sangh worker visited my home. Revered Guruji also visited our home many times.”[14]

From point of view of Sangh, the people who influenced Rajju Bhaiya’s life and thinking most were Bapurao Moghe, Bhaurao Deoras, Deendayal Upadhyaya and Nanaji Deshmukh. He learnt a lot from them. People outside Sangh circle who influenced him most were Purushottamdas Tandon, referred to by most as Rajarshi Tandon, Lal Bahadur Shastri and Sant Prabhudatta Brahmachari.

People raise questions many a times about the historical period of 1942 and role of Sangh and swayamsevaks during his time, though in the biography of Dr. Keshav Baliram Hedgewar, the founder of RSS, N.H. Palkar has given detailed account with news reports and book references of those times. Lot of information is also available from Shri Guruji’s biography, anecdotes shared by old swayamsevaks of that time and memoirs of prachaaraks of those times. We note that Rajju Bhaiya’s entry into the Sangh in 1942 happened after the incidents of Quit India movement of 1942 or rather due to failure of this movement. When he was asked about this period, he shared his personal experience—

“I joined Sangh quite late, after 1942. Therefore, I do not know much about whether Sangh helped 1942 movement or not. But it seems that whatever decision Sangh took about this movement was correct. Congress leaders passed the resolution about ‘Quit India’ in 1942. All the leaders were arrested and put into jails. There was not one leader in the entire country who could give direction to the nation, to the society or the people of this country. All the big leaders – Nehru, Tandon, Kripalani – were members of the Working Committee. If they thought that British will not arrest anybody after this resolution was passed, one can only say that leaders of the time didn't apply their mind and lacked understanding. There was no plan for the people and what the leaders not in jail and were free, would do. Only Ram Manohar Lohia and Jaiprakash did some work.

Sangh had felt, and felt rightly, that Congress was the prime organisation for the Hindu society of the nation. Congress's actions touched the Hindu society. Cow protection, Ram Rajya, Gram Swaraj (village republic), educating people in Bharatiya languages, simplicity etc. – all these things attracted Sangh and the Hindu heart more. Gandhiji had seen that small number of Muslims, who had joined Congress were isolated by Jinnah. After Congress leaders were sent to jail, there was no leadership for the Hindu society. After this, Muslim League and Communist people, who were always traitors, would have harassed and confused Hindu society so much that they would have lost heart to put up any fight.

Sangh said that those who wish to take part (in Quit India movement) should do so in their personal capacity. Swayamsevak should think that Sangh is also a Hindu power, and he should try to help, save and support Congress people and people who think of well-being of Hindu society, in every possible way. And, also expand Sangh work rapidly. How rapidly Shri Guruji expanded the work, can be gauged by the fact that while there were 25-50 prachaaraks till 1940, another 200 prachaaraks joined their ranks in 1942 itself. Punjab, itself saw addition of new 125 prachaaraks. Large numbers also came out of Maharashtra. There was no pessimism; there was no sense of hopelessness. Mantra was, organise, learn discipline, learn patriotism and take responsibility to free the country. Many people may not be aware that the Sangh oath at that time read, "I have become member of Sangh to free Hindu Rashtra." (Now this sentence has become – "for all round development") Objective was clear – to gain independence, to work as per our inherent nature after we gain independence, find our own path and not copy the West in a stupid way, the way it is happening now.

Many old Congress members joined Sangh after 1942. Big leaders were still in jails. Not only me, but with our joint efforts many others like Ram Prakash, Mahadevi Prasad, Manmohan and many students joined Sangh. Only such young people used to join RSS at that time. Senior citizens felt that Sangh was not meant for them. Sangh grew in a big way in next 2-4 years. There were around 500-700 shakhas in Uttar Pradesh itself. People in larger numbers could have joined but there were not enough teachers. There used to be Sangh Shiksha Varg. Every year numbers raised by two to three times. In 1946 the number of shakhas rose to 1,000. (This was also the time when Hindus began leaving Punjab and responsibility of taking their care with compassion too came on Sangh.)

Just a year before that, Sangh Shiksha Varg had begun in North Bharat. 1942 Varg was held in Lucknow, 1943 in Kashi. Swayamsevaks from Bihar and Bengal too joined this Varg. There were 500-600 trainees. Bapurao (Moghe) was the chief instructor for physical training. He is the one who taught us the preliminary things about Sangh and physical programme. Bhaurao (Deoras) was present in this Varg. Ashok Singhal, his brothers Anand, Ravindra and Bharatendu were also present as trainees. Since, I couldn't bear the hot summer, I used to escape to the hills during last 5-6 years where my father was posted. Therefore, I was not comfortable in the Varg. There was one team that had senior swayamsevaks of that time. Laxmanrao Bhide was the instructor for this group. Anant Ramchandra Gokhale, Kshirsagar, Rajabhau Savargaonkar were also to help him. Things were organised with lot of affection, in a cheerful atmosphere. I learned a lot; lots of doubts were cleared. I saw and heard revered Guruji for the first time there. I heard his famed, highly impactful lecture on 'Shivaji's letter to Maharaja Jaisingh' there only.

My result of M.Sc. was declared when I was a participant in the Kashi Varg. I stood second in merit by scoring first class marks. Guruji asked me, "What will you do after this?" I replied,

"So far, I am thinking of being a teacher if I can do research in Prayag and be a teacher too." Guruji gave his assent to the idea and I returned to Prayag."[15]

It was after his return from this Sangh Shiksha Varg that Rajendra Singh's journey as a teacher and as a Sangh worker began and Rajendra Singhji became lecturer Rajendra Singh.

References

1. Apne Parampujaniya Sarsanghchaalak, Vijay Kumar
2. Vichar Pravaah Visheshaank, December 2003, Page 88, Kashi Vishwa Samvad Kendra, special issue dedicated to Rajju Bhaiya
3. Recording of Rajju Bhaiya, Audio file no. 5A (Rajju Bhaiya spent his later life in Kaushik Ashram, Pune after retiring as the Sarsanghchaalak. He recorded his own memoirs in audio tapes there. These audio recordings have been used in this book and readers will find audio file numbers in other references in the book) Received from RSS Documentation Centre, Jhandewalan, Delhi. There are many audio files and they have been marked as he recorded them
4. Vichar Pravaah Visheshaank, op. cit.
5. Audio file 4A, op. cit.
6. Ibid
7. Ibid
8. Vichar Pravaah Visheshaank, Page 76, op. cit
9. Padmakar Mishra, email, 23 October, 2013, (Rajju Bhaiya was State Pracharak of Uttar Pradesh, and later Kshetra (regional) prachaarak from 1970 to 1975. Padmakar Mishra was a prachaarak in that area during those years. Now he stays in UK.)
10. Audio file 4A, op. cit.
11. Shridhar Damle, conversation on phone October, 2013 (Co-author of 'Brotherhood in Saffron' with Walter Anderson, resident of USA)
12. Vichar Pravaah Visheshaank, op. cit. p. 4, 61)
13. Vijay Kumar, Joint Editor, Rashtradharma publications, Vichar Pravaah Visheshaank, op. cit. Page 57
14. Audio file 5A, op. cit.
15. Audio file 1A, op. cit.

□

2

Initial years in the University

Second rank in M.Sc. in the University was to bring a huge revolutionary change in Rajendra Singh's life. It could make him a successful scientist and bring laurels to him as a researcher. Choice of path for his life was in his hands. Any other young man would never have even imagined rejecting the proposal of Professor C.V. Raman's to join him as a researcher.

Jyoti Swaroop, former kshetra prachaarak pramukh, writes about this incident, "Nobel prize winner C.V. Raman (Venkatraman) was his examiner for the practical examination. He was so impressed with his experiment based on his own theory of 'Raman Effect' that he gave him 100 out of 100 marks. It had never happened before. He invited this talented student, Rajendra Singh, to do research under him in Bengaluru. He had stood second in M.Sc. and his friend and colleague Harishchandra stood first. When the Principal consoled Rajendra Singh about it, he said, "If, I had stood first, I would have repented my whole life, because Harishchandra truly deserves it." His friend, Harishchandra, went to Dr. Bhabha for research. He became a famous researcher and went on to occupy the famous scientist Einstein's Chair. Rajju Bhaiya, known for nurturing his relations throughout life, had very nice relation with him till the last. When he heard of his death on radio, Rajju Bhaiya cried, did not eat that night and went quiet."[1]

Despite Shri C.V. Raman's invitation to join him in Bengaluru, Rajju Bhaiya wished to become a teacher and do research with his guru Professor Krishnan. He did not wish to leave Prayag. Hearing his decision, C.V. Raman told his guru Prof. Krishnan, "I have never seen such a practical boy in my life."[2]

He shared the secret of his being a good teacher. It was inspiration of Shri C.V. Raman. He spoke of this incident much later in life in 1973-74. Rajju Bhaiya asked him once, "Sir, despite being such a great physicist, you teach very basic things to new students every year again and again. Don't you get bored?" He had then replied, "Rajendra, when you take interest in every learner, opening a new window to the sky of knowledge, you never get tired. You have to admire and enjoy every learner's spirit to explore." He imbibed these words and led his life as a teacher with this thought and went on to become his students' most loved teacher.[3]

It was widely speculated that had Rajju Bhaiya not dedicated his life to Sangh, he would have been amongst one of the few top-rated scientists of India. But Rajju Bhaiya would simply brush aside such a discussion in his humble way with a smile. Understanding his nature and character, we can understand that denying such a talk was only his nature of extreme self-abnegation. He said once with a smile, "There are many misgivings and myths. For example, I would have been a great scientist if I had not been in Sangh. Or Bhabha had told Guruji that you kept a person away from science who would have been suitable for a Nobel Prize. This is not true. Nuclear physics was in its infancy. I was spectroscopy specialist which is a branch of light. My examiner was C.V. Raman. Harishchandra stood first and I was second. He was my good friend. He was a little weak in practicals but was ahead of me in theory. He used to say, "I am afraid of you. You know less than me, but you write in such a way that examiner would think, you know better!" Professor Krishnan, who taught us Raman Effect, was part of Raman's team. Therefore, Ramanji came to Prayag many a times and was also our examiner. He was very happy with the good photograph I could take of Raman Effect during practical and he invited me to join him for research. My friend Harishchandra had decided to do research with Bhabha. Though Raman had invited me, Prof. Krishnan stopped me from leaving Prayag and asked me to do research with him." When asked about the source of this 'rumour', he felt this idea must have spread because of an article written by Ramchandra Malhotra.[3]

It is nothing but humility of Rajju Bhaiya that he negated and brushed aside this talk about his being a very good researcher. But it is a fact that if Rajju Bhaiya had not become a prachaarak, he would have been a renowned scientist. Some years back Ravi Iyer, a prachaarak of Hindu swayamsevak Sangh, had asked him about some talk about his discussions with Homi Bhabha and whether it was true. Rajju Bhaiya then told Ravi Iyer about this story. In 1947, when Homi Bhabha suggested to Pandit Nehru that India could be a leading country in nuclear research, Nehru gave him permission to move ahead. PM told him to recruit best scientists and get best infrastructure without worrying about budgets. Dr. Bhabha asked Sir C.V. Raman to suggest some names of good scientists. Shri Raman told him, "There is a young man in Prayag who is highly talented. He had not agreed to join me in Bengaluru and now he teaches there. If you can bring him in, it would be great." He was talking about Rajju Bhaiya. Rajju Bhaiya was invited but he did not agree. He told Bhabha, "I teach only three days a week, and give all other time to Sangh. I cannot give less time to the society. Therefore, I cannot take up a government job where I have to work 6-7 days every week." When Bhabha told Nehru that this talented scientist was not agreeing to join, Nehru told him, "How can it be? Offer him whatever salary he wants." Bhabha then told him, "This is not the issue. His priorities in life are different and they have nothing to do with money." This is how this story came to a close. Thus, there is reason to believe that when Homi Bhabha met Guruji, he told him, "Bharat lost one of the best scientists because of you."[4]

Rajju Bhaiya recalls his friendship with Dr. Harishchandra, 'I had gone to America in 1982 and met him there. Workers of Vishwa Hindu Parishad requested me to suggest a good name for a programme there. I told them, "Bhai (brother), I don't know anybody here." Then I remembered Harishchandra, so I called him on phone and invited him to be special guest for the programme. He then told me that he was not well and doctors had told him not to go anywhere. He expired within a year. I had stopped him from going to US and told him, "What is there for him? Our nation is about to become free, do research here, construct a theory in your name, something like Harishchandra effect. Finally, I persuaded him to join research under Bhabha sir. He did good work there. He went on to become National Professor of Mathematics and was nominated as FRS (Fellow of Royal Society of UK). He was considered to be among the top 4-5 mathematicians."[5]

He always kept himself abreast of nuclear science. Shridhar Damle shared his own experience in this regard. In the tour mentioned above, he was surprised to the core when he arranged his visit to world renowned 'Fermi lab' near Chicago and saw him discussing various topics with the scientists there. He had a strong hold on the topic even after leaving teaching work for years. People there were highly impressed with his knowledge.[6]

His progress as a teacher in Prayag was quite rapid. One could call it coincidence spurred by his love for teaching and deep affection for students. Pushed by the situations around him, his journey as a brilliant teacher progressed rapidly. His insistence on fair play and ethics can be seen even in those years. He tells us about his initial years of teaching, "Dr. Krishnan called me as soon as I landed in Prayag. It was already decided that I will do research under him and when I came to know that I had been appointed as a lecturer too, I was happy. I liked teaching. It was my hobby to explain subjects to the students. Other students in research, like Dr. Ajit Ram Verma, had joined one year prior to me. Dr. Devendra Sharma had joined prior to him. Both of them were research scholars. When I received the appointment letter as a lecturer, I felt that both of them were senior to me and it was not a good development. I told this to respected Professor. But, Prof. Krishnan said, "No, this is alright. Both of them receive scholarships. Both of them wish to finish their thesis at the earliest. When I was convinced about this, only then did I accept lecturer's post."[7]

We can say that he had inherited his dedication to the society. Rajju Bhaiya told Amarnath about his first salary, 'I received the first salary of rupees 190/- in 1943. I asked my father, what do I do with it? He told me, "Go, ask your mother." There had been floods during this period. Sir Tej Bahadur Sapru had appealed to the society to co-operate and help. I too felt that my first salary should be used for some sacred cause. After deciding this, I went to my mother and told her, "Pitaji (respected father) used to give me 500 rupees for my studies. I have received my first salary today and I wish to donate it for flood relief fund." Mataji (respected mother) said, "This is, indeed, a very good thought." I then went and handed over my salary to Sir Tej Bahadur Sapru."[8] He further talks about his life as a teacher—

'Teacher for the first year was supposed to take two-three practicals and tutorials. In tutorials students used to come to solve their difficulties. I used to enjoy taking practicals. My first appointment was as a demonstrator. I used to work very hard for the tutorials. I began making them interesting and mixed up with the students very well. There was not much of a difference between students' age and mine. These tutorials became very popular. Instead of 10 students, my tutorials would attract 30 students. Thus, I got good experience to give lectures within first year itself.

An unexpected incident gave me another opportunity that was not an easy task for a junior lecturer. There was a senior professor who used to bring books in the class. His teaching was monotonous and he used to speak in a flat tone. Students used to be a little scared in the first year and hence would remain silent. But, by the second year they would become clever and they behaved the same way with any teacher, the way he behaved with them. Students began harassing him in the second year. Whenever he turned his back, they would throw chalks at him and make mischief. One day he said in a teachers' meeting that he would not take classes on 'Heat' for the second-year students as these students were very mischievous. The Head of the Department said, "Then it seems, I will have to take the lecture. Students need to be controlled and taught. It will be difficult for anybody else to teach the students who have made a professor run away." He then asked, "Is there anybody else ready to take up the task? If there is anybody, please let me know." I raised my hand and said, "I can try. I have experience of giving lectures to a big class. I have good relations with students too. You can try it on experimental basis." This is how I began taking classes for second year in my first year itself. I reached the college with flickering heart on the first day, but due to good relations with the students and because of confidence, I could manage the class well.

I could speak both in English and Hindi so students found it easy to understand. When I got a chance, I would tell them about the lives of our earlier and ancient Indian scientists. This used to make the topic interesting. I also used to tell stories of western scientists. That class was full of bright students, who did some great work later years. Gopal Swaroop Pathak went on to become the Vice President. His son R.S. Pathak became Chief Justice. Shanti Bhushan became the law minister in 1977. All these were students of that class. Even now, when they meet, they talk about how I taught them even a boring subject like Science in an interesting way."[9]

Ex-Prime Minister V.P. Singh was also his student. In his homage to Rajju Bhaiya, he wrote how he used to make even uninteresting subjects interesting.[10] His teaching colleagues and past students have time and again talked about his close affectionate relations with students.

During 1945 to 1952, he used to stay in his home 'Anand'. He would always guide his students. Apart from lectures, he would also guide them in laboratory in their practicals. He would tell them how to study and which career to choose, with great interest.[11] One of his students, staying in Canada now, Dr. Bharatendu Shrivastava emailed, "When he was a student of M.Sc., Rajju Bhaiya taught him as well as guided him in the laboratory. He was not only a teacher of highest calibre, but he was also compassionate and helpful. He used to give clear and right advice on any subject. He experienced the worth of Rajju Bhaiya's guidance a number of times. For example, when he was going to Canada for his Ph.D., Rajju Bhaiya called him and told him that seas are rough in September and he could get sea sick, should take required medicines with him. Though he had never been outside Bharat till that time, he had found this information out to help his student." When Rajju Bhaiya went to Canada, he went to his home in Toronto and also went to see Niagara Falls with his family. Even after years, his relations with his student remained as warm.

Another student reminisced, "When he was checking our sheets while sitting in laboratory, he used to teach us about usage of a language. He would read each sentence and tell us how to make a good English sentence. It was rare example of a Physics teacher teaching his students also about finer points of English language. Nobody was comparable to his ease of explaining something in Hindi. He could explain even the most complex subjects in simple way. Once, while teaching in M.Sc. the word 'sieve' was used and asked one student out of 40 students to tell the meaning of sieve. When he couldn't explain, he said, "See, if we don't insist on teaching Science in English, how easy it would be for people to understand it!"[12]

When a teacher couldn't teach a topic, there would be a call for Rajju Bhaiya (who was a lecturer at that time.) He had the post of a reader who didn't do Ph.D. but many of his students received a Doctorate under him. Many students used to come from faraway South, insisting that they would study Physics only from him.[13]

Students had immense respect for him. Padmakar Mishra, a prachaarak at that time, was witness to many incidences. He writes, "A public programme had been arranged in 1973-74 in Dumraon town. Respected Rajju Bhaiya was Joint-Regional prachaarak of Bihar-Uttar Pradesh of that time. He was the keynote speaker on the day. A local kaaryakarta and I went to hand over an invitation to the Managing Director of a Textile Mills in the same area belonging to the Maharaja of Dumraon. The guard at the gate took our invitation card, sent it inside and sent us back from the gates. We had hardly gone some distance with a sense of disappointment when that guard called back us loudly. The director hosted us with warmth and respect in his room and told him that Rajju Bhaiya was Head of the Department of Physics in Prayag University when he was a student and he was the most respected teacher. He was the only teacher who used to teach 'Polarisation of Light'. He became emotional on seeing his name on the invitation. He came for the programme and we were happy witness to the bond of love between the teacher and the student."[14]

Rajju Bhaiya would always go to meet students in hostels and talk to them personally to encourage them to study well. He never liked the idea of a swayamsevak being left behind in his study. He told them that whatever responsibility a swayamsevak accepts, he must do it skilfully and with honesty. He had homely contacts with his students. Because of this, even members of students' families used to lend support to Sangh work at local level and participate in its activities. He maintained very good relations with ordinary people as well.[15]

Due to his excellent teaching and his affectionate relations with the students, senior office bearers of the University wished to hand over bigger responsibilities to Rajju Bhaiya. Rajju Bhaiya talks about it in his audio memoirs—

"Chancellor of the University, Shri Amarnath Jha used to send more active teachers to NCC. He called me one day and said, "Now you have joined the University, so you should take up this responsibility." My experience with NCC was not good. When I was a student, I had joined NCC. My experience was that students who came there, used uncouth language which I didn't like. So, I had left NCC within two days, disgusted with their language. I explained to him that apart from teaching, I am also involved in a national mission that I like very much, therefore I cannot take this responsibility. I do not wish to do this work, still if you insist, I cannot refuse. But, I can resign from the job. Then he sent a message, "You have understood me wrong. You have been a good student and a good teacher, that is why I had made this suggestion."[16]

Vishwambhar Dayal Gupta, an erstwhile student of Rajju Bhaiya and former senior Professor of Prayag University recollecting about his Sangh work told that he would go to the classes directly from station after finishing his tour. But, quality of his lectures would never suffer. What was the secret behind this? Prof. Gupta says, "I was coming with him once from Delhi. He was preparing his lecture for the next day till late night. He did his morning ablutions etc. in the train and went directly to the university to teach."[17]

He had a very sharp memory. Head of the Department of Physics, Prof. Gopal Krishna Pandey remembers, "When I got a chance to teach, I had a problem of a stammering. Some senior professors found me unfit as a teacher for this reason. Then, one day Rajju Bhaiya called me and said, "From tomorrow you should go to teach the classes. I have heard you five years back in Sampoornanand Lecture series." I was speechless! I didn't even remember that lecture. But, Rajju Bhaiya was present in that lecture as a judge and he remembered everything. He had come to Prayag one year before his death in 2002. He came to my department. He couldn't see properly, but he took a round of the department and met everybody very affectionately. As soon as he met me, he asked me affectionately, "I hope, now you don't stammer." He remembered everything even then!"[18]

Many people have called Rajju Bhaiya as 'Teacher par excellence'. Even students who were not from his department, would come to listen to his lecture. He used to tell his colleagues, "A careless teacher can spoil hundreds of lives - Don't destroy the lives of others."[19]

He always used to guide new teachers, how to teach and how to win hearts of the students. He inspired and motivated large number of teachers in his career as a teacher. He would treat his junior teachers as his friends and showered his love upon them as they were his younger brothers. He would go out of way to find solutions to problems faced by the students and encourage them to read text books. He would insist about all round development of the students.[20] Prof. Sushil Kumar talks about his nature of going out of way to help others—"I came back to Prayag after getting post-doctoral degree from America. I needed money to carry out research. When Prof. Rajendra Singh came to know about it, he stopped me one day in university corridor and said, "We have sanctioned 10,000 rupees for the research. If you need more in coming times, please let me know."

Padmakar Mishra writes via an email, about an incident that Rajju Bhaiya shared with him about Prayag University. Students of the hostel used to bring gifts for their very dear teachers. Rajju Bhaiya told them with love, "Have you paid any attention to some of the self-respecting brothers of yours who are struggling hard to study without any resources? Can you support them in some way without hurting their self-pride? When you get a shirt stitched you can get one more as a gift for your friend who has only one shirt. This way, he used to teach lessons on sensitivity and views about life while teaching his subject."

Though he was such an impressive and popular professor, he was increasingly focused on Sangh work. Therefore, he refused promotions at various times when opportunities were offered. We find one example in his audio memoirs—

"Because of my warm relations with the students, Vice Chancellor Shri Tarachand told me, "I hear that you have excellent relations with the students. People listen to your views and accept them. If you take up the job of Proctor of the University, wouldn't it be great?" I told him, I have special relations with a typical kind of students, therefore whatever decisions I will take, people may connect them to my political and cultural views. So, I can help you in this work, but I cannot become Proctor."[21]

Prof. Sushil Kumar, Head of the Science department of the Prayag University spoke very touchingly about Rajju Bhaiya's life as a teacher and his personality, "I can say from my clear conscience that I did not see any blemish in Rajju Bhaiya in my entire life. He had no shortcomings that we see in ordinary human beings and that are taken as normal human frailties. We learned from his life, what kind of devotion one needs to have for any work that one takes up."[22]

Due to his affectionate behaviour like an elder brother and his readiness to always help students in the initial years in the university, students began calling him 'Rajju Bhaiya' instead of 'Sir'. This is how Rajendra Singh became 'Rajju Bhaiya'. His journey as a successful teacher and his growth as an excellent kaaryakarta began during this period.

References

1. Vichar Pravaah, commemorative issue, p. 16
2. Devendra Swaroop, Gomant Shakti, 10 April, 1998 issue
3. Rajju Bhaiya's audio Tape 1 B
4. Ravi Iyer, personal conversation, 16 October, 2013 (Ravi Iyer was joint convenor of HSS)
5. Audio file 1 B, op cit
6. Shridhar Damle, conversation on telephone, 22 October, 2013
7. Audio file, 1 B, op cit
8. Vichar Pravaah, op cit, p. 88
9. Audio file, 1 B, op cit
10. Panchjanya, 27 July, 2003
11. Dr. Narendra Kumar Singh 'Gaur', Vichar Pravaah, op cit p. 27

12. Prof. Jagmohan Singh Rajput, Vichar Pravaah, op cit, p. 78 (former director NCERT)
13. Virendra Kumar Singh Chaudhary, Vichar Pravaah, op cit, p. 5
14. Padmakar Mishra, email, 23 October, 2013
15. Dr. Rajendra Agrawal, Vichar Pravaah, op cit, p. 48
16. Audio file, 1 B, op cit
17. Prof. Vishwambhar Dayal Gupta, Vichar Pravaah, op cit, p. 73
18. Prof. Gopal Krishna Pandey, Vichar Pravaah, op cit, p. 71
19. Prof. Vishwambhar Dayal Gupta, op cit
20. Prof. N.K. Bishnoi, Vichar Pravaah, p. 75
21. Audio file, 1 B, op cit
22. Prof. Sushil Kumar, Vichar Pravaah, op cit, p. 67

□

3

Life dedicated to Sangh

The two dimensions of Rajju Bhaiya's life – of becoming a teacher and dedicating his life to the society through Sangh, ran nearly parallel for 23 years. His time and contribution to Sangh kept on growing during this period. His natural habit of taking care of everybody around him was also part of his Sangh work. In his words, his earlier 3-4 years of life went along joyfully. The routine of meeting new people regularly, connecting them to shakha, touring neighbouring villages and the entire district went well in initial years. He talks about his life as a teacher and increasing maturity and understanding as a Sangh kaaryakarta,

"I got to learn and know a lot in the initial years. Being a senior in age, I had to learn everything very fast. I gained experience in work too. I got a chance to learn as I visited the neighbouring areas. I was appointed as the Nagar karyavaah (city secretary). Prayag had 3 shakhas. When 1-2 shakhas were established in the district too, I was appointed Jilaa karyavaah (district secretary). This was my achievement in the first year from Sangh point of view.

Being a Sangh kaaryakarta, I used to visit student hostels. I would talk to new students, and help students if required. I used to solve students' difficulties. Therefore, I became very popular as a teacher who worried about students and solved their problems with affection. I used these relations to bring students to shakha. Out of 100 students, 20-25 students would join shakha." Rajju Bhaiya, in his own inimitable humble and humorous manner says, "People talk big about the help I gave. Yes, I used to help a little bit, but I didn't really help in a big way. A teacher would hardly have that much money!"[1]

However, it is a fact that right from his first salary to his last moments of life, helping people around him, helping different organisations to the best of his ability, that too with humility and without making any show of it remained a part of his dignified personality.

It was usual for people, known and unknown, to walk into his bungalow 'Anand' in Civil Lines in Prayag. Once in a while it so happened that they walked away with some objects from his house. If his mother got upset, Rajju Bhaiya used to say, "Bear with cheating. But, never hurt a heart." Living life smilingly, bearing the pain of being cheated had become a part of his mental makeup.[2]

Bharat Singh 'Saadhak' shares his experience about Rajju Bhaiya's compassion, "I went to Musafirkhana, a tehsil of Sultanpur district as prachaarak. I fell sick there. Doctors told it was TB. Respected sanghchaalak Shardaprasad Dwivedi took me to Rajju Bhaiya in Prayag. My treatment began in a room of his bungalow. I would get food cooked by respected mother and two students of the university would come to clean my clothes and utensils. I was cured slowly due to this affectionate care. During this time his father Shri Balveer Singhji, taking a walk with me once, asked me, "Bharat, do you know for whom I have built this bungalow?" I said, "No". He said, "For your Rajju Bhaiya. He is a lecturer in university and gets good salary. But he spends all his money on young people like you for their security and well-being. So, how will he build a home for himself? That is why I have built this bungalow for him." We know that Rajju Bhaiya donated even this bungalow for Sangh office later.[3]

Shri Devendra Swaroop, tells something more about this episode. It tells us about his compassionate nature and his father's big heartedness. During those days, family of Adv.

Virendra Pratap Singh also used to reside with their family as their bungalow next to their house was under construction. Their children were much younger at that time. Mother got worried that the children may be exposed to risk if kept in company of a TB patient. She shared her concern with Rajju Bhaiya's father. When Rajju Bhaiya returned from his tour, father asked him, "Rajju, can't Bharat be taken care of in a sanatorium?" Rajju Bhaiya told him, "I have tried at many places but there is no vacancy in any sanatorium. There is waiting list there too. I will take him there as soon as I get a place." Father then told him, "Is not possible that we take a separate room for Bharat Singh and arrange for his regular nursing?" Rajju Bhaiya responded promptly, "Pitaji, suppose if I had been afflicted with TB, then what would you have done?" Father understood the feelings immediately and said, "It is ok, now Bharat Singh will stay here in the outer room. I will take his care personally. This door will remain shut. No child will come from this side."[4]

A swayamsevak of Prayag who worked with him for long tells this story. "It is an incident of 1945 Sangh Shiksha Varg. I fell seriously sick. It turned out to be scarlet fever. There was an injection that was very costly and difficult to get. People searched for it in different cities, but it was not available. But Rajju Bhaiya would not give up so easily. He kept his search on. Finally, the injection was procured by Shri Ramkrishna Sevashram from England. He kept awake for three days and night taking my care." Senior Sangh workers talk about his compassion for swayamsevaks and affection. This swayamsevak tells us that a prachaarak wished to give up his prachaarak life and return home to serve his unwell parents and to take care of two younger brothers' studies. Rajju Bhaiya not only relieved him from his responsibility but remembered his difficulty. He arranged a teacher's job in a school for him.[5]

In the earlier years, it was not easy to import materials due to India taking part in World War with British. Therefore, laboratory materials like photographic plates had to be made by the students and department in-house. Thus, not much research could be done. Then he decided that he will focus on Sangh work and teaching, not on research. And he went on to become one of the favourite professors who took different subjects easily.[6]

He began devoting entire spare time after teaching hours into Sangh work. Rajju Bhaiya reminisces that he had learnt public speaking on Sangh related topics as he was invited to many RSS programmes because of him being a university lecturer. During this time, Shri Bapurao, Bhaurao, and Pandit Deendayal Upadhyaya played a key role in imparting knowledge about Sangh. Ramchandra Gokhale also used to be in touch, though all of them were prachaaraks in different areas.[7]

Apart from these Sangh prachaaraks, Rajju Bhaiya developed close relations with many families. It was a quality of Rajju Bhaiya that even in those days of difficult communications, he could keep in touch with his old colleagues, friends and students over long periods. Rajju Bhaiya believed firmly that distinguishing feature of Sangh is its family relations and he could experience this wonderful quality many a times in his life. He remembers a few incidents of those days—

"Annual festival of Azamgarh shakha was considered a well organised programme. This festival used to see good number of lawyers and court employees attending it. A senior young lawyer Shri Pratap Narayan's responsibility was to take care of the shoes in full Sangh uniform. He would pick up the shoes and arrange them in proper order when people took them off to sit down on mats. A colleague passed a remark, "You have got a good job." He answered, "Bhagwan Shri Krishna also got this responsibility during the Yagya conducted by Yudhishthira. Now I have got this opportunity." No job is big or small in RSS, members do whatever responsibility is given to them with full alertness.

Once, when Shri Shriprakash came for an RSS festival, he saw shoes arranged properly in lines. He was so happy that he remarked, "I have seen people sitting in disciplined lines, but never saw shoes in proper line. An organisation that can do this, can surely instill discipline."[8]

Shri Anant Ramchandra Gokhale used to be regional prachaarak at that time and he was senior colleague of Rajju Bhaiya. He highlights another quality in Rajju Bhaiya. He says, "I had gone from Prayag for a programme to Kanpur. While chatting, I told him that Shree Guruji can count number of swayamsevaks sitting in front of him while he gives his lecture even if they number around 1,000-1,500. In the next year's state level meeting when he met me, he told me that he also practised this art and he too can count the number of people sitting in front of him and when the chief instructor (mukhya shikshak) comes to tell me the count, I am more or less correct. Such was the talent of Rajju Bhaiya. He would collect information and also share information while chatting with people."[9]

Keeping expenses low, to keep full account of funds of the society and Sangh, using them carefully was a part of his nature. He would not only follow this conscientiously but insist on others too to be as careful till the end of his life. In 1946, Devendra Swaroop went to receive Rajju Bhaiya when he went to Ballia for his Sangh tour. He looked for him in first class, then second class and finally in interclass. But then he saw him coming out of third class with his prachaarak jhola (cotton bag) on his shoulders. He had booked a second-class ticket for Rajju Bhaiya's return. Rajju Bhaiya got him to return that ticket and gave his own money to book a third-class ticket. He tells us that he always used to spend out of his pocket from his salary for all his travels. During travels he preferred low-cost railway platform food rather than trouble swayamsevaks to bring home cooked food, though this was the norm during that time. He knew good and cheap eating place at different railway stations and bus depots. He would contribute whatever was saved from his salary, to Guru Dakshina. When he was operated upon for prostrate, he bore the entire expense and refused to accept it from Sangh.[10]

Sangh work was progressing in a big way in 1946-47. In 1947, Sangh Shiksha Varg was held in Prayag and Faizabad. The attendance in each was around 600 each. When number of shakhas increased to 30-40, he needed motorcycle to move around. Rajju Bhaiya tells, Pitaji (father) had one condition, "Drive motorcycle carefully and with less speed," and gave him a motorcycle. That very year there was a big accident. As Rajju Bhaiya put it, without falling you can't learn to drive![11]

Looking at his work, it was decided to increase his responsibilities. He says, "That year something important happened. Guruji called me and told me that Andhra needs a state level prachaarak and we have selected Bapurao for it because his English is good. Who will take care of Prayag? If you can give 10-12 days in a month, you can take up this responsibility. I agreed to fulfil the responsibility and I was appointed prachaarak for Prayag Vibhag."[12]

When Rajju Bhaiya was Vibhag prachaarak of Prayag, he met lots of people, came in touch with some outstanding personalities. Rajarshi Purushottamdas Tandon's son used to study with him. He met Lal Bahadur Shastri in his house. He met Acharya Kripalani in Congress office. If there was a programme in Anand Bhavan, he would meet leaders like Rajagopalachari and Sitharamaiyya. Relations can sour because of difference in viewpoints, but not in his case. He went to Anand Bhavan where he heard Netaji Subhashchandra Bose. According to him, Netaji had an effulgent character and speech too used to be intellectually satisfying. It was in his nature to have good relations with many leaders of the Congress.[13] Rajju Bhaiya describes atmosphere around that time—

"Though the nation was moving towards the partition of the country after 1946, we believed that Gandhiji will not allow this to happen as he always sides with the Truth. He has said that Pakistan will be built upon his dead body so he will definitely follow the path of truth. But Congress was in a hurry to get power. We felt that a few Congress leaders are keenly interested in gaining power, they may not take part in satyagraha. But we believed in Gandhi. We felt that even if Congress did not go along in satyagraha, Sangh swayamsevaks will surely do this as it was a question of life and death for them. We felt that Congress and Sangh could work together and be able to preserve the unity of this land even as we gained independence. But unfortunately, Congress passed such a resolution and it received approval right in front of Gandhiji. Swayamsevaks were deeply pained. Congress created an atmosphere that those who were opposing partition were opposed to independence too. Congress has the monopoly of independence struggle. Congress got a bad name because it agreed to partition due to hunger for power."[14]

It was a responsibility to rescue people who were suffering due to partition. Atmosphere was full of anger. Sangh work had increased hugely during these days as it was felt that we will have to go to jails for independence. This expansion slowed down due to these reasons. This period of 1947 was full of such incidences. It had huge impact on the nation, such was this decisive year.[15]

Rajju Bhaiya's views on education were well crystallised. He had presented his views on different occasions while on tours during 1945 to 1952. His view was that education should be within easy reach of people till middle level. It should be free and compulsory in the long run. Syllabus too should be such that when a student finished his school level education and jumped into the practical world, his heart should be brimming with independent courageous thoughts and full of pride.[16]

About Swadeshi industry, he felt that they could be made strong only with competition inspired by mindset based on consumers' requirements. If our feeling of swadeshi gives some support to local industry, then they could face competition with regards to pricing and quality in coming times.[17]

Rajju Bhaiya enjoyed sports and music too. He used to play violin. But, as his devotion to Sangh increased, these hobbies got left behind gradually. He has not even talked of his hobbies in his own audio memoirs. But, Advocate Yateendra

Singh of Prayag tells us, "Rajju Bhaiya used to play squash and tennis in earlier days in university. Later he began discussing tennis more. Whenever he found time, he would go to watch big games of tennis in Prayag. Ilie Nastase was playing in a match once. He asked me, "Why does Nastase use top spin so much?" I answered, "It is his practice. His ball drops only after clearing the net." He then explained to me how it happens as per Bernoulli's principle. Then he also explained how the ball swings in cricket and in football and also explained how airplanes fly.

...Tokyo Olympics of 1964 was on. One day, while reading newspaper, he said, "Have you noticed something? Why is 100-meter race time more than the 100×4 relay race? How is it possible?" I thought there is some printing error and checked other newspapers. They had the same data. Then he explained to me that maximum time is lost in reaching the peak speed, that is, in initial 15 meters. In relay race, baton is exchanged after 15 meters run therefore it saves time."[18] Sheshadri Chari also noticed his deep knowledge of sports. He used to keep track of the players and their scores. He used to study every subject from a scientific perspective."[19]

Yateendra Singh tells us that he used to ask lot of questions and was keen about solving riddles, that too related to science. Some years back when the rumours of Shree Ganeshji's statue drinking milk spread all over the country, he explained that there was no miracle in it. It was not. It is possible due to surface tension. He also said, "God cannot be so merciless that he would drink so much of milk while millions of children go to sleep without a drop of milk."[20]

References

1. Audio file, 1 B, op cit
2. Dinesh Kumar, Vichar Pravaah, op cit, p. 40
3. Bharat Singh Sadhak, Vichar Pravaah, op cit, p. 41
4. Panchjanya, 27th July, 2003
5. A swayamsevak of Prayag, Vichar Pravaah, op cit, p. 32
6. Audio file, 1 B, op cit

7. Audio file, 1 A, op cit
8. Tap 1 A, op cit (Shri Shri Prakash was a freedom fighter and a politician who was part of government many times. He was ambassador in Pakistan, and Governor of Assam, Madras and Bombay states of that time
9. Anant Ramchandra Gokhale, Vichar Pravaah, p. 55
10. Devendra Swaroop, Panchjanya special homage issue, 27th July, 2003
11. Audio file 1 A, op cit
12. Ibid
13. Ibid
14. Ibid
15. Ibid
16. A swayamsevak of Prayag, Vichar Pravaah, op cit, p. 35
17. Ibid
18. Adv. Yateendra Singh, Vichar Pravaah, op cit, p. 85
19. Sheshadri Chari, Vichar Pravaah, op cit, p. 7
20. Adv. Yateendra Singh, op cit

□

4

Moulding of personality in the hands of senior prachaaraks

Rajju Bhaiya was a brilliant student and a popular, successful teacher. He was growing in Sangh also due to his outstanding work. But he always remained in humble learning mode. He kept learning from everyone who could teach and imbibed those learnings in his life. According to him, there were some Sangh kaaryakartas and prachaaraks who left deep imprint on him. He learnt a lot from them and absorbed knowledge and philosophy of Sangh in his awakened intellect.

A few of his words about the Sangh prachaaraks and workers who taught him a lot and inspired him are quoted below. I am presenting them as it is without any of my own remarks. People who knew him will remember him as they read these words and those who didn't know him would come to understand his personality better. We will be able to understand the hard work and tapasya of the first-generation RSS prachaaraks to some extent.

"When I joined Sangh, **Bapurao Moghe** was our Vibhag prachaarak and he resolved many of my initial queries about Sangh. Bapurao belonged to a well to do family of Indore. He was sent to Kashi to become a doctor. But it was mandatory to be a domicile of Uttar Pradesh therefore he couldn't get admission there. So, he chose to do B.Sc. in Biology. Though he met Guruji twice as his room-mate was a swayamsevak, he did not become a swayamsevak at that time. When he went to Lucknow to do his M.Sc., he came in touch of Bhaurao Deoras. Bhaurao had come to do B.A. and Law in Lucknow and also to expand Sangh work. Feeling that being from Maharashtra it may be easier to have company, he sought out Bapurao. Both became fast friends. Bapurao became a swayamsevak then. When family refused to support him after finishing M.Sc., he began taking tuitions along with Sangh work. After all he became a prachaarak and initiated Sangh work in many places."

"He understood the key elements of Sangh and used to give very satisfactory answers to various questions. His conduct was very impressive. He was not a tall person, only about 5 feet. But he used to wear good clothes and impressed people with his conversations. I got in touch with him in 1942 and was close to him till 1946, At that time he was Prayag Vibhag prachaarak before he left for Andhra Pradesh as Prant prachaarak. He had an extraordinary hold over English language. There was not much of Sangh literature at that time, just a short biography of Dr. Hedgewar. But I read many books recommended by him. For example, I read Fundamentals of Unity of India by Dr. Radhakumud Mukherjee. Similarly, '*Bharat ki ekta ke adhaarbhoot siddhant*' (Fundamental principles of inherent unity of Bharat' by Vasudev Sharan Agrawal, 'How they ruined our trade and commerce' by a famous writer of Bengal and '*Hindu Padpaadshahi*' of Savarkar. All these books gave me lot of clarity. It also helped me realise clearly that it is most important to work for Hindu society and that a person can do every other task only after this task is accomplished."

"After this period, we had a new Sangh kaaryalay. University students used to come there around 3-4 p.m. Bapurao had good relations with all of them. All the students were under his thrall. So, people used to come to chat with him to understand various issues and would stay there till 5 p.m. I was also one among them. I had begun teaching in the University and began understanding Sangh work too. I saw from close quarters how tough his life was. But he never talked about it. He understood how to utilise limited means, keep clothes in good shape without ironing and washing clothes well with hands. During initial days, he would make khichdi without much of roti and vegetables. He fell sick twice or thrice during this time. I helped him a little, tried to understand the emotions deep in his heart. I could see how deep his bond was with Sangh. It resulted in big changes in my life too. I couldn't learn much from him about reading and writing, but I could definitely learn the art of speaking and responding to questions, because I would find it difficult to give long lectures in my initial days. I could meet Bapurao during some meetings of Sangh. We also kept in touch through letters."

Though I had met respected **Bhaurao Deoras** once, I came close to him in 1943 during Sangh Shiksha Varg. I heard his lectures there and also had discussions with him. I could see how he made all the arrangements. He used to give lectures on history, historic necessity of Sangh and history from 1857 CE to the period of foundation of Congress in 1885. His lectures used to have strong logic and based on deep study. I used to get his letters on and off that used to provide guidance. My relation with him grew over time.[1]

One of the important jobs of Bhaurao was to explain fine points of Sangh work to prachaaraks. Anant Ramchandra Gokhale had come to Kanpur by then. Vijay Munje had taken up responsibilities in Lucknow. Nanaji (Deshmukh) had come earlier to Agra then Gorakhpur. Bapurao Moghe had been appointed in Lakhimpur Vibhag and then in Prayag Vibhag. Laxmanrao Bhide had also come to U.P. All of them used to receive guidance from Bhaurao. Though there was no major difference in age of these kaaryakartas, one can appreciate Bhaurao's ability to provide guidance. There used to be special programmes for prachaaraks where good positive discussions used to take place. We would also keep in mind that Bhaurao was respected well outside the organisation as he was the person looking after the organisation at state level.

Bhaurao used to travel across the state twice in a year. Once, in the beginning of the year when programmes for the year were being chalked out and at the end of the year when we were making preparations for Sangh Shiksha Vargas. He used to stay at the home of a famous Kashi personality Shri Dattaraj Kalia, though there was Ram temple that was utilized as Sangh Kaaryalay in Godhuliya at that time. The temple belong to Nagpur Prant Sanghachalak Respected Babasaheb Ghatate. Dr. Banerjee was the sanghchaalak of Kashi at that time. All the families used to have close relations. Apart from these families in Kashi there were other families like those of Barrister Narendrajeet Singh in Kanpur, Pandit Shobharam in Agra and Singhals' and our families in Allahabad. He used to guide through letters he wrote to important kaaryakartas. The credit for the foundation of good Sangh work in UP goes to Bhaurao.

Deendayal Upadhyaya also became a prachaarak during his term. After helping him go through various experiences, Bhaurao recognised his talent in writing and independent thinking. He got him to write articles for newspapers and periodicals. It was Bhaurao's motivation that saw him write his first book 'Samraat Chandragupt' and second book 'Jagadguru Shankaracharya'.

He could understand a person quite well. He met people like Hanuman Prasad Poddarji and Prabhudatta Brahmachari regularly to discuss issues to seek their opinions. It was his speciality to recognise peoples' talents and give them the right kind of work. If somebody made a mistake, he would counsel the person, that was his style. But he would not criticise a person there and then as he took care that a person's self-pride should not be hurt. He would explain to the person about his mistake when there was nobody around. He used to study every issue deeply. Therefore, Vanvasi Kalyan Ashram and Saraswati Shishu Mandir used to run with Bhaurao's advice. In politics too, Deendayalji would consult him.

Bhaurao's health deteriorated in the intervening period. Political scenario did not evolve as he had thought. Therefore, he focused his attention on Shishu Mandir from 1954 to 1960. He worked with his good friend Murlidhar Tulsyan in Chhindwara to study how to run a good school. He decided to guide Shishu Mandir to help it run well. There was a huge programme of school children in 1977 after the ban on RSS was removed. Around 12,000 children from around the country took part in it. This programme was organised by Bhaurao. We got to know Babu Jagjivan Ram better during this time.

Bhaurao was afflicted with heart trouble. He had been troubled with this problem two-three times earlier too. He remained an advisor to Shishu Mandir till his last years. His understanding of the working of Shishu Mandir and politics was very good. But he did make a mistake in politics. He made Deendayalji fight an election in 1968 though Deendayalji had refused repeatedly. He was saddened deeply due to this defeat. After the death of Deendayalji in 1968, he took great care of a school and a college running in his memory. Today, Saraswati Shishu Mandir is a big organisation and Bhaurao's contribution played a big role in it's growth.

His full name was Murlidhar Dattatreya Deoras. His father was a government employee and a bitter critic of Sangh. One of Bhaurao's brothers was in police, second one was a doctor and third one was a lawyer. He fervently wished that Balasaheb and Bhaurao too should enhance the dignity of the family with similar achievements. But both of them were one among the best swayamsevaks of Dr. Hedgewar. Balasaheb became a prachaarak and was sent to Bengal while Bhaurao went to Uttar Pradesh. Bhaurao used to stay at Ghatate's Ram temple. His father too used to visit Kashi sometimes to stay there. Bhaurao used to feel disturbed due to his nature and used to avoid meeting him. Once, he came to know that his father was coming to Kashi. He requested a kaaryakarta named Ramkrishna to take his care. He made good arrangements. His father's trip turned out to be enjoyable. Once, Mr. Nene heard him speaking to the priest of the temple – "I have five sons. Three are well settled. Earlier I used to be happy about them and upset with these two. But my respect has increased all over Bharat due to them. My arrangements in Kashi were good because of Bhaurao. Now, I appreciate them a lot." When Nene talked about this conversation to Bhaurao, he was very happy that his father was changing. But he could not talk to his father openly till the end. His mother always encouraged both the brothers.

There is another very senior kaaryakarta of Sangh with whom I have very old relations. He is **Nana Deshmukh**. (When he was recording his memoirs, Nanaji was alive.) Nanaji completed his education with great difficulty. He had lost both his parents. Therefore, he completed his education till Inter with lot of hardships. He used to work for a year and study for one year. He had taken admission to study in Engineering College of Pilani in Rajasthan in 1940 and had already gone there. However, in the same year Dr. Hedgewar died. Babasaheb Apte went to bring him back and told him to stop his education and become a prachaarak; and he accepted it. He stayed in Agra for a few days. Another prachaarak was arranged in Agra, so he was sent to Gorakhpur.

He was very strict with himself regarding discipline. So strict that once he fell seriously sick. He suffered from serious diarrhea. He underwent treatment in Prayag for 2-3 months too. Still dysentery troubled him for long. Finally, he was cured with Ayurvedic medicines.

Nanaji had special knack of becoming friend with famous people and talking to them boldly. He was able to make friends with high-ranking people very easily. He, then, used to discuss issues with them on equal level. He had highly gifted brain and could understand any subject easily. He was offered Industry Ministry in Morarji Desai's cabinet in 1977 in Janta Party Government. However, there was a discussion with him that there should be someone to take care of the organisation too.

So, Nanaji declined the offer and became General Secretary of the newly born party.

Nanaji had very good relations with Bhaiji (Hanuman Prasad Poddar) in Gorakhpur. He started the first Shishu Mandir with his inspiration. Then, he was sent to Bharatiya Jan Sangh. He had warm relations with Shyama Prasad Mukherjee and Deb Prasad Ghosh. If somebody wished to convey something to them, they used to go through Nanaji. Nanaji was very skilled in tackling big personalities. A big leader of Congress, Shri C.B. Gupta used to call him Nanaji Fadnavis. Once he told me, "You people have nominated Raja Saheb of Pratapgarh Ajit Prasad Singh for Rajya Sabha. But, you have only 17 votes, how can you win?" I told him, "Nanaji must have thought of something. Chachaji, let us see what does he do." He actually needed 36-37 votes to win. He got 40 votes and reached Rajya Sabha. C.B. Gupta said, "Your Nanaji is very clever, I have no clue from where he collected these votes!"

Once, K.K. Birla filed nomination for Rajya Sabha. At that time Jan Sangh had 42-43 MLAs in Uttar Pradesh. Nanaji was worried that he might 'purchase' many poor MLAs. He told Birlaji, "You can try your tricks on others, but on Jan Sangh MLAs." He assured Nanaji that he would not do so. Next day, Nanaji told him, "You have not followed your promise." Birlaji said, "It is not true. I have fulfilled my promise." At that very moment, Jan Sangh MLAs were sitting in a room in that bungalow. One MLA came outside and told Nanaji that they had been given 10 thousand each by his manager. Word spread. Everybody gave votes openly. Jan Sangh did not face any loss, and K.K. Birla lost the election.

He had deep knowledge of politics; therefore, he had good relations with Jai Prakash Narayan. He had warm relations with Congress leaders too. But, after experiencing that the country cannot be pulled out of problems with politics, he took 'sanyas' from politics without discussing the decision with anybody; saying that improvement is not possible through politics. Only I received the news. He was asked why he didn't inform anybody. He said, "Because, everybody would have dissuaded me. After retirement from politics he kept focus on rural upliftment and social work. He has aged a lot, but he is still as enthusiast. He still has urge to learn new ideas, new things. He always enthuses people and retains his idealism; therefore, our friendship still thrives.

Such were his relations with important people that he could cut jokes with them. He once told Nani Palkhiwala, "How are you Nani?" Then added after a pause, "I need to keep this information with me so when people ask me, how is Nani; though I have no Nani, I can atleast talk about Nani Palkhiwala's health." Mankikar came close to Sangh after his retirement, he came to Lucknow once. He decided to take a round of Lucknow and do some shopping. When he met Nanaji next day, Nanaji said, "Arrey, you went for shopping but didn't take me along? What do you know about what women are interested in? I could have told you and requested some ladies to accompany you. Next time, take me along." And imagine, this was the first time he had met him!

Whether Ratan Tata, or Nusli Wadia or Nausherwan Wadia – he has friendship with all of them and it is a friendship of equals. He advised me actually to keep away from Delhi after my retirement from Sangh responsibility and to stay in Pune keeping in mind its weather. He has a role in this plan of mine.

Babasaheb Apte played biggest role in creating prachaaraks. I doubt if there is anyone who has contributed more. He was highly dedicated to the goal. He had worked for a few projects, but Doctorji could judge him well and made him head of a small Sangh office, where some students used to stay. He was just a high school pass. But, he self-studied so much that he was wiser and knowledgeable than many highly learned scholars and was immeasurably dedicated to the Sangh objectives. I had taken him to meet my mother to show that there are senior people too in Sangh. He stayed in my house many times. He would ask me to bring books from library every time and would read till one in the night. He had a great liking for reading and insisted on gathering knowledge, an urge that I doubt if I saw in any other person I know. Many people did M.A. in Sanskrit due to his inspiration. It was his motivation that led to intellectual training sessions in Sanskrit in Sangh Shiksha Vargas. Many senior people from different social fields joined Sangh due to his inspiration. Nanaji, and Gokhaleji too became a prachaarak as they could not say no to him.

He went through lot of physical hardships in earlier years of Sangh. So much so, that people who moved with him, would fall sick. When Sangh did not have enough resources in Kanpur, it was normal for him to walk around 20-30 miles each day. He missed the last train once as meeting got extended, so he took along Bhaurao and Deendayalji and walked 14 miles at night to reach the next destination. Due to these tireless physical hardships, his health deteriorated and he left this world early. I felt very sad that old people like me are surviving but he died just around 70 years. He had another speciality – his dress and spectacles. He looked elderly from beginning and this personality of his proved to be useful for Sangh work.[2]

When I was studying, **Pandit Deendayal Upadhyay** was studying law in Prayag, but I was not a part of Sangh then, therefore, I couldn't meet him at that time. Later I found in him a person who was a true example of simplicity who never bothered about himself and had wonderful knowledge about many fields.

Rajju Bhaiya chuckles in his audio memoirs as he talks of one of the incidents. He tells us, "We had invited him to an I.T.C. camp in Faizabad. I found that he didn't have even one clean dhoti. When I pointed this out, he produced another dhoti from his cotton bag. Even that was dirty. Then, he said, "Should I wear this?" and added "People will come to listen to my speech, not to see my dhoti, isn't it?"

He was an original thinker. Therefore, it was a pleasure talking to him and analyse various issues. After he was sent to politics, once Guruji opened up a new subject, and it was our demand too; that it will not be sufficient to create an organisation or a political party. There are two ideologies currently – one is Communism and Socialism where the government has all the powers and an individual follows it as a person has no other option. Second is Capitalism where an individual is everything, there is no worry about the society. We will have to present a third ideology that is in sync with basic nature of Bharat. He enunciated the principle of *'Ekaatma Manav darshan'* (Integral Humanism) in the field of economics and social science explaining how it will take shape in different dimensions of social life. This is what gives a unique identity to Bharatiya Janata Party now. There are many incidents in Deendayalji's life that tell us of his straightforward, simple nature, deep knowledge and his way of conversing with people. He was a person who taught and explained many things in life to people and I too learned a lot looking at him and hearing him.

If there was one person whose life was orderly and disciplined, that was **Madhavrao Deshmukh.** Madhavrao had a very attractive personality. Fair complexion, big moustache twirled upwards, and to top it all, an interesting way of conversing. His talks would attract people. He was a Sanskrit scholar and had knowledge of astrology. His speeches used to have lot of stories and events that would impress any person. I learned Sanskrit quotes and shlokas from him. He was an expert in washing clothes. His clothes always seemed to have been washed by a washerman and pressed though he washed them himself. His letters used to be short but carried deep meaning. His other two brothers, Keshavrao and Yadavrao were also Sangh prachaaraks. Yadavrao became editor of Panchjanya later and also secretary of *Deendayal Shodh Sansthaan* (Deendayal Research Institute).[3]

References

1. Audio tape, 5 A, op cit
2. Ibid
3. Ibid

□

5

Assassination of Gandhiji and ban on Sangh

The period of 1947-48 was very tough for the nation from historic point of view and had long term impact. Partition of Bharat, the terrifying human tragedy arising out of it, killings of thousands, displacement of millions of people that history cannot forget; followed by Gandhiji's assassination, ban imposed on Sangh by Congress out of jealousy, atrocities on the swayamsevaks, extraordinarily peaceful and incomparable satyagraha by the swayamsevaks, lifting of ban on Sangh and then, and in the words of revered Guruji, *'Punahshcha Hari Om'* (making a fresh beginning), re-establishing Sangh work. Such was this period. Many outsiders and Sangh's historians have written about it.

Rajju Bhaiya looked after the Prayag Vibhag of Uttar Pradesh in this period. It comprised of 14 districts under it. In his memoirs he talks more about his personal experiences and experiences of swayamsevaks of this particular part of UP. Even in his young age, his calm demeanour, affectionate but royal personality used to impress swayamsevaks and the Government officers who met him and also the convicted prisoners who were in the same jail. This section is very useful to understand the atmosphere of that time and his committed and duty-bound personality. The following part contains his own memoirs, and also the experiences of swayamsevaks who worked with or under him during those testing times.

'By December, the atmosphere of the nation had become very tense and angry because people who had arrived from Punjab had shared their experiences about horrifying atrocities perpetrated on Hindus in Punjab. It was hair-raising to listen about incidents of killing women, kidnapping them, atrocities on men, women and children. Heads would reel in shock and horror. An urge to take revenge would rise in people's hearts.

In such an atmosphere, a Punjabi young man even tried to attack Gandhiji in January 1948. After this, Sardar Patel had naturally appointed a CID person to keep an eye on people. When people complained about it to Gandhiji, he got this person removed. Thus, anybody could walk into the prayer assembly. Such was the scenario.

Sardar Patel gave speeches in Lucknow and other places during these days that were very important from the point of view of Sangh. He had praised Sangh in these speeches and had said that "it is an organisation with nationalist views that has worked a lot for security of the Hindu society. Therefore, you cannot talk to them with dandaa (wooden staff), we can put them to welfare work for the nation with love and affection." Therefore, we thought that Congress members must also be thinking on same line, that perhaps we could help in progress of the nation.

In this atmosphere, on 30th January, a major incident took place, in which Nathuram Godse killed Gandhiji with bullets during his prayer meeting. Entire nation sank into grief. People did not cook on that day and spent the entire night with a heavy heart. Pandit Nehru gave a highly aggressive and angry speech the next day. This gave me an idea that there is going to be some big action. He announced a ban on Sangh on 4th February. Naturally, at that very moment, I made all the preparations because as a karyavaah I would have to go to jail. Other senior workers too prepared themselves to be imprisoned. When the station officer and the commissioner came home at 8 in the morning, he found me ready. He told me that he would put me in a room in the police station till the time I was shifted to jail. In a little while, 4-5 swayamsevaks too came there. Police van took these 5 swayamsevaks to Naini jail. Because of small numbers, we were kept in a barrack that housed thieves and robbers. Throwing invective and swearing was a common thing there. At 4 in the morning these prisoners shouted choicest and dirtiest abuses on the police personnel. Slowly, as the numbers increased to 60, the superintendent vacated a barrack to house swayamsevaks.

On the very second day after we landed in jail, a prisoner facing life term, who was had become leader of all the prisoners, came to me and told me, "Babuji, don't worry about anything. You will get whatever you need. You will have to pay just 25 per cent over the cost. Because, that is our expense to get these goods and we have to pay in some places. You will get whatever you need for eating or reading." I was quite surprised that one can get everything in jail. Slowly, our numbers in jail increased and we decided that all of us will stay together and also organise programmes in the mornings and evenings to spend our time well. We wrote Sangh poems on paper, drew plans for playing Kabaddi. Soon, the numbers swelled to 200, of which 100 were university students. So, we planned for their studies too. We used to hear different news from outside informing us of kind of allegations being thrown at Sangh and also how members of Sangh were fighting against such accusations."[1]

Swayamsevaks were stuffed into jails after Gandhiji's murder. Rajju Bhaiya who was in Naini jail at that time, was offered 'B' grade. But he was not ready to leave company of swayamsevaks in 'C' grade. His presence worked like a whiff of life-giving fresh air for swayamsevaks in the jail leading a hellish life. Officers and prisoners too were humbled by his simple and dignified conduct. A younger colleague of his, recounts, "I was busy removing insects and pebbles from rice in my barrack. Rajju Bhaiya was inspecting the barrack from one end to another. When he reached me, he stopped. I looked up and he said, "What are you doing? Whatever you get is a prasad from God," and moved ahead. From that day, whatever food I received turned into God's prasad for me."[2]

Shri Shambhunath Dixit says that Congress leaders wished to send Rajju Bhaiya in another cell or in a different jail. But, with a strong feeling that 'we will not allow separation', all the swayamsevaks would form a human chain around Rajju Bhaiya, holding hands; so that if anyone tried to reach Rajju Bhaiya, he would have to walk over their bodies first. When Bhandari, who was supposed to be strict jailer, saw this scene, he refused to listen to Congress leaders' directive and let him stay with us. Environment inside the jail was like that of a Sangh Shiksha Varg. When Ram Nagar prachaarak, Shri Surendra died of small pox, Rajju Bhaiya was crying incessantly for a long time. He used to sing a song and ask us to sing, "Cost of loving the country is our life, let us see who pays the price."[3]

Rajju Bhaiya always considered swayamsevaks to be members of a large family. Shri Ramgopal Sand writes about his affectionate nature thus, "Whenever Rajju Bhaiya's mother came to meet him, she would bring jaggery for him, because sweets were prohibited as per jail rules. Rajju Bhaiya used to distribute this jaggery to all of us. I had lost my job because of imprisonment. After being released after 8 months, Rajju Bhaiya asked me, "What will you do now?" For me there was darkness all around. In those times of hardships, Rajju Bhaiya got me a job of tuition with a friend's family. This allowed me not only to take care of my family but also to do my B.Ed."[4]

Rajju Bhaiya remembers some other incidents of those times, "I specially recall three incidents. First one happened when the Parliament Secretary came to jail barrack to inspect our barrack. He had written a book about Doctorji (Hedgewar) and Nazi techniques. In this book, he had presented a laughable idea that Doctorji had learnt the technique of running RSS from Hitler in Germany. This gentleman was Govind Sahay. His son Krantiveer had been my student. Therefore, Govind Sahay told me, "Now you would have understood how dangerous this organisation is and this must be the organisation that hatched the conspiracy to kill Gandhiji." I told him, "I don't know about it, but you seem to know it. And I am sure matters will be clear in coming days and you will realise that Sangh had no hand in killing of Gandhiji." He said, "Ok, let us see," and walked off.

Second incident is about Commissioner's visit to the jail. We were standing in a line like in a parade. Commissioner began walking in front of the row. He cracked a joke on a teenage swayamsevak, hardly 14-year-old, saying, "So, young man, you have become a leader at such a young age!" He never expected to get a sharp repartee from this teenager. This swayamsevak retorted, "Commissioner saheb, have you seen small red pepper? Is it strongly pungent or big black eggplant?" Officer walked off in a huff. Such brave young boys were working fearlessly during those times.

Mataji (mother) used to come to jail to meet me. Heat had increased by the month of April. We wished to sleep outside. We sent an application. Finally, one copy was sent to Lal Bahadur Shastri and one to Govind Ballabh Pant, who was the Chief Minister. When Mataji asked us, we told her we wish to sleep outside but we are cooped up inside the prison from 6 in the evening. My mother said, "I will meet the leaders." She was very courageous. She went and meet Govind Ballabh Pant and Shastriji and told them, "You have lived in prisons, you understand the issues of prisons. These boys are not going to run away anywhere, then why are you taking such a long time to decide?" And we got permission to sleep outside.

After about 5 months, my mother asked my father, who was the Chief Engineer in U.P. Government, to go and meet his son. While coming to the prison Shastriji and my father were in the same bogey. Shastriji asked him, "Where are you going?" Pitaji (father) told him, "I am going to Prayag, my elder son Rajendra is in jail. I am going to meet him." Shastriji said, "Your son is a senior worker of Sangh. Keep him away from dangerous organisation like Sangh." My father paused for a while and told him, "I do not know Sangh, but I know my son very well. I can say with full conviction that if my son is in that organisation, it cannot be a bad organisation." Then, Shastriji told him, "Tell him to write me a letter explaining me a little about Sangh." When Pitaji told me about this, two-three colleagues and I sat down to write a long letter to Shastriji. 5-6 of us were released within 2-3 days of this letter sent to him. This letter was later published in Panchjanya weekly. Detention period of 6 months was about to end; therefore, others were also being released slowly.[5]

During this time, new ways were found to keep in touch. Prayag used to have a Swadeshi exhibition. We set up a shop selling sweets in this exhibition that sold laddoos made of 'sangeera'. All of us used to collect there every evening. We would hardly purchase sweets there but spend most of the time in discussions. Our swayamsevaks in Lucknow opened a tea shop. Our people would get together there and meet each other as they passed by the place. In this way we could exchange information and instructions.

What did Guruji write in his letter? When is the judgement expected? All such news would be collected from these centres and would reach swayamsevaks in small meetings (baithaks). The judgement was out on 14th November and Guruji reached Delhi. Nehruji refused to meet Guruji. He had a meeting with Sardar Patel. Guruji was never interested in a clash with Congress that could increase distance between Sangh and Congress and then lead to non-cooperation with each other. Therefore, when there was pressure to organise satyagraha, even in that situation, he tried his best to see that such a situation be avoided. Finally, it was decided to offer satyagraha from 9th December."[6]

Just as very few people know about Rajju Bhaiya's deep interest in sports, not many people would know about his courageous and bold nature and his skill in horse riding. Shri Mithilesh Narayan 'Mithilesh' shares his experience about this through an incident that took place during the period of ban before the satyagraha began. "Rajju Bhaiya had an adventurous and courageous spirit. There was a ban after Gandhiji's assassination. A secret meeting had been organised in this regard in Manaskawan Upadhyay khed in the home of Laxmikant Upadhyay. Rajju Bhaiya was to attend this meeting. 10-12 Sangh kaaryakartas began their journey from Manaskawan station on horses with Rajju Bhaiya. The horse that Rajju Bhaiya got was a little mischievous. He behaved well for some time after Rajju Bhaiya was astride on it. But, after some distance he began to neigh loudly and lift his rear legs and try to throw Rajju Bhaiya off every now and then. All of us were very scared. But, Rajju Bhaiya told us in a loud voice, "Don't worry, I know how to tame mischievous horses. If I cannot correct this horse, how can I correct the society?" From then on it was a struggle between the horse and Rajju Bhaiya to win this battle of wits. Rajju Bhaiya took full control of the reins hard and made him gallop through fields. Finally, the horse gave up his games and came under control of Rajju Bhaiya. For the first time, we came to know that he was such a wonderful horse rider![7]

Sangh finally decided to organise satyagrahas across Bharat to force the government to lift the unjust ban. The nation saw satyagrahas across the entire country as per Sangh plan. The format of the satyagraha was very simple. A leader of a shakha would inform the local police station about his and his team's plan to offer satyagraha. As a part of satyagraha, shakha would be organised in an open place or a ground. The satyagrahis would offer Sangh prayer and then full team would offer arrest to the police. The next day this team would be presented before the court.

Rajju Bhaiya tells us about the satyagraha, "Government had expected the satyagraha to die down soon. It had asked for state wise figures. The reports said there were about 30,000 Sangh detainees in jails earlier. They might be demoralised. Therefore, at the most only 3 to 4 thousand people may offer satyagraha. So, the government put its foot down. When the satyagraha commenced, it was but natural that as the Vibhag karyavaah (district secretary), I would lead the first batch. Fifteen swayamsevaks organised shakha in Mohammad Ali Park to offer satyagraha and we were arrested. Similarly, some more groups from Mirzapur from Prayag district and some others from other areas reached the Naini jail, numbering more than 500.

Courts used to be organise in the jails for us. There was a SDM who used to charge us with legal sections. The court proceedings used to be short. He would ask us, "Did you try to organise a shakha at x place on y day?" The leader of the team would say, "Yes, because no charge has been proved on Sangh, but still there is this ban. We have insisted on the truth and as a protest we organised shakha." And a jail term of 4-6 months would be announced. Magistrate was a nice and favourable person. Therefore, he would award jail terms of three months to students from lower standards and not more than 6 months to university students. Only people like me, who were supposed to be leaders, would be awarded higher sentence. In fact, I told the court that I should be given maximum jail term as I was the leader and I prepared them for this satyagraha. I was given 15 months imprisonment. All others got about 6 months. All these people were to be released by May. But, by 26th January, there were around 50,000 prisoners already in jails. In Uttar Pradesh, around 12,000 had entered prisons.

The education minister at that time, Dr. Sampoornanand was a big-hearted man. He talked to the Chief Minister and suggested that they should not waste students' entire academic year and all the students be released. Govind Ballabh Pant agreed to this suggestion. So, government announced via a gazette on 26th January informing that all the students would be released unconditionally. Satyagrah was suspended from 26th January across India to create an atmosphere of goodwill and restart a dialogue with the government. I feel that if the satyagraha had not stopped another 10-15 thousand would have taken part in it. Some people were ready to offer satyagraha again after being released. Thus, government's estimates that only 3000-4000 people would take part were proven totally wrong."[8]

Talking about Rajju Bhaiya's qualities that were worth following, and his affectionate nature, Ramkripal Mishra writes, "This incident is from satyagraha in 1948. All of us were inside Naini Central jail. Rajju Bhaiya would chat with many prisoners routinely. Many of them were influenced by his nature. A prisoner, who was supposed to be the leader of all other prisoners, became a devotee of Rajju Bhaiya. Once, Rajju Bhaiya's watch vanished from his bedside. He made his informers run around. He brought a prisoner to him, beating him on way. Rajju Bhaiya got this prisoner released from the grip of the leader, offered him jaggery and advised him not to tell others about this theft."[9] To continue with Rajju Bhaiya's own narration,

"Numbers decreased in a big way after 26th January. In our barracks, numbers decreased from 500 to 250. So, we tried to organise ourselves in a way so that we could have better facilities and live a little comfortably. But, all of us we're not from the same category. During this time, we also had quarrels with the jail superintendent Bhandari 2-3 times. He separated our group and quality of food deteriorated too. So, the relations which were nice, initially, were soured to some extent. Slowly, many more were released. Finally, only 15 of us were left. We were entitled to 'B' grade. We decided to ask for B grade and live comfortably. There was a big difference in the facilities between B and C class. While C class prisoners were entitled to an allowance of 8-10 annas, B class prisoners would get around 1.25 rupees. Quality of food was better. So, the few that were left in the prison, stayed in this comfort for nearly 3 months and our time in jail was well spent. We would have oil massage, do exercises, play chess and study every day; and time passed quite happily. We also kept receiving news from the outside that talks were going on, or they were stalled. I am not much aware of what happened at that time. I do know that the ban was lifted on 9th July and we were also released."

Rajju Bhaiya reminisces about the days after the release. "We had to do jobs which we had never done normally. Like taking out processions, wear garlands etc. It was done to assure people that ban was lifted and we could begin running shakhas again. We were not habituated to this kind of work, but we had to do it as a necessity. We had to go to public receptions, get garlanded and give speeches in a language which we generally never used."[10]

Rajju Bhaiya was released after five and half months. He kept working till July 1949 as Vibhag prachaarak. He had to face a new problem on being released. In his words,

"When I went back to the university, I came to know that when I was in jail for five months in the first phase, no action was taken as I was under detention. But I had been jailed the second time as I had offered satyagraha. Therefore, the executive council had dismissed me from my job.[11]

I thought that it was good riddance and I could give full time to Sangh work. But, many teachers from the University came to meet me and told me that if University kept throwing people like this then other people too might be dismissed on smallest of pretexts. "You are the people who can fight for such a cause and you should fight." We had a good system in the University. A person could demand for a tribunal in case the person did not like a ruling of the executive council or the vice chancellor. The tribunal would have a representative of the complainant and one of the vice chancellors. I knew a retired justice quite well. I chose him as my counsel and my case was presented to the university. They felt that since the ban was lifted and I had been released, there was no justification for removing me from the job. Therefore, the vice chancellor called me and told me that he would take me back but will not give me my due seniority. I told him that I didn't really need the job. I had been released with honour and the ban too had been removed. Therefore, I should get my due seniority. Only then would I join back. Finally, the university agreed to this too and I was reinstated with due seniority.

Since, I got reappointed after so much of legal battle, it was not easy to resign. But it was my heartfelt wish to stay in Sangh Kaaryalay and learn Sangh work by being full time into it. So far, I was giving only 15 days a month to Sangh work. Therefore, as soon as I was appointed permanently, I took two-year leave from the university and told Prant prachaarak Bhaurao Deoras that he could appoint me anywhere, explaining, "I am free from the university fully for two years."[12]

This is how the terrible period of Gandhiji's assassination, ban on Sangh, satyagraha and lifting of the ban got over finally. And, Rajju Bhaiya's life as a full time worker (Sangh prachaarak) began.

References

1. Audio file, 1 A, op cit
2. A swayamsevak of Prayag, Vichar Pravaah, op cit, p. 34
3. Shambhunath Dixit, Vichar Pravaah, op cit, p. 65
4. Rajkumar Sand, Vichar Pravaah, op cit, p. 30
5. Audio file, 2 B, op cit
6. Audio file, 2 B, op cit
7. Mithilesh Narayan, Vichar Pravaah, op cit, p. 64
8. Audio file, 2 A, op cit
9. Ram Kripal Mishra, Vichar Pravaah, op cit, p. 54
10. Audio file, 2 A, op cit
11. Ibid
12. Audio file, 2 B, op cit

□

6

Formal beginning of the life of a prachaarak

Respected Bhaurao appointed Rajju Bhaiya as the Lucknow Sambhaag (division) prachaarak. Nanaji Deshmukh points out that Rajju Bhaiya's decision to become a prachaarak, leaving aside all the attractions of a comfortable life was a little different from other prachaaraks. He belonged to a very well to do family. He was habituated to all the facilities and luxuries of life. He was a lover of music. Violin was his favourite instrument. He used to play violin well. But he left all this and devoted all his energies with full commitment for Sangh work. It was a speciality of his character that he could work with people and co-ordinate activities well. He could recognise qualities in his fellow beings and judge well where a person could be of good utility. His strongest quality was that there was no trace of ego in his personality or in his conduct.[1]

Rajju Bhaiya reminisces about this new kind of life—

"Respected father held the post of Chief Engineer of Uttar Pradesh at that time. Bhaurao had given some good thought about my appointment in Lucknow. I had three Vibhags under me – Lucknow, Sitapur and Prayag. Lucknow Sambhaag (division) consisted of these three. The other sambhaags were being looked after by Bapurao, Laxmanrao and Deendayalji during those days. After coming to Lucknow, I stayed at home and asked Pitaji, "Can I stay at home and carry on Sangh work?

I hope you have no objection." He told me with a laugh, "I have no objection. But this is a government house. There is no problem if you work from here and meet your friends. But, do not organise meetings in this house." I agreed to his condition.

Both the kaaryalayas (offices) in Lucknow had been sealed. Because, these were government allotted places and they were newly allotted to other people. Sangh had no place for its office. I was given the responsibility of finding a place for Sangh kaaryalay (office). The Commissioner, Chaudhary Harpal Singh, was a very good friend of Pitaji. I went to meet him and told him, "You have allocated our kaaryalay to someone else and we have been left with no place. What should we do?" He then told me, "You go and find a vacant house. I will allot it for your work. It is your right. Your kaaryalay has been allotted to somebody else by mistake." We began the search for the kaaryalay and finally found a good place. Rent for the place too was not very high. It had been allotted to a police officer who had been transferred. We gave this information to Harpal Singh. He told me, "Yes, this is a very good place. Our minister Guptaji too had asked for it. Can I ask him once?" I told him, "This is not right. You had agreed that when we find a good place you will allot it to us." He said, "But, Guptaji will be upset." I told him, "Why are you afraid of his unhappiness? You are not doing anything wrong. What will Guptaji do? At the most, he will transfer you to Hamirpur. He cannot demote you from the post of Commissioner and make you 'patwari'. You officers should work with courage." He was a nice, straightforward person so he told me," Okay then, bring the papers, I am going to allot it to your name immediately. I will bear with any consequences." This is how the first Sangh kaaryalay in Uttar Pradesh came up and all of us moved into it. Even today, this kaaryalay is useful for different Sangh activities."

I had three Vibhaags and 14 districts under me. I got very good experience in practically working there on the field. Jay Gopal was a very good practical prachaarak there. Mahesh, Bhalla and Ramprakash Gupta (he was UP Chief Minister when Rajju Bhaiya recorded his memoirs) were the Vibhag prachaaraks. I learnt a lot while going to different programmes with them and interacting with kaaryakartas. And I could also stay with my father at home. I stayed in Lucknow till the end of 1951 and beginning of 1952. Therefore, I came in good contact with many new people in engineering department. Due to these good relations, we could help get back jobs of many people who had been removed from their jobs due to the ban.

I returned to Prayag in 1951 and began working in the University again. I was entrusted with an additional responsibility. The Indian constitution had just been accepted and first General Elections were to take place in 1952 January or February. Pandit Deendayalji was given the responsibility of finding right people for Bharatiya Jan Sangh in Uttar Pradesh. I was asked to think about it and find out such names. I placed as much information and suggestions that I had about the state to Pandit Deendayalji.

The first idea put forward was to pitch great Sant Prabhudatta Brahmachariji against Pandit Nehru to oppose Hindu Code Bill. All the kaaryakartas cooperated very well in this regard though we had very limited resources. Brahmachariji's personality was such that nobody could behave improperly with him. Secondly, he wished to bring to people's attention that if Congress did not have a right to change laws about Muslims and felt that it had no right to tinker with Christian laws, then who gave it the right to change laws pertaining to Hindus? They should have discussed the matters with scholars of Hindu Dharma. Election was fought on this issue. Pandit Nehru, at one time had said that I will not visit my constituency even once, I don't need to. People know about my work. But, because of Brahmachariji he had to visit every assembly seat within his constituency and address meetings. He had to admit that he had no intentions of designing a Hindu code bill and the Parliament that was to be elected by the people would decide about it. This is the story of that dare to challenge, or success of our bold approach to put forward our views in front of the society."[2]

Rajju Bhaiya was appointed as Uttar Pradesh state karyavaah (secretary) in 1952. He did his second year Sangh Shiksha Varg in 1954 in Bareilly. Bhaurao Deoras had returned home. So Rajju Bhaiya was designated as Uttar Pradesh State prachaarak too till 1957.

Sanghchaalak of Kashi prant (a part of political state of Uttar Pradesh), Dr. Rajendra Agrawal, gives an example of open hearted and compassionate nature of Rajju Bhaiya. "Picnic of Dehradun students with Rajju Bhaiya proved to be a landmark programme. It took place in Manaksiddh Temple. Rajju Bhaiya was to arrive at Dehradun bus depot and I went to pick him up. He came out of the bus. I had a very lean physique. Looking at me and my bicycle, he asked, "Would you be able to carry me on this cycle?" I blurted out, "No, Rajju Bhaiya." He said, "Ok, then sit in the front." With me on the cross-bar, he cycled me double seated for 15 kilometers to Manaksiddh temple. He sang Sangh songs, narrated stories and experiences all the way." [3]

In 1957 Rajju Bhaiya did his third year training in Nagpur. He was in a team that was being trained by Shri Sudarshanji. Sudarshanji recalls, "He was State Prachaarak, but still he was very keen to learn everything and would prepare well. Why did he need to do preparations? But his nature was that one must learn whatever one is learning, with full focus. Just as he was an excellent teacher, he was also an excellent student."[4] Incidentally, Sudarshanji went on to become fifth Sarsanghchaalak after Rajju Bhaiya relinquished his post as Sarsanghchaalak.

Rajnath Singh 'Surya' talks about his all-encompassing personality. "Despite difference of opinion, there would be hardly anybody who had not felt his compassionate and affectionate nature. Everyone would be impressed by his intellectual depth and his unconditional love for all. Incidentally, I was fortunate to be in his company during 1957

Nagpur training camp. He was Prant prachaarak and I was a student. Despite himself being a trainee, he would keep a sharp eye over the trainees from Uttar Pradesh. One day, we were chatting before entering the dining hall with our utensils and then went ahead and sat in the dining row. It was the normal routine every day. But, when we sat down, we realised that we were sitting in a row opposite to where swayamsevaks from South India were sitting. We realised that there was a lesson for us from Rajju Bhaiya. We used to feel a little reluctant to sit with them due to their eating style and used to avoid sitting with them. Rajju Bhaiya cleared our minds without saying a word."[5]

By the time of 1952 General Elections, the political atmosphere in the country had changed a lot. Though Rajju Bhaiya never took direct part in politics, he was quite aware about it and had deep understanding of politics. It is but natural that politics will cross your path somewhere or the other when you are working in social organisations. It is not easy to keep oneself aloof from party politics. Therefore, where the situation demanded, he would work like an unattached Karmayogi and moved away from the situation as soon as that necessity was over. Let us hear about the situation of that time in his own words—

"Elections of 1952 and period following it proved to be very important from the point of view of the nation. Pandit Nehru had become the most powerful person in the nation. After independence, Gandhiji had said that Congress should be dissolved and people should form their own parties as per their ideological inclinations. This was absolutely true. Congress was a platform where people of every political view came. Leaders from Hindu Mahasabha to leaders with Communist views would come on this platform. This platform had Krishna Menon and it had Dange too. It had Malaviyaji and it had Rajendra babu too. Thus, it was just a platform; and people like Jai Prakash and Lohia had thought about forming a party on ideals of socialism. They formed a separate bloc of Congress leaders with a more pragmatic approach and Communists moved into different direction. Sardar Patel had formed a labour union, INTUC, and in a clever move, it was separated from Congress. But Congress wished to exploit the goodwill and the name used for the movement to free India and profit from it. Therefore, they did not agree to Gandhiji's advice.

Many people had also begun to think after independence that Sangh too should form a political party. Guruji was not in favour of this idea though Congress attitude towards Sangh during and after Gandhiji was not good. Still, he felt that Congress will remain a large political platform in the country and there may be a time when Sangh swayamsevaks could work with Congress.

Such a condition did appear possible when Purushottamdas Tandon became Congress President. He had become President of the party despite Pandit Nehru's opposition but due to Sardar Patel's wish. When Nehruji was out of India, Congress working committee passed a resolution that was supported by Sardar Patel. Sardar Patel asked the members, what was their view about Sangh. People said, "Yes, it is a good organisation. We should take in their members." "Should they be permitted to join Congres or not?" Every delegate said, "They should be." Thus, the resolution ws passed. But, when Pandit Nehru returned from his foreign tour, his friends told him that Purushottamdas Tandon, Patel and their collegues had passed the resolution. They expressed their worry that if RSS people were to join Congress, they would slowly take control of Congress. Therefore, RSS people should not enter Congress. Unfortunately, during this time, Sardar Patel passed away. Purushottamdas Tandonji was harassed so much that he left Congress with a heavy heart. Even Kripalaniji preferred to leave Congress.

Thus, after Gandhiji's assassination most senior leaders had left Congress; while Sardar Patel had left this world by this time. Therefore, there was nobody who could stop

Jawaharlalji, and it was clear that he would do as he wished. He even got a resolution passed that the person who would be the Prime Minister, will also be the President of Congress. This is a strange idea that two very important posts can be managed by one person. Congress was now in his hands completely and turned in any direction that he wished it to.

I recall two incidents clearly. Vishwanath Das had been Odisha State President of Congress and was the Governor of Uttar Pradesh too. His son Harihar Das had studied with me till B.Sc. So, I had friendship with him as well as Vishwanathji. I went to meet him once. I asked him, did Congress have not even one member who could have reasoned with Nehruji that Hindu Code Bill was unjust? When we are not making any changes in religious matters of Muslims and Christians, nor changing their succession rights; then how can we change laws for Hindus without asking any Shankaracharya or religious scholars? He then told me that he had raised this issue in Congress working committee once. Nehruji interrupted him and told him that people like him had no place in Congress. People like him should join Ram Rajya Party.

Second incident was about Congress decision to introduce co-operative farming. Nehruji was a great supporter of this idea because Russia was implementing co-operative farming. But Chaudhary Charan Singh had done in-depth study of the topic. He had data about how farming is done in cooperative and government farms, how is the productivity there. How the quality of produce is much better in personal farms because farmer loves his land. And, in India where there is shortage of land, cooperative farming is not a good idea for agriculture. He had all the data on this issue. Therefore, when proposal of cooperative farming was mooted in Congress, he was very sure that he would be able to oppose it with his factual arguments and change the policy. He had talked to 5-7 people about it. When he began speaking about it in the meeting, Nehruji interrupted him and said, "Does anybody else wish to express his views?" Nobody rose. He immediately got voting done and stopped Chaudharyji's speech. He was stopped as if his views had no relevance.

Thus, it became impossible for Congress to be run except by Nehruji's dictate. It was proven much later that the friends and advisors of Nehru gave him wrong advice or just agreed to whatever Nehruji thought. All those people harmed our nation in a big way. One can think of Sheikh Abdullah, V K Krishna Menon and Pratap Singh Kairon etc. in this regard.

By 1951, only yes men of Nehru were left in Congress. At this time many swayamsevaks felt that it was possible to create their own space in politics. This view carried lot of weight in Delhi and regions around it. They felt, since Sangh had done so much for Hindus during Partition, it had made a very good place for itself in the Hindu society. Therefore, if they form a party, they could succeed in a big way. Dr. Shyama Prasad Mukherjee had resigned from the Central cabinet due to Nehru's policies for Bengal and had formed a separate party in the name of Bharatiya Jan Sangh. He requested respected Guruji if he could give him some people who had interest in political field. Guruji acceded to his request and at that time people like Pandit Deendayal Upadhyay, Balraj Madhok, Bhai Mahavir, and Vasantrao Oak went to work with him.

Preparations were done with lot of enthusiasm. People had big hopes from Uttar Pradesh, Madhya Pradesh and Rajasthan. But the results of 1952 elections were much against the hopes of our people. Uttar Pradesh gave only two seats. Only four Members of Parliament were elected from all over the country, including prominent names like Shyama Prasad Mukherjee and Barrister Trivedi. Probably around 20-30 members were elected in assembly elections. It was a big shock. But, slowly and steadily this organisation rose on firm grounds by picking up right issues over years. After some years, it could succeed well.

We can say that Sangh work received a setback in 1952 that might be considered bigger than the setback it received after Gandhiji's assassination. A little confusion resulted in serious harm and number of shakhas dropped in Uttar Pradesh in 1952."[6]

He talks about his work in Sangh during this period, "I was given the main responsibility at state level for the Sangh Shiksha Varg in 1952 held in Prayag. I began to work as assistant to Bhaurao Deoras in the state because Bapurao and his senior colleague Deendayalji both went out of UP. Bapurao went to Andhra Pradesh and Deendayalji had become general secretary of Jan Sangh. Bhauraoji worked in UP from 1952 to 1954. He stayed in Chhindwara from 1954 to 1960; and left all the responsibilities on my shoulders. I may not have been able to carry out this responsibility properly, but I had very good colleagues in the state. Madhavrao Deshmukh looked after one 'sambhaag' (division of state), Laxmanrao Bhide looked after another while Vishwanath Limaye looked after the third sambhaag. With such wonderful colleagues Sangh work struck strong roots again. People realised that in independent India, it was as important to organise Hindu society and raise its self-confidence to create a base for politics based on Hindutva, as it was earlier. Respected Guruji used to tour all over the country regularly."[7]

There seemed to be a vacuum at the top in the absence of a senior prachaarak in Uttar Pradesh after induction of Deendayal Upadhyayji into Jan Sangh. There were senior and very high quality prachaaraks like Bhaurao Deoras, Bapurao Moghe, Laxmanrao Bhide and Vishwanath Limaye; but they were from Maharashtra. Rajju Bhaiya filled this vacuum. During his time RSS work spread in cities, towns, district centres and also penetrated in remote areas in villages.

By this time his two year of leave from the University was over and he was managing his responsibility as a teacher and prachaarak with dexterity and intelligence. Prachaarak in Prayag at that time, Veereshwar Trivedi writes about his busy schedules and commitment to his work thus, "Rajju Bhaiya used to be so busy in his round the clock work of inculcating patriotism, discipline and character in the youth through

Sangh that sometimes he would come on his scooter from a Sangh tour, park his scooter in front of the class and walk in to lecture in his RSS half-pant or dhoti."[8]

Rajju Bhaiya could get even difficult work done easily due to his straightforward nature and affectionate relations. Putting forward his views with clarity and firmly was his forte. It didn't matter if the person on the other side was someone junior or a very senior leader. Virendra Kumar Singh remembers, "It is an incident, possibly of 1952. Revered Prabhudatta Brahmachari was running his Gorakshaa (cow protection) movement in Uttar Pradesh. I was the general secretary of the organisation. Revered Prabhudattaji, Rajju Bhaiya and I went to meet the Chief Minister Govind Ballabh Pant. Pantji had great pride and affection for the son of the first Indian Engineer head of irrigation department and Rajju Bhaiya had huge respect for Pantji. When the discussion about Cow Protection legislation began, like an experienced and clever politician, Pantji told him, "Rajju, what do you know about difficulties faced in preparing a legislation? What are the points to be discussed? A law can be made only by taking into account view of all and working out a consensus." Rajju Bhaiya wished to make his point but Pantji refused to budge from his position. Finally, Pantji said, "See Rajju, I am twice your age. When you reach my age, you will understand how to make people agree and create consensus. One can't do it in a hurry." Rajju Bhaiya responded off the cuff, "Pantji, I live my life at twice the normal speed." Pantji laughed aloud listening to this argument and said, "Ok Rajju, you win. We will make a law." And Uttar Pradesh government brought in a Cow Protection law.[9]

He could make anybody his own with his soft spoken and pleasant nature, and everybody thought of him as his own. Whether it was about a possible marriage or about university affairs or questions by swayamsevaks, he would give his opinion frankly; even to leaders of the stature of Purushottamdas Tandon or Ram Manohar Lohia. We can witness many such incidences in his life. This was the reason why everyone respected his opinion.

Period of 1952 to 1960 was very important for another reason too. Rajju Bhaiya had crossed 30 years of age. He had gained good experience of teaching, doing Sangh work on the field and grappling with different situations. He had gained confidence of doing a good job in different situations. He had decided that whenever possible, he would give full time to Sangh work. He was sure that he would not get married and live his present life only.[10] Let us listen to the story ahead in his own words—

"Respected father had returned to Allahabad after retirement. Firstly, he thought of living with his two younger sons. Then, he felt that Prayag was a better place for him and he had many friends there. Designing interiors for people's homes and also get his own house built as per his wishes would keep him pretty busy. I had left Prayag for two years on leave for Sangh work. So, Sangh had called a very well to do lawyer from Banda, Advocate Virendra Pratap Singh to Prayag for Sangh work. He was staying in a house next door to where I used to live. He had set up his legal practice with lot of hard work. When I returned to Prayag, I stayed with him in the old house. Father purchased a new plot and began building a new house. My father did lot of experiments in this new construction and also had many new experiences. He constructed about 5-6 villas in Prayag and supervised many constructions. For a person who had built dams worth crores of Rupees, he got very interested in this work. During this time he was also elected as a member of the Executive Council of Prayag University and had close interaction with the university. Therefore, when I used to go out on tour, he never felt lonely. It took him some time to mix-up with friend circle in Prayag but he began enjoying Prayag.

I had developed good relations with Prabhudatta Brahmachari during elections. He developed excellent relations with Guruji during this time. They also had similar nature, so they used to meet each other with joy and affection. He used to call Guruji his younger brother. Guruji developed good relations with nearly all the good people in UP like Hanuman Prasadji Poddar. During this period Saraswati Shishu Mandirs were also established with Poddarji's help.

Activities grew very fast in education, student and political fields in Uttar Pradesh. Even in the hilly regions, mountainous areas, districts where there was less work, projects and plans were chalked out to expand work. Though Bhauraoji was not in UP for 4-5 years, I used to be in constant touch with him. He used to tour the state once in a while. By 1960, his health improved significantly and he began work enthusiastically again. Guruji then asked me, "Where should he be sent?" I told him, "His state is always waiting for him with open arms. Please send him to UP whenever you wish. I am just managing the situation in his absence." He returned in 1960 and was appointed as the kshetra (regional) prachaarak. There was no concept of kshetra till then. UP and Bihar were organised as one kshetra. Many prachaaraks were sent from UP to Bihar. Number of shakhas in UP had crossed one thousand. Sangh Shiksha Vargas began to have more than 1,000 trainees now. There was enthusiasm all round. We could cultivate good relations with well to do sections of the society too."[11]

In 1962, the attack by China destroyed whatever legitimacy Nehru's rule had. Krishna Menon too lost his job. Wrong decisions of Nehruji began to bear bitter fruits by 1962. Before this happened, Chinese had persuaded Nehruji to raise slogans of "Hindi Chini bhai bhai" and declare that Tibet was a part of China. China sent its troops who walked into Tibet and annexed it. To avoid arrest their religious and temporal head of Tibet, Dalai Lama, had to escape to Bharat and take asylum in Bharat. Tibetans became refugees leaving behind everything. Rajju Bhaiya describes the atmosphere in that period—

'This incident did not open Nehruji's eyes. The popular feeling amongst government and its supporters was that

China will never attack Bharat as it is a socialist country and socialist friends cannot attack another socialist. I recall that our university professors used to talk like this. When Guruji toured Bharat, he clearly said that we have big faith on China but this faith will prove to be wrongly placed. China will attack Bharat one day. My socialist friends told me, "Your Guruji is making such irresponsible statements. China is our close friend; how can he talk about it like this?" I told them, "If Guruji is speaking like this, he will definitely have some evidence." And, that year entire nation and the whole world were badly shaken when China attacked India. They claimed that British had drawn wrong boundaries and they named many areas they claimed were theirs, and attacked us. Because Bharat was not prepared, we lost face badly and lost the war. Hundreds of our people died because our Indian forces had to retreat from many areas. This defeat affected our standing in the world. Communists in our country, named CPI, too faced infamy because they made some comments which were against the feelings of the nation. They went to the extent of saying that let us first find out who attacked first.

Thus, 1962 proved to be a difficult year for Nehruji. He had to drop Krishna Menon. He also suffered physically. He could not speak effectively. He would doze off while sitting with journalists. We could not read any statement from him for many days. His close friends disclosed that he was badly broken. He passed away in 1964. Lal Bahadur Shastri became the Prime Minister. But, before this another incident took place.

For the Republic Day parade of 1963, Nehruji expressed a wish that people from the society should also take part in the Republic Day parade along with Army and para-military forces. The DMO and SP tried hard to find people who would take part in the march past but they could not find the right organisation. They then asked Nehruji, "Can we invite RSS people? Because, everybody is saying 'No'. No one else but Sangh can take part in the march past as others don't even know how to march." Nehruji told the DM, "Sangh members too are patriot and disciplined, what is harm in inviting them for the parade?" On receiving the invitation, around 2500 swayamsevaks took part in the parade with complete musical band of RSS. This was a pleasant surprise for all of us that how these people were allowed to take part in the parade despite Nehruji."[12]

Shantanu Raghunath Shende, a Vidya Bharati prachaarak shared his memories about Rajju Bhaiya treating all workers like an elder brother. It was his first meeting with Rajju Bhaiya. "I am talking about an event that took place in 1962-63. I had gone to Prayag for all India convention of Akhil Bharatiya Vidyarthi Parishad. Our room was in the Hindu Hostel in the university. It was cold winter of January. I was preparing my bed at night after day's programmes got over. At that moment, respected Virendraji and Rajju Bhaiya walked in. It was my first face to face meeting with him. He was Prant prachaarak at that time. He told us casually, "If anyone here has a problem, he can come to my home for sleeping." I raised my hands immediately and he took me home. We went in Virendraji's car. Upon reaching home, Rajju Bhaiya's mother offered me a glass of hot milk and gave a cotton quilt of about 5 kg. I had seen such a heavy quilt for the first time. I woke up in the morning and took glass of hot milk. By this time, Rajju Bhaiya came in and asked me, "Do you know how to cycle?" I said, "Yes." He said, "Come we have to go to shakha and there is a 'bouddhik' there. I reached Azad Maidan shivering in cold. It is the ground where great revolutionary Chandrashekhar Azad was martyred. Shakha had been organised there. Bouddhik was by Rajju Bhaiya himself. I had heard him for the first time. He told us about Sangh ideals, duties of students, vision of Vidyarthi Parishad followed by atomic power and his views about Bharat. I came to know for the first time that he is a scientist and my respect for him doubled. Later I used to receive his guidance in managing Pandit Deendayal Upadhyay Vidyalay and in many programmes."[13]

Rajju Bhaiya faced a serious problem in 1961-62. He tells us, "Though I was quite young, a few of my seniors in the university retired together. So, apart from my teaching, which was of great value to students and was very useful for the university, I was also appointed as the Head of Department. I wished to avoid the responsibility. But my colleagues insisted, "If you were not to take responsibility, the university will suffer. We have great faith in you. How can you leave this department that you have served so well?" I was thinking about leaving the university at that time. Vice Chancellor then suggested that if I could bring in a qualified and able person for the post, he could relieve me. There was an old colleague, who was very senior and who was making a name for himself in America, Dr. Kundanmal Singhvi. I requested him. I evoked his love for the nation, his affection for Prayag University etc. and persuaded him to take up the responsibility. He agreed and returned to Bharat to take up the responsibility. But he lasted only two years. He said, "I have only a few years for research and Prayag is not upto mark for it." This presented a new problem for me. I, then, decided that I shall leave the university anyway.

Respected Pitaji's health was not good. He had talked to Guruji that he might appoint Rajju anywhere but his centre should be Allahabad; and allow him to stay in Allahabad for a few days. But this arrangement did not work for a long time. He left for his heavenly abode at the age of 65 years. I decided at that moment that I will leave the university and work for Sangh for my entire life. My respected Mataji had gone to Roorkee to stay with my brother. She too did not survive for long."[14]

Rajju Bhaiya decided to resign and become a prachaarak formally. He was already living the life of a prachaarak unofficially. But, on Guruji's insistence he stayed back in the university. The reason was that Prayag was to host a huge conference for Vishwa Hindu Parishad in 1966. He was to look after all the arrangements along with Murli Manohar Joshi. He remained in the university till January 1966. He resigned from the university in the same month and was appointed as Saha Kshetra Pracharak for Bihar and UP, the region that was looked after by Bhaurao Deoras. He describes his new responsibility and the work he did during the period—

"Bihar and Eastern UP have similar nature. Therefore, Bhaurao took many of the workers from Eastern UP to strengthen the work in Bihar which was not developed well. After I became assistant to kshetra prachaarak, I called many workers from UP who would be useful in Bihar like Govindacharya and Shankar Tiwari. Bhideji used to look after Sangh work in areas around Nepal. Wonderful workers like Rajabhau Sarvagaonkar created lot of enthusiasm in activities in Bihar. They began making bold plans for districts in Bihar where there were 50 shakhas.[15]

Bhaurao also insisted that people with high standing in the society and who are supporting Sangh work should also be given responsibilities. In 1966, we were introduced to respected Babuaji and we came closer and enjoyed warm relations. He had been appointed as sanghchaalak by Doctor Hedgewar himself. He was the successor of an estate, but he never showed it in his conduct. He was a Hindu Mahasabha worker and had come in contact with Doctorji in 1938-39 when he had gone to Pune for the congregation of Hindu Maha Sabha's youth wing. Then Babuaji came to Nagpur and knew Sangh. He went to jail in many agitations. Savarkarji was to come to Gaya for a lecture in 1942, but he was arrested in Bhagalpur. Babuaji read out his speech then. There are plaques in his home indicating where Savarkarji sat and where Doctorji sat. With due advice from him and Guruji, prestigious members of the society were given responsibilities. I was in touch with him till the year 2000. I had great respect for him. He used to give his entire time for serving the society. His business is now looked after by his son.

I came into contact with Madanlal Agrawal during the same time. I stayed at his home in Dhanbad. I also saw his colliery. Over the years I developed close relations with the family. I was in touch with the family till the year 2000. He did lot of good work for Sangh. He gave full support to Shyam Gupt's Ekal Vidyalay project in the initial stages."

"This way, I developed close affectionate relations with sanghchaalaks and kaaryakartas in all the places. I toured a lot and because of these visits to each district atleast once a month, Sangh work took a sharp upward turn. Atmosphere became positive and enthusiastic as more and more workers joined the Sangh work. Slowly, shakhas in Bihar too touched almost one thousand and work reached to new heights.

During those years, Bhaurao was given the responsibility of the two regions that included Assam, Bengal, Odisha, Uttar Pradesh and Bihar. Major part of his time used to be spent in the three states of Assam, Bengal and Odisha. He used to tour Kashi and Lucknow etc. once in a while. In those regions too his area of interest used to be in the dimensions outside normal Sangh work. For example, he used to take special care of Shishu Mandirs and other activities."[16]

Patron of Vidya Bharati, Shri Jay Gopal believes that he could mould his colleagues the way he wished to even as he took them along with love. He shares a memory, "I had come to Prayag from Kathmandu in the year 1967. By that time, Rajju Bhaiya had gained fame due to his personal qualities as a model teacher and a highly skilled organiser. As we see even today, teachers in universities would get divided into caste groups. I drew Rajju Bhaiya's attention to this problem. I still do not know what he did after this, but the pleasant result was that caste wise groupings ended slowly. Rajju Bhaiya was able to bring them together, including their leaders."[17]

Padmakar Mishra gives another example of Rajju Bhaiya's knack of cultivating good qualities in workers and guiding them in the right direction, "On a late night of a Saturday, Vibhag prachaarak Govindacharya gave me the responsibility of receiving Rajju Bhaiya and take him to Shri Babuaji's residence for rest. Only then, was I supposed to go to the Vijay Niketan Sangh office for sleeping before attending next day's teacher training workshop. I was shivering on the platform due to unexpectedly cold night, waiting for the train. As soon as he got down from the train, he advised me, "There is always a chance of train getting late. You should have kept a blanket and a bed sheet with you. Taking trouble and pain is not sacrifice and not correct. While we were on cycle rickshaw, he asked me some simple questions. While answering I was making noises between the words. He corrected me, "Not speaking in clearly is a sign of old age, avoid this habit." I had key to the room in Babuaji's home where he was to stay. After making proper arrangements, I was about to leave. It was already 2 a.m. He, in a way, gave me a command to sleep there itself. He made a small point, "Just like avoidable pain, unnecessary labour is also not called sacrifice." I was tired and went into deep sleep. He woke me up early in the morning at 4 a.m. to leave for the training workshop. I then realised, that all this activity from station up till that moment was just to teach me three lessons."[18]

Rajju Bhaiya was a wonderful example how a senior should listen to a junior worker carefully, if there was a problem then solve it and create the right environment by putting full faith in him. Jay Gopalji tells another anecdote, "When I was appointed as the Prayag Vibhag prachaarak in 1967, I found that whenever I asked a colleague to do a certain task, he would respond, "First ask Rajju Bhaiya." I resented this attitude. I shared my pain with Rajju Bhaiya one day. Rajju Bhaiya called a meeting of senior workers without telling me anything. In the meeting he told in clear words, "There is no need to seek my advice in matters related to district or Vibhag. Now we have Vibhag Pracharak and district prachaarak. It would be in the best interest of all to listen to whatever advice or opinion these people give. It does not suit this great organisation to put off a decision by taking my name. Only on state or national level issues, you should seek guidance from senior workers." Whatever I had explained to Rajju Bhaiya, understanding my feelings, he gave directions exactly the same way. He did not feel bad at all about my views and did not even bring it up in future."[19]

In words of K.N. Govindacharya, who had joined in as a new prachaarak, "There was no difference between his image and his responsibilities. You could keep tapping it to find some cracks but there was none, his was a concrete personality. He was a living ideal of life-long dedicated practice. Self-abnegation was the specialty of his personality. He used to teach from life itself, not by simply telling. I reached Patna in 1966 as a prachaarak. Rajju Bhaiya came on a tour after a few months. He found that I was not as natural with celebrated personalities as with students. I would feel inadequate and thought how can a 22–23-year-old worker like me explain Sangh to them? Before leaving, he told me that next time he came I should seek appointment of some famous people in different social areas and be with him when he met them. Next time, when he came, he took me to meet an industrialist, a body builder, a professor and an editor of a newspaper. He told them about Sangh work, adding some things of interest to them and helped them understand better. All of them gladly showed readiness to do something or the other for Sangh. At the end of the day, he explained to me, "If we take interest in people, they come closer to us, they understand Sangh and then also become swayamsevaks; not just by speaking with them." Thus, he explained to me the key quality of a good organiser with practical experience. I also understood Sangh's way of improving the capacities and skills of workers."[20]

Whatever be the area of interest of a person he met, Rajju Bhaiya would speak about it in depth. Once he told in a kaaryakarta meeting, "Don't keep speaking yourself, about yourself. If you collect information to the best of your capability about the area in which people work, it proves useful in having affectionate relations. Padmakar Mishra speaks about his own experience in this regard, "My father, Pandit Jaykant Mishra was a famous journalist. He was also once the President of All India Editor's Association. In his programme to meet eminent people, he came to meet my respected father after shakha. He had a deep and authoritative discussion with my father about running a newspaper organisation, its department wise issues and circulation related issues of various newspapers of Bharat. My father and I wondered whether he was a journalist or a Sangh Pracharak? It is worth mentioning that he did not utter a single word about Sangh in that chat. I experienced this dimension of organisational skill in person. I heard about its impact on my father after many years. He was accompanying Rajju Bhaiya during his tour of a rural area. He had stopped somewhere in a home for an overnight break. There was only one narrow cot. Both of them slept on that single cot. He had brought my father so close to Sangh."[21]

Rajju Bhaiya was a very compassionate person. Whom-so-ever he met, his/her happiness or pain were his happiness or pain, and he helped them. There are many such living examples. An ex-prachaarak Sunil Sahay writes that Rajju Bhaiya relieved him from his role as a prachaarak because his sister was to get married and his father was alone in making arrangements. He did not stop there; he made arrangements for a proper job for his sister and took care of worries of his family.[22]

Arun Kankani tells how Rajju Bhaiya's personality would leave a deep mark on the person he met. His was a character worth emulating. He tells us, "During my college days, I had read the interview of a prachaarak who was working at Nanaji Deshmukh's Gonda project. He told in the interview that he ate only once in the day and then told the reason that goes back to the first ban on RSS. The organisation was suffering from huge shortage of funds. Many prachaaraks were told to return to their homes because Sangh did not have enough funds to take care of the prachaaraks. Rajju Bhaiya was looking after the prachaaraks' arrangements. He called a meeting of the prachaaraks and explained to them the problems being faced due to shortage of funds. He reasoned, "We spend next to nothing as prachaaraks. But, if we can save some money somehow, then it could help Sangh activities in a big way."

Everyone could understand the gravity of the situation and they were wondering how they could reduce the expenses. I (then a prachaarak) also thought a lot and then I questioned myself, is it really necessary to eat twice a day? And I began eating once a day. I realised that I can work by eating once a day. I am carrying on with the same practice even today." Arun understood the real meaning of *tapobal* or strength of penance. A person is ready to sacrifice anything, inspired by the words of such a person. He becomes victorious even over basic human needs like hunger.[23]

He had the heart of a deeply affectionate person and it always radiated from his persona. He could make a person from any station of life as his own. Whenever he went to market, he would buy something or the other. He was fond of shopping. Respected Sureshrao Ketkar, another very senior prachaarak, tells how he whould buy a towel or a sweater and give it to Ayodhya Prasad in Delhi and sweater to Ramesh, the driver of Sangh office. When he reached Nagpur, he would gift a dhoti to the chief kitchen in-charge Mangal Prasad. It was a routine for him."[24]

It was his second nature to keep himself fully informed about the kaaryakartas in his area of operation and beyond too. Vyankateshwarji tells us that after he was appointed Nagar sanghchaalak, Rajju Bhaiya came to Prayag and he was informed about his meeting with Rajju Bhaiya. Rajju Bhaiya was staying at Chandramohanji's home. Light hearted chat was going on with the people who had come to visit him. Rajju Bhaiya had never met him earlier so Vyankateshwarji requested Joint State Secretary, Nigamji, diffidently to stay back. But, when he was introduced, he immediately said, "Yes, I know about him. You have been a government officer before retirement." He appreciated my work and so on. "I was surprised and was a bit embarrassed to note how he keeps himself informed about workers."[25]

We may recall that he had met Guruji during his first training camp in Prayag. However, he could watch Guruji closely during the first national conference of Vishwa Hindu Parishad. Later on, he had lot of occasions to work and travel with Guruji. He recounts a few of his experiences of these interactions:

"I had an opportunity to watch respected Guruji closely during 1966 VHP conference. It was the conference for which Guruji had asked me to stay back in Prayag. I could get in touch with many great saints and sadhus. It was an extraordinary programme. I saw the active personality of Guruji interacting with various sadhus and saints. Everyone who attended the conference could experience his multifaceted personality closely. All the saints agreed that the conference was a great success because of hard work put in by Guruji and due to his great personality. I also got introduced to many great personalities."[26]

Next year he got another chance to be in his august company for a long period when Guruji undertook a yatra of Kedarnath on insistence of Prabhudatta Brahmachari. This pilgrimage took place in September in 1967. Rajju Bhaiya was entrusted with all the arrangements for the pilgrimage. He has been quoted extensively in Guruji's biography where he talks about profound character of Guruji.[27] After he retired from Sangh responsibilities, he told Nana Neurkar in Pune about his travel with Guruji in Assam when he drove the car for him on hilly roads.[28] He cherished all these special moments, though he regularly interacted with him in official meetings.

After retiring from the university, Rajju Bhaiya held the responsibility of Kshetra from 1966 to 1975. In 1975 other eastern states were also added to the same Kshetra. Bhaurao Deoras moved to the central team. We are told that Rajju Bhaiya also held the honorary post of director of Rashtradharma Prakashan from 1966 to 1970. He had excellent personal relations with every junior and senior employee of the publication. Whenever he visited the publication's office, employees not only discussed the work but also their personal problems and their moments of Joy or grief. The publication went into serious deficit once. He then contributed his own pension to rebuild it. Even when he became Sarkaryavaah and Sarsanghchaalak, he would not forget to ask about the well-being of the employees of the publication and other workers in Lucknow.[29]

Shri Vijay Ganesh Kulkarni, who was Bengal Prant Sangathan Mantree of Vidya Bharati during those days of Rajju Bhaiya, remembers his stay in Kalyangarh. He talks of his personality as that of a soft hearted and egoless person who would always praise a worker's qualities. He tells, "There was a Sangh Shiksha Varg in West Bengal in Kalyangarh. A young teenager Swaroop Kumar, who had just given exams for tenth standard, had come for the training camp. He would always seek introduction of all the people –young or old. Once he stood in front of respected Rajju Bhaiya and asked him, "Please introduce yourself." Rajju Bhaiya, without batting an eyelid, simply introduced himself formally, "My name is Rajendra Singh and I am Sarkaryavaah of Sangh. In the night, he took a meeting of organisers and training instructors that ran upto 12 in the night. He asked questions in great details. Then, he took 3-4 names and said you have good shikshaks (instructors or teachers). I was one of those named. I had been a teacher in these camps for nearly 10-11 years, but no one had ever called me a 'good shikshak'. He was a large-hearted saint like person who would see good qualities in a person and talk about them and raise his confidence further."[30]

Due to his innate urge, he would take every chance to enjoy the nature in his busy life. Whenever he found time, he would try to fulfil his urge to enjoy the nature. Vijay Kulkarni talks about one of those trips. "Rajju Bhaiya travelled to Darjeeling and Sikkim as per his official *pravaas*. I was a District prachaarak and accompanied him in the tour. Prant sanghchaalak Shri Madanlal Agrawal, his son and Veerendraji of Prayag were also in the group. He told us on the way, "Once a year, I take out 5-7 days and visit some good places worth viewing. From my pension I contribute to Guru Dakshina and also manage such trips." There were some meetings, visits to some schools and lecture programme for poor young children. Entire period was joyful. Watching beautiful greenery and mountains, he began singing a Bangla song in his beautiful musical voice—

'Dhan dhaanya pushpe bharaa aamoder ei vasundhara,
Taahaar maajhe aachhe desh ek sakal desher sera."[31]

Rajju Bhaiya had surrendered his all to the nation. He gave away even his house that his father had built for him, for a school. Inspired by his act, many other people in the society, too, donated their properties for sewa projects.

While describing this donation of his property, he says, "During this period there was some thinking about the house in Prayag that was lying vacant. It is quite large. Senior workers suggested that this home be given to Shishu Mandir. I agreed. And for a nominal rent of 200 rupees I gave it to the school. This rent was charged so there was no issue about expenses on routine maintenance of the building. Name of my respected Mataji was given to this Shishu Mandir. I kept one room for myself so that whenever I visited the city I could use it or other visiters could stay in the room. Rooms had not been designed for school rooms. A large piece of land was lying idle. A new school building was constructed and the old home building began to be used slowly for State office and finally it was handed over to Sangh. Watching this, many other friends too decided to act similarly. Family of Himmat Singh Maheshwari donated their property for Ved Sanskrit Education to Vishwa Hindu Parishad. Big house of Ashok Singhal in Prayag too is being used by Vishwa Hindu Parishad."[32]

The news of respected Guruji being struck with cancer was a big blow to the swayamsevaks of Sangh. As the successor Sarsanghchaalak nominated by Doctorji, he had nurtured the sapling into a huge banyan tree that had spread its roots and branches all over the nation with his untiring efforts of 33 years. This happened in 1970. Rajju Bhaiya shares the feelings of the workers of that time,

"We received the painful new of a cancerous gland on the left side of his chest for the first time in 1970. Guruji completed all his tours across Bharat with firm resolve and refused to stop his tour programmes. Though Abaji Thatte was with him and various Ayurvedic and indigenous medicines were tried, it was clear that this disease was going to take its toll on Guruji. The last programme of that leg of tours was in Bihar. We could see that he would get acutely breathless. Weakness could be seen clearly. The all-India meeting in Nagpur takes place only after the camps in May. Guruji got admitted to Tata Hospital in Mumbai on directions of his advisor. Guruji was not keen on any treatment. He would say, "Even Doctors say that one can live only for another 4-5 years after the surgery. I would stay alive this long anyway." However, the surgery was successful and our annual meeting with Guruji was organised in Mumbai in July 1970. He was present throughout the meeting. He worked with the same energy for three years. There was a big camp for senior level of workers in October 1972, named '*Disha Darshan*' or 'Viewing the direction' or path. This was to clear any doubt and give satisfactory answer to any query. This camp was held in the ashram of famous Saint Pandurang Athawale (of Swaadhyaay Parivar). We could sense that it was painful for Guruji to speak. After the meeting, Guruji went through radiation therapy. But Guruji could not come out of this disease. The year of 1972-73 was very painful. But one has to bear with the pain that cannot be avoided. We had to harden our heart and see our dear Sarsanghchaalak leave us. This moment of pain came upon us during the Sangh Shiksha Varg of 1973 when he was in Nagpur. He was going weak gradually. He left this world on 5th June 1973."[33]

Thus, the second Sarsanghchaalak and a leading light (*yug purush*) in the history of Sangh, a guide to all the swayamsevaks, workers and specially that of prachaaraks – Revered Madhav Sadashiv Golwalkar completed his journey of Mrityu Lok. Shree Guruji had actually set up proper systems, processes and working guidelines for the prachaaraks. His life, like that of a Rishi, was a source of inspiration for all. Therefore, the news of his leaving for his heavenly abode disturbed every heart in RSS. It is a very special quality of the seed planted by Doctorji and nurtured with utmost care and caution by Guruji that can be seen today. This was evident once again to its critics as well as supporters when they saw Sangh grow from strength to strength even in his absence.

Thrift was a quality ingrained in Rajju Bhaiya while dealing with money. His clear direction was that swayamsevaks' money must be spent with great care for good purpose only, must be spent for the society. He would show this concern in his own conduct and chats. Dr. Gaurinath Rastogi tells us that he never used even a paisa for his own upkeep from Sangh funds. He always spent his own salary and pension. It was his habit from the earliest days to help the deserving students. He would help Bharatiya Kalyan Ashram and Saraswati Shishu Mandir routinely. He would buy fans etc. for helpers in Sangh offices out of his pocket.[34] He would donate for poor students and organisation from his salary. He would also ask about the expenses in a camp or monthly Sangh Shiksha Varg. He would advise colleagues from where to get cheaper and good quality grains, cereals or vegetables. Before leaving this world, he donated whatever funds he had to organisations working in tribal areas and for leprosy affected people.[35]

Harishchandra Shrivastav tells us that while he went to Varanasi station once to board a train, he found Rajju Bhaiya eating aloo-poori from a handcart. 'After paying my respects, I asked him, "Did people in Kashi not know of your journey?" His answer was, "I am going to Prayag. I don't think it is proper to ask workers to bring meals, unless there is specific requirement. I can get poori for one rupee, vegetable is free. I had it and I feel satiated now." Saying this, he boarded the train in third class.[36] He would always insist that he will travel in third class and so should Sangh workers. He began travelling by first class on request of senior workers only when he became a senior office bearer at national level.

Rajju Bhaiya went to Kerala on official tour for the first time after his appointment as Sarkaryavaah. A grand programme was arranged in Kollam in his honour. Rajju Bhaiya paid respects to the memorial of great Sant Narayan Guru. The programme held in the evening saw very impressive attendance and it was grand. There was a meeting in the night with the workers. Every kaaryakarta was mildly surprised when Rajju Bhaiya in his inimitable affectionate style gently chided them. He said, "Why lights were on before there was dark outside? Our programmes should not be show offs. We should spend minimum as per our requirements. We should take care that the programmes should be excellent in every way, not spend on decoration and showing off. If you had not switched on the lights when there was enough natural light, you could have saved a few thousand rupees."[37]

His habit of using everything properly could be seen anywhere. When he became Sarsanghchaalak and went to Delhi for the first time, lot of well-wishers came to meet him with rose garlands. After two days, his personal assistant was seen washing the rose petals and depositing them in a glass jar. When asked, he said that this will make pure 'gulkand' and could be used in kitchen to be served to people who came for lunch.[38]

He would keep an eye on prices of vegetables and worry about inflation. This habit of his was alive till his last days. When he visited Shridhar Damle in USA in 1982, he asked him to take him to grocery store. While making a round there he looked at the cost of vegetables and other eatables. He was accompanied by Laxmanrao Bhide at that time who told Shridhar that it was his old hobby. "Wherever he goes, he visits the market there and finds out the rates of vegetables and grocery to understand how inflation is working." Whether it was railway budget or general budget, he would listen to it carefully to understand how it would affect the budgets of Sangh if prices would rise. He had seen Sangh struggle with very limited resources and how it affected Sangh work. So, he would be careful that there was no waste of funds anywhere. Bhideji tells us that when Motherland daily was launched, Mankikarji was appointed its editor. He had worked in big newspapers and was habituated to air-conditioned room. So, air conditioner was installed in his room. When he left his job, Rajju Bhaiya said, "Now there is no need for an air conditioner. Please remove it now."[39]

In the overseas tour mentioned above, he also visited Netherlands. He went to the training camp of Hindu Swayamsevak Sangh there. Koenraad Elst came to meet him one day and was there till lunch. After lunch, the guests went for washing their hands. As per western culture they were offered paper napkins. But Rajju Bhaiya refused and took out his handkerchief from his pocket to dry his hands. Arun Kankani sharing this incident, says, "He told us that using paper napkin is against ecology, because this requires cutting of large number of trees and also lot of energy to manufacture them." After this incident Arun, too, became very conscious and always used his handkerchief though it is no more a habit to carry handkerchieves in USA. He would inspire people with his own personal conduct without any fuss. Thus, it was not just about saving money wherever possible, but he was always careful that natural resources are not wasted.[40] We are talking of 1980s when such issues were not on the top of collective human mind.

Arun Kankani shares another example about his careful attention to use of money—"It is an incident of 1990 when Dr. Hedgewar Centenary celebrations had just concluded. Rajju Bhaiya finally found time to take care of his urological problem. He was admitted to Dr. Phadke's nursing home in Dadar, Mumbai. I was doing my MCA in VJTI. I was deputed to look after Rajju Bhaiya's arrangements. This was the first time I had an occasion to spend a good deal of time with Rajju Bhaiya and watch him from close quarters. I had worked as a student vistaarak (short-term full-time worker) in Mumbai for ten months by then. For the first time, I had to keep account of my expenses for Sangh work. It was around 300 rupees per month for me and my Sangh work. Once I was surprised to see Rajju Bhaiya making notes of his expenses in a diary. He was Sah-Sarkaryavaah (Joint general secretary) of Sangh. It was beyond my imagination that a leader of his status was following this discipline. Then, I glanced at his expense sheet. I was shocked beyond belief to note that his expense was nearly that of mine. Then I realised that his cloth bag in which he carried his clothes etc, was very old and it had been repaired in a number of places and had lot of patches. Then, I looked at his belongings and I found that his clothes and other materials were old and frayed. Then I understood the real meaning of 'मन वचन कर्म एकरूपता', that is, mind, speech and action were all aligned. There was complete harmony in his words, in thoughts, words and deeds."[41]

Bimal Kedia remembers another incident. 'This incident may be around 1974-75. There was a telephone call one day. It was a call from Sangh office. I was told that Rajju Bhaiya was going somewhere by air. But there were some technical problems with the aircraft and flight would not take off. Rajju Bhaiya was standing outside the airport with his jhola (cotton bag) and he has to be brought home. I had a scooter at that time. I immediately rushed to the airport, very close to my home. I met Rajju Bhaiya and told him, "We will go by taxi." He then asked, "How did you come?" I replied, "I have come on scooter." He said promptly, "Then, why do we need a taxi? I will sit on pillion and we will go by scooter." We drove home on scooter. After some time, a car from RSS office came and he went to Kaaryalay in car. His simplicity left a mark in my heart without saying a word."[42]

He also liked to see the same simple conduct in his swayamsevaks. Once, the ex-Maharaja of Jaunpur was to visit the Sangh office for the first time. Workers desired to spread a carpet and make better arrangements in keeping with his prestige. But, Rajju Bhaiya told them that arrangements should be made in keeping with the Sangh's culture of simplicity and there was no need for any special arrangement. Simple clean mats were spread, ordinary biscuits and tea offered. His parting reaction after the visit was, "Sangh is such a great organisation. If they wish they can run their organisation in an opulent manner but the atmosphere here is so simple!"[43]

He explained in beautiful words to Mithilesh Narayan 'Mithilesh', how the nature of a prachaarak and his views should be. He had moved to Jan Sangh and had come to seek his blessings. He tells us, "In 1971 I was deputed to Jan Sangh." Rajju Bhaiya then advised him, "Prachaarak's nature should be all encompassing, touch everyone and he should be popular. He should be pure like Triveni (confluence of three rivers in Prayag). Just as Triveni does not stop anyone from taking bath, and cleanses every one of their sins; prachaarak should have this kind of nature and you should keep this nature alive even in Jan Sangh."[44]

Rajju Bhaiya's college friend and a senior professor, Devendra Sharma, of Prayag University reminisces that despite keeping busy with so many issues, being connected with colleagues and friends and having close relations with their families, was his special quality. He would be part of their happy or sad moments whenever required. For a self-sacrificing person who had given up all physical comforts and even his own property, having such affection for people around him was a surprise.[45]

His affectionate close relations were not just limited to his activities in Sangh. His relations outside this sphere too were as sweet. He had good relations with people and leaders of different social and political organisations. His polite manner to respect every one's view, at the same time, put forward his views firmly, resulted in these long-term relations. Though he was a scholar, he always had an approach of a student and was ready to learn from anyone.

References

1. Nanaji Deshmukh, Vichar Pravaah, op cit, p. 8
2. Audio file, Tape 2 B, op cit
3. Dr. Rajendra Agrawal, Vichar Pravaah, op cit, p. 48
4. Sudarshanji, former Sarsanghchaalak, Vichar Pravaah, op cit, p. 1
5. Rajnath Singh 'Surya', Vichar Pravaah, op cit, p. 21
6. Audio file, 2 B, op cit
7. Ibid
8. Veereshwar Trivedi, Vichar Pravaah, op cit, p. 24
9. Virendra Kumar Singh, Vichar Pravaah, op cit, p. 6
10. Audio file, 3 A, op cit
11. Ibid
12. Shantanu Shende, letter received 5th October, 2013
13. Audio file, 3 A, op cit
14. Ibid
15. Ibid
16. Audio tape, 4 A, op cit
17. Jay Gopal, Vichar Pravaah, op cit, p. 44
18. Padmakar Mishra, email dated 24th October, 2013
19. Jay Gopal, op cit
20. Govindacharya, Vichar Pravaah, op cit, p. 16
21. Padmakar Mishra, op cit
22. Sunil Sahay, Vichar Pravaah, op cit, p. 36
23. Padmakar Mishra, op cit.
24. Suresh Ketkar, Gomant Shakti, 10th April, 1998
25. Vyankatesh, Vichar Pravaah, op cit, p. 26
26. Audio tape, 4 A, op cit
27. Ranga Hari, Guruji Golwalkar, Jeevan Charitra, Biography, Shri Bharati Prakashan, p. 364-368
28. Nana Neurkar, letter received October 2013
29. Vijay Kumar, Vichar Pravaah, op cit, p. 57
30. Vijay Ganesh Kulkarni, letter received 5th October, 2103
31. Ibid
32. Audio file, 4 A, op cit
33. Audio file, 3 A, op cit
34. Dr. Gaurinath Rastogi, Vichar Pravaah, op cit, p. 23
35. H.V. Sheshadri, Vichar Pravaah, p. 7
36. Harishchandra Shrivastava, Vichar Pravaaha, op cit, p. 31
37. Memories shared by Kerala swayamsevaks via email dated 15th July, 2013
38. Arun Kankani, email dated 21st October 2013
39. Laxmanrao Bhide, telephonic conversation on 22nd October, 2103. (Laxmanrao Bhide was his colleague in UP and was first Hindu missionary who worked for Hindus in Kenya and other countries for many years

40. Arun Kankani, op cit
41. Ibid
42. Bimal Kedia, Keshav Srishti Samachar, August 2003 edition
43. H.V. Sheshadriji, Vichar Pravaah, op cit, p. 7
44. Mithilesh Kumar 'Mithilesh', Vichar Pravaah, op cit, p. 64
45. Devendra Sharma, Vichar Pravaah, op cit, p. 71

□

7
Relations with people outside Sangh

Rajju Bhaiya had the fortune of meeting many great people as a social worker, and building good relations with them. He also received their affection. He believed that it was possible because he had decided to give a certain direction to his life. As these were personal experiences, I present his memories in his own words.

"When I went to Prayag, Dayasagar was my colleague and he was son of **Rajarshi Purushottamdas Tandon.** I began visiting their house frequently. Tandonji had a soft corner for me as a good student who always thought about the nation and who thought a lot for Hindi. Tandonji had this feeling for me. When I became a teacher in the university, I used to discuss many issues with him. Tandonji and Brahmachariji helped the movement for cow protection a lot and then they came in touch with Shri Guruji too. These three used to come together during the Cow Protection Conferences.[1]

Lal Bahadur Shastriji used to visit Tandonji very often. I think, he was working in some creative field, but he was also involved with Tandonji for Peoples Society for India that had been formed by Lala Lajpat Rai. He was an important worker in it. So, I could meet him on and off when he visited Tandonji. He was a very short and a thorough gentleman. Because, I had limited relations with him, I will begin from him.

When Congress leaders came out of jails in 1945 and political activities began again, Shastriji was asked to fight for the assembly seat of Prayag. Here is a small example about how straightforward and affectionate relations he had. He came to meet Tandonji once and met me there. He told me, "Bhai, you have a prachaarak named Raj Narayan in this area and he sings very well. He has also memorised many wonderful patriotic songs. My workers have told me that he is able to keep the audience in thrall." Raj Narayan had been posted in Jaunpur as a new prachaarak and he, indeed, was gifted with such qualities. Shastriji added, "We in Congress have no such system of singing songs and I get late many times in reaching public meetings. Why don't you give us Raj Narayan for a month? He will be able to create the right atmosphere before the meeting." I responded, "Surely. I want you to get elected with good margin and if Raj Narayan can be of any help, then I will send him to you." This shows that there were no differences between Congress and Sangh.[2]

I had second serious contact with him when we were in jail due to Gandhiji's assassination. Shastriji was the home minister of UP at that time. My mother used to come to jail to meet me every month. Once she told my father that he too should make time to meet Rajju. Coincidentally, Shastriji was travelling in the same train in which my father was travelling.[3] *(I have mentioned about their discussion about Rajju Bhaiya, and his long letter on behalf of Sangh earlier in the chapter on ban on Sangh – author.)*

When I became a prachaarak, I was told by Bhaurao to keep meeting Shastriji. He believed that it would help remove many misgivings and confusion that he may have. It is your duty. I kept meeting Shastriji on and off. We would have light hearted banter too. Once he said, "You hold so many meetings." I replied, "We talk about number of swayamsevaks who came, what were the special programmes and what are the future programmes. We also discuss about special invitee for a programme." Shastriji laughed and said, "Don't you talk about what is the number of Muslims in a particular area, where are their huts and what mischief can they play?" I responded with smile, "Shastriji, you are welcome to visit any of our meetings – whether it is for local team leaders or prachaaraks, we shall welcome you." He brushed aside the suggestion with a smile. During this time, respected Guruji came to Lucknow. I went to Shastriji and requested him, "We have organised a programme for people from outside Sangh. Guruji will be present there and will respond to any question. If you can come for this programme, it will be great." Then he shared what was in his heart, "You can roam around with me anywhere. Your people have full faith in you. Nobody will say that you have become a congressman. But, if I attend your meeting, I will be stamped as a RSS man. This is the difference between you and us." I asked him with surprise, "Doesn't your party have this much confidence about a senior worker like you? And you are the home minister. It is your job to understand about different organisations and activities." Shastriji, however, responded in negative. It was then that I realised the confidence level within political parties.[4]

Lal Bahadur Shastri improved his relations with Sangh after he became the PM. When Pakistan attacked Bharat in 1965, the only social leader he called apart from political leaders was Guruji. This event generated lot of discussions. Guruji told him in the meeting, "Wherever police or paramilitary forces are used, for example stations or traffic police, we could deploy our swayamsevaks. Our swayamsevaks are trained and they can do it. You can send the police on the front. If Pakistanis enter our land, then we should have no problem in going across the border and attack them." As the meeting got over, Shastriji told him that he had briefed the generals accordingly that they can enter Pakistan and respond to it. Unfortunately, he did not survive for long. When Guruji came to know about Tashkent meeting, he wrote a letter to Atal Behari Vajpayee to ask Shastriji not to go. But, by then he had left for Russia. It is unfortunate that people who were close to him knew that the room in which he was sleeping had no phone or alarm bell to call someone in case of emergency. When he had pain in the heart, he had to get up and go out to get help. Therefore, it was felt during those times that there was a big conspiracy in Russia to kill Shastriji. But, to preserve good relations with Russia that we had developed, this issue was buried.[5]

The person whom we saw with huge respect was Babuji, **Purushottamdas Tandon.** He was a man of Satvik nature who did wonderful work for Hindi. When Babuji retired and moved to Prayag near Hindi Sahitya Sammelan office, we could see his simple Khadi attire. He would keep repairing his old clothes himself. And he did not wish to take any help from his son. When he was not an assembly member, he used to face serious problems in travelling around. He suffered from phlegm and cough. The people who invited him would be worried about his health. He used to object to drinking cow's milk and honey. So, when he received Ayurvedic treatment, his vaidya would face this difficulty. He had an effulgent persona and he was very strict with himself too. He had warm relations with Prabhudatta Brahmachariji. Brahmachariji used to joke with him, "You are now 75, and you should go and stay in an ashram. Which Hindu scripture has told us that after 75 one should stay at home?"[6]

I remember an incident well. I had a chat with him after the murder of Dr. Shyama Prasad Mukherjee in 1953. When I informed him about the entire episode, he released a very strong statement that Nehruji should order an enquiry against Sheikh Abdullah and the circumstances that led to his death. It is necessary to win confidence of the people. He made a couple of more such strong statements.

Congress feared that an upset Babuji can leave Congress. So, they sent him a proposal to go to Odisha as Governor. I think Maulana Azad had sent this proposal. All the friends of Tandonji advised him to give assent to this very good proposal. He could go to Odisha and it would also improve his health as he would be looked after well. He could also serve

Hindi's cause in a non-Hindi state. During this time, I landed up at his home during one of my informal visits. He asked me, "Rajendra, you tell me what I should do in this matter." I told him, "I am too young to advise you. But, since you have honoured me by asking this question, I would say frankly that the offer of Governor's post is a sweet Rosogulla offered to you to keep your mouth shut; so that you will not be able to make any statement against Congress. Otherwise, Governor's post is not very important. If Congress believes that you are still an important person, they can offer you many other important posts." He said, "You have spoken the truth. I also believe the same." Thus, the clever idea of Congress failed and Tandonji refused that offer.

Everyone knows about my relations with respected **Prabhudatta Brahmachariji.** I don't need to add anything more. But I was highly impressed with his personality when he was fighting election against Nehruji. Prabhudatta Brahmachariji was incredibly courageous. I have rarely seen such courage in true sense. He was persuaded to stand for elections because the society had huge respect for him and Congress goons would not dare to disturb his meetings. But, when Maharajji reached Sirsa to address a meeting, there were around 3000 to 4000 people in the meeting. Just as he reached the meeting ground, goons began hurling stones at him. Other sadhus sat down quietly holding their shawls on their heads. But, Brahmachariji threw down his shawl and tying his dhoti around his waist; he stood in the centre of the ground and challenged thus, "I, Prabhudatta Brahmachari, stand here in the centre of the ground. Whoever wants to hurl stones at me, come on." I could visualize him as Shivji, as drawn by Raja Ravi Verma, standing with head held high to let Ganga flow down into his matted hair! All the stones and pebbles stopped. Then he roared, "Those who have no arguments throw stones. We have a tradition in this country to listen to others' arguments." When we were about to leave the meeting ground, some of our supporters came to meet us and told us that there was going to be an attack on our group and we should not go from that path. He asked them, "Are these people with two arms or four arms?" "Swamiji, with two arms", they replied. He told them, "Then, we will take care of them. If they had four arms, we might have worried." I drove him out with two swayamsevaks standing on the footboard of the car with lathis. No one dared to do any mischief.

Maharajji had abiding faith in Eeshwar (God). There are many such times during the campaign when we felt we had no funds. At that very moment Hanuman Prasadji or such other devotee would send 500 rupees for the election. I saw his persona as a devotee when he undertook an 80 day fast for cow protection law. Having fasted for so long, lack of salt in the body would make his head turn hot. He would not be able to sleep at night and would keep murmuring something or the other in anger. People had called me there as he generally listened to me. He became adamant one day that I must call Guruji. Guruji was on tour of Tamilnadu or Kerala. We sent a telegram to Guruji and he came down to meet him, cancelling all his meetings. He met Maharajji with great affection, understood the situation and also reasoned with him. When he was about to leave, I told Guruji, "Guruji, if this continues, he may call you every second or third day. I then explained to Maharajji how troublesome it would have been for Guruji to make this visit. "You will again call him after 2-3 days. If you keep calling Guruji like this, all his tours will get disturbed. We need to find a way out." He immediately agreed and said, "What you say is correct." Then, he gave me a simple solution. "I will keep his shawl with me. Whenever I remember him and feel like meeting him, I will smell it and feel his closeness with me. He need not come himself." You will find very few ennobling examples of such a brotherly feeling; such was their deep affection."[7]

Guruji was suffering from Cancer during 1972-73. Brahmachariji wrote a letter at that time to Guruji, "When it was clear that he had to leave this world, Shukdevji narrated

Bhagwat to Parikshit. I also wish to narrate Bhagwat to you." Guruji wrote a letter with love, "They were all great people. Please do not take this trouble for me. If you insist, I will listen to some parts of Bhagwat Katha every day. But, please do not trouble yourself." This incident tells us about the close bond they both had.[8]

Brahmachariji was very transparent in his views. He never felt uneasy about speaking with anybody. He would speak with the richest and powerful people with open heart. While returning from a very rich man's Yagya in Uttar Pradesh someone said something that his driver heard, "Hey, there is no difference between them and us. Both have excellent arrangements for food and every kind of comfort." Brahmachariji came to know of this talk. Next day, when Sethji came, he told him, "Look Seth, do you wish to see the difference between a family man and a sacrificing sanyasi? Then, watch this. Let us get up from here and move on. Everything will be left behind. When there is sense of surrender in heart, a human being is ready to drop everything. It doesn't matter whether it is a loin cloth or a palace. If you have reached that state of quietude and surrender, you too will become a big man. Difference between a Sanyasi and a domestic man is only this much, that a sanyasi is left with no longing for anything." I have so many memories of Brahmachariji, there are so many incidents. I have learned so much from him that this topic will have to be closed here.[9]

Another person, whom I met for a very short time but who impressed me a lot, was Dr. **Shyama Prasad Mukherjee.** I met him first when he came to Prayag for a programme. He stayed at the home of my teacher, Professor A.C. Banerjee. There was a press conference in the evening. The way he responded to questions from the press showed his clarity of thoughts. I was impressed with his intellectual prowess and control over language. One quality of his was that he would agree to any request from workers without any fuss. He told Nanaji (Deshmukh) at Banerjee sir's home, "Nana you will kill me! I am not a man who can do six-six programmes in a day. I can just do three programmes easily in a day – one private meeting, one public meeting in the evening and a press conference in the afternoon or evening. Nanaji replied, "You are going to fight with Nehruji. Nehruji does eight programmes in a day. If you are unable to do six programmes in a day, then how will it work out? You will have to do three programmes in the morning, take rest in the afternoon and do another three programmes after taking rest. He surrendered, "Ok baba, I will do as you tell me." Then Nanaji told him, "You will also have to give speech in Hindi. No English speaking person can become the leader of this nation. If you can't recall a word, use a Bengali word." Shyam babu agreed to this suggestion and he acquired an entirely different image due to his speeches. He spoke in Hindi all over the country after this.

My last meeting with him was during his Delhi-Kolkata train journey. His train reached Prayag in the morning. Deendayalji had asked me to arrange for his breakfast and tea. So, I reached the station with tea and breakfast. It may have been a pleasant surprise for him. Generally, no one takes care of their political leaders like this. I asked him a short question at that time. Four or five unhappy legislators of Congress were about to join Jan Sangh. I asked him, what is your opinion about their transfer of loyalty. He laughed and said, "Let us ask the young professor the answer. What he would do in such circumstances?" I replied, "I do not know much about politics. But those who are coming to Jan Sangh as a reaction to something; may return after that action is over. A party cannot be built up with such people. In the initial stages we must take in such people who are strong in their beliefs and who may not desert us on small pretexts." He told me with a smile, "Rest assured, this is what I am going to do." We all know about his clarity in thinking, how he managed to organise the Kashmir satyagraha. His dress sense was so simple and straightforward that one would be surprised. He had a chipped mirror for shaving. He used to say, this small piece is enough to shave.

Like his scholarship and ideological clarity, his life too was simple and Satvik.

Other great personalities with whom I had a chance to meet and understand their views, **Acharya Kripalani** is one of them. Dada, that is Acharya Kripalani, was the General Secretary of AICC (All India Congress Committee). He used to stay at Swarajya Ashram in Prayag. This place was given to Congress by Pandit Motilal Nehru. He had excellent relations with the students and kaaryakartas of Prayag. I got to meet him during my student days before independence. He used to be ready to go for any programme. Being a professor, he used to take lot of interest in moulding students. He used to speak in a satirical style and major part of his speech would be in the form of questions and answers. Because, students would participate in them directly, they would remember most of the things he taught.[10]

He came to address our student union once. He began by asking, "Who teaches you at the university? With whose help and money are you taught?" Students gave straightforward answer, "Father or guardian or family teaches them." Then he asked with a smile, "Do you know how much fee you pay?" At that time the fee was twelve rupees per annum. He would then laugh and ask, "Do you think that twelve rupees can take care of such a huge college, library and professors? If you go for tuition, the college would charge you fifty rupees for one hour. Then, how can they teach you for twelve rupees?" At that time, per student expense used to be around hundred rupees. "You pay only twelve; balance is arranged by the government. And from where does the government bring the money?" We would be informed that government collects taxes. Then he would ask, "Who pays the taxes? These are paid by common citizens. So, actually, you are studying with the help of those taxes. Therefore, it is not your father but the society that takes care of your teaching. You think so much for the person who has paid fifteen rupees for you, but the society that actually helped you study and spent money on you, why don't you think about it? That society has a right over you." This was the way he would explain and also scold the students. He used to say, "We are the salt of the nation, but if you don't have saltiness, how will it work? If youth of today do not think about the society, then how society will work? Thinking about nation has been forgotten."

Acharya Kripalani used to tell us about his student days in Pune. He was like a dedicated disciple of Aurobindo Ghoshji. He told us, "A periodical of Aurobindo Ghosh used to be published from Calcutta. We used to reach Pune rail station early in the morning so that the limited copies of the periodical may not be sold out. The periodical was read one by one. If you read about good people, you will get inspired to do something in life."

I became a teacher in the university later. Meeting him became a bit irregular. Then, I had another chance to meet him. There were serious incidents like Gandhiji's assassination, satyagraha etc. Then, the ban was removed in 1949. He had become a critic of Nehru due to his working style during those days. He had very good friendship with Prof. Bhattacharya of Law department. I met him in his Seoni home in 1949. I asked Dada, "Dada, you know about Sangh and also know that all the allegations against RSS were false. Sangh used to respect Gandhiji. It didn't like his Muslim appeasement, that's all. Our swayamsevaks had made security arrangements in Delhi when he was staying there. Therefore, there is no question of Sangh having any hand in the entire episode. You know all this. What are the issues on which we need to think?" After pondering over my question, he replied, "I know that there were many people in Congress against you. But I also know that you are not that kind of people. I believe that in the changes that you think of, it is necessary that you should speak about Bharatiya nation not Hindu nation. I then said, "Dada, what you say is right. But we actually do not see any difference in Hindu and Bharatiya. Both are different names of concept of the same society. But, tell me, what is such a specialty of Bharatiyata that is not a Hindu specialty? You might say, Truth, non-violence, importance of positive *(satvik)* qualities, respect for all faiths, spirit of co-operation, sacrifice and living simple life is Bharatiyata. But all this is contribution of Hindu thought. Both are same. What is that one quality out of these that is taught by Islam or Christianity? So, because they want to abuse us, they call us communal. They might invent a word for you tomorrow. You are running a big Socialist party now. They may allege against you that your party is a party that creates conflicts and a party that fights. They may call your party a lackey of another party. We simply believe that we should speak with clarity. We believe in our *Sanskriti* and consider it as the prime goal of our national life and culturally, Bharat is Hindu Rashtra." He said, "What you say is correct. Now your struggle will be around this argument only." This is how, this discussion closed.

But he went on to be closer to us. When Sucheta Kripalani became the Chief Minister of Uttar Pradesh, we used to meet her many times. Nanaji had good friendship with Suchetaji because she used to take his advice on many issues. When we used to go to their home, we would find Dada reading something or writing something. Looking at Nanaji he would laugh and say, "Yes brother, you must have come to meet Sucheta. Who will come to meet me, an old man?" Though he joked like this, due to his nature he would get into minutest of details and speak out his mind with boldness. Therefore, when three seats of members of parliament went vacant in 1968, three common candidates were nominated to fight the elections. He was one of them. Jan Sangh had good amount of ground work in all the three. Dr. Ram Manohar Lohia stood from Farrukhabad, Acharya Kripalani from Moradabad and Deendayal Upadhyaya from Jaunpur. Very negative propaganda was done to consolidate the votes of Muslims and Mullahs came together. They carried out lot of propaganda against Acharyaji. After coming back from a public meeting, Acharyaji said in a lighter vein, "Congress has managed to collect all the mullahs with long beards. You can imagine how many people had come there because the rates of chickens have risen by two rupees!"

Our relations became so good that I invited him for a lecture on the platform of Deendayal Vyakhyanmala (lecture series), of which I was the Chairman. We brought him from Delhi to Meerut by car. Programme went very well. He appreciated all the aspects of the programme. But I was surprised with one thing. When we invited him for dinner as per arrangements, he said, "Arrey Bhai, Sucheta is sick. Her health is not good. But she does not take dinner till I return. She must be sitting on some sofa. If I go by your arrangements, this will get over by 10-11 p.m. You better drop me earlier. I don't feel good that she has to wait for me long and hence can't sleep at a proper time." So sweet were his relations and his love for Suchetaji.

Acharya Kripalani's sense of humour did not desert him till his end. Dada had to undergo an operation and a food pipe was inserted on his side. Dr. Jain used to come every day to change the dressing. Nanaji could not go to meet him for nearly three months. After he came from Delhi Nanaji and I went to meet him. He saw us from a distance and said, "Arrey, is this Nana? Arrey Nana, I thought so many months have passed since we came here, but you did not come to meet us. I thought you are dead; otherwise, you would have surely come to meet me. Did you really die? Nanaji smiled replied, "No, Dada. I am here only, but was bit busy with work." "Arrey Bhai, you are the only one who has taken care of Dada for such a long time." Nanaji then told him that he was getting news about his health regularly from Dr. Jain. I have not met many people with such non-acquisitive nature, a simple man who had no desire for himself in his life and who had such a sharp intellect and quick repartee. He invoked respect.[11]

A famous man, for whom you felt respect when you saw him from close quarters, was **Dr. Ram Manohar Lohia.** My first contact with him was in 1962 when he had come to Prayag to request Brahmachariji to fight election against

Nehruji again. Brahmachariji explained to him, "It was a different matter earlier. Cow protection and Hindu Code Bill were the issues which were important for us. There are so many issues now and there are many policies on which you can work better. I suggest that you fight from here." Lohiaji was surprised. Brahmachariji explained, "Whichever seat you fight from, whichever seat your followers gave you, it will be a good seat. Wherever you stand you will lose. Then, why should you not stand against Nehruji and explain your point of view, why you are fighting against Nehru?" But he did not have much base in the seat that they were talking about. "And we don't fight where we have poor work on ground," he reasoned. Then Brahmachariji added, "There is a young man, Rajendra, who teaches in the university and works for Sangh. You should meet him. I will inform him and he will meet you." Thus, I received messages from both Brahmachariji and Lohiaji who was put up in Civil Lines. This is how I met him for the first time. We exchanged notes on how Brahmachariji's election was fought, what were the issues, how did we got votes, what problems came up; all these points were discussed. I said, "Nehruji has become much weaker now. Therefore, there can be good fight between you two." He laughed and said, "We don't even have our committees in two-three places. We hardly have talks with Jan Sangh too. In such a situation, who will work for me?" I told him, "You need not worry. We have around sixty shakhas in this area. They are running quite well. Young people and boys come there, play and exercise, participate in physical and intellectual programmes. Their intellect and maturity is much beyond their age. Therefore, we have two or three people in every village with whom we have good contacts. If they agree, we can take advantage of their contacts in sixty villages. And if you stand for elections then they won't find it difficult to work for you because our work is about supporting good people." Hearing this, Lohiaji was very happy and said, "If you have contacts in sixty places then it is good enough. Please send out message to all the places. Ask them to make a group of two to four people and they can take along people who are opposed to Congress." Lohiaji fought from Prayag and fought well. Pandit Nehru was unable to get his deposit forfeited. This is how we met for the first time.[12]

After this discussion, we met at his place many times and discuss various issues. He was an open minded person. Once he said, "I find you very liberal and progressive in thoughts. Which topic do you teach in the university?" I told him, "Physics." He laughed and said, "I used to think that people in Sangh are from ancient history and philosophy. But you are teaching modern subjects. I told him with a smile, "Our Sarsanghchaalak is M.Sc. in Zoology and we get more people from science in Sangh."

I found him to be very close to Hindutva and Bharatiyatva. He used to say, "See, I look at this issue from another viewpoint. I present the subject in a different way. You talk about Akhand Bharat, that Bharat should not be broken. It is a matter of reverence. Bharat is mother. Hindu has a good quality of investing. But we need Muslim labour. Wherever you see, skilled labour is Muslim, he is a good mechanic." I said, "Yes, this is true." He then added, "We cannot work without both. So, I say, both are necessary for each other and say that Bharat and Pakistan should be unified." He would also invent new words in his speeches. He would not use English words. He went to the extent of calling PSP as – Lakwa Maar Party – Paralytic Socialist Party. He used to speak in a sitting posture in the Bharatiya way. He used to talk calmly. He started Ramayan Mela in Chitrakoot. He went on to say that character of Ram is equally important for every citizen of this country. Similarly, he had great devotion to Swadeshi and deep love for Bharat.

He began a campaign in 1967 that Congress wins even with minority of votes. Jan Sangh, Socialist Party and other parties lose because they do not come together. He began to campaign for their union. Because, he began this movement, people took it seriously. He met Guruji during those days. Guruji had come to Delhi for Sardar Patel Vyakhyanmala (lecture series). It had a lecture by Guruji and also by Lohiaji. When both of them came out, they were holding each other's hands. I asked Guruji later about what they had discussed. Guruji said, "Lohiaji said that opposition parties should have an alliance. I told him, ok, please talk to Deendayal and his team." He then said, "I know that they will not take any decision without taking advice from you. This is why I am meeting you." Later on, both developed good relations.

His campaign in 1967 was quite successful. Haryana, Uttar Pradesh, Madhya Pradesh, and Bihar saw SVD (Samyukta Vidhayak Dal) governments. They also included a faction of Congress that was not happy with its leadership. These governments had Socialist Party, PSP, and Jan Sangh members. Lohiaji had lost elections in 1967. But, in 1968, common leaders were chosen to fight by-elections from three places. Everybody worked together and he won by 1,000 votes from Farrukhabad. He always had quicksilver responses. When he attended Lok Sabha, Congress members taunted him, "What was your winning margin?" Congress had three hundred members then. Lohiaji taunted, "I have won with much bigger margin than the numbers of Congress sitting here." He used to have close relations with party workers. He would behave in a friendly manner with workers and would have coffee with them. His conduct was simple and straightforward. He would take care of sisters and Bhabhis who work and take care of leaders. He would find time to chat with sisters preparing food and be one with them like family. It was misfortune of this country that he met untimely death. He was operated upon for prostrate but there was no proper care.[13]

Women don't attend shakhas, but they are part of Sangh. That is, they are actively present in other programmes of Sangh or Sangh inspired organisations. Women hold great importance and they are given their due place with lot of respect. Rajju Bhaiya talked about this aspect in his audio memories. He says, "I did not have many occasions to be in touch with women in course of my work or in my life. Still, I found that the women with whom I came in touch are second to none in terms of intellect, fortitude, courage and bravery in any way."[14]

Rajju Bhaiya's close and affectionate relations with great personalities having different ideologies tell us about clean political and social life of those times. At the same time, they also reflect the selfless and straightforward nature of Rajju Bhaiya. We can witness intellectual qualities of his character here. We see, how he had healthy exchange of ideas with senior political leaders even at that young age. His readiness to learn, to express his views unhesitatingly, offering co-operation in politics in national interest but also remaining unattached to party politics and keep doing his Sangh work. We will note how his nature to have warm relations and affection for every person without any sense of bias impacted the history in future.

References

1. Audio file, 6 A, op cit
2. Ibid
3. Chapter 5 of this book
4. Audio file, 2 A, op cit
5. Audio file, 3 B, op cit
6. Audio file, 6 A, op cit
7. Ibid
8. Audio file, 3 A, op cit
9. Audio file, 6 A, op cit
10. Audio file, 6 B, op cit
11. Ibid
12. Ibid
13. Ibid
14. Audio tape, 4 B, op cit

□

8
Changing national scenario & emergency

Rajju Bhaiya referred to the big changes in political scenario while talking about Ram Manohar Lohia. This was a result of Indira Gandhi becoming the PM after sudden demise of Lal Bahadur Shastri in 1965, her deteriorating relations with the Syndicate, decreasing Congress influence and coming together of opposition. As wheels of time moved, liberation of Bangladesh, big victory of Indira Gandhi and rising anger against corruption saw the movement for Sampoorna Kranti or Complete Revolution under the leadership of Jai Prakash Narayan. All these inter-related events saw the announcement of internal Emergency. It was followed by struggle to restore democracy in which Rashtriya Swayamsevak Sangh played a major role.

Rajju Bhaiya played a critical role in this fast-changing national scenario. Rajju Bhaiya was earlier appointed as Sah Sarkaryavaah in 1977 and after the demise of Man. Madhavrao Mulye to the top post of Sarkaryavaah. This itself shows his leadership qualities. When we look at these events, we see once again that whenever there is a national crisis, Sangh does not mind getting into politics, though not in party politics. After such compulsions of the time, Sangh gets itself unattached from politics after its role is over. It is also natural that due to historic situations many times, being a humongous national organisation and due to its presence in nearly all dimensions of socio-economic life of the nation, it has to take a stand.

In this chapter, we will get to know about the history of those times and also details of some incidents during the time. He notes,

'After Shastriji's death, Indiraji was selected by the highest body of Congress as the Prime Minister. After nominating Indiraji in 1966 as the PM, Syndicate realised that she would not listen to anyone and she was going to rule the nation as per her own wishes.[1]

1967 General Elections were held under the leadership of Indiraji. In absence of Nehruji and in absence of any major issue, Congress lost heavily and returned to power with a much less majority. If opposition parties and communist parties were to come together, the government could have fallen. Therefore, Indiraji extended a hand of friendship to communist faction known as CPI. On the other side she also brought in people like Ashok Mehta from Socialist party. Mohan Kumarmangalam and Ashok Mehta joined Congress during those days. Thus, there were sufficient number of people who came from outside into Congress.

At this very moment, Dr. Ram Manohar Lohia began insisting on opposition parties coming together to fight Congress. Opposition formed governments in many states with bridge building by leaders like Deendayal Upadhyaya and Nanaji Deshmukh. These governments known as SVD (Samyukta Vidhayak Dal) were formed where Congress was once the dominant party. Unfortunately, Deendayalji was murdered in 1968 and entire responsibility fell on the shoulders of Atalji. By 1969 Congress became very weak and Indiraji was in no position to take any major decision.

During this time, the problem of Bangladesh, (then East Pakistan) arose. Sheikh Mujibur Rehman of Bangladesh was imprisoned and Ayub Khan became absolute dictator of Pakistan. He put all intellectuals and scholars behind bars.

People who raised their voices against this oppression had to escape to Bharat including millions of refugees. Thus, the crises became acute. All of us know how the 1971 war was the result of Bangladesh crises and Bangladesh was separated from Pakistan after the defeat of Pakistan. After this famed victory, Indiraji gained a very special place in India. Her image became that of a victorious lady who had broken Pakistan to pieces. Finding this situation favourable, she called for mid-term elections in 1971 and returned to power with huge majority. For the first time elections to the Lok Sabha and state assemblies did not take place simultaneously. Indiraji came out very powerful from these elections. And, after 1971 she morphed into a person who wished to control every activity of the nation. She was against the opposition and was trying to destroy it. She created division within the Congress and got V.V. Giri elected against Sanjeeva Reddy who was the official candidate and took complete control of Congress.[2]

The way she was moving, it was felt that everyone should come together to create a common front. First to come together were student organisations. They raised their voice against the rulers. Vidyarthi Parishad and youth wing of Socialist party raised their voice in Uttar Pradesh and Bihar. Later Jan Sangh, Charan Singh's party at that time and many other parties in Bihar began to join hands. Slowly, the opposition to Congress gained strength.

Though, Lohiaji was no more on the scene; persons like Ram Bahadur Rai, Govindacharya, Nanaji Deshmukh etc. played important role in bringing Jai Prakash Narayan closer and then persuaded him to lead the agitation. Jai Prakashji led a silent march of students. These activities brought Jai Prakashji closer to Sangh and he came to Delhi to take a closer look at Sangh by visiting the Sangh Shiksha Varg there.

The news of opposition coming together and Jai Prakashji leading them had an impact at many places in Bharat. Gujarat agitation, specially, picked up steam. As a test case, Indiraji dissolved the Gujarat assembly and announced elections there. All the parties fought this election under the leadership of Morarji Desai. Opposition parties came together to form the government in Gujarat. Babubhai Patel was chosen the leader. Congress went down. Congress also realised that if opposition comes together, it ensures its defeat.

Indiraji had won with a big majority in 1971. During this time, petitions were filed against certain results. Indiraji too faced a petition. Judgements began coming out soon. Everyone was surprised to find that Raj Narayan had won the appeal against Indiraji. Judgement on his petition was declared on 12th June 1975. Indiraji appealed in the Supreme Court but everyone felt that she will not resign. It was felt that there was bound to be some trouble. But, no one had imagined that she will take such a harsh action."

In 1975, my karyakshetra (area of work) became even wider. Bengal, Odisha and North East became part of my karyakshetra. Bhaurao was moved to the centre. Before I could commence my tours, Sangh was banned.[3]

We are aware that there was cruel attempt to crush democratic rule in 1975 and Indiraji declared Emergency. The reason given was that Jai Prakash Narayan was instigating the army and police not to follow the orders of the government and that entire nation was facing a dangerous situation. Leaders and workers of other political parties were moving freely without any control but Rashtriya Swayamsevak Sangh was banned.[4]

When Emergency was declared, it was decided that senior workers will return to their own region to take care of work there. So, Bhaurao returned again to look after Odisha, Bengal and Assam and I, who had just taken charge of entire region, returned back to take the responsibility of Uttar Pradesh and Bihar work with full focus.[5]

The story of 19 months is very interesting, which I have shared in other places also. But Bharat presented an extraordinary example of peoples' power defeating government power. Sangh too got an opportunity to meet and talk to all the leaders and show its readiness to undertake any struggle."

A conspiracy was hatched in 1975 to end the rule of law in the republic and Indiraji declared Emergency. Police was told to arrest all the opposition leaders. We shall look at that period and learn about the fear and courage of many people who struggled for democracy in the words of Rajju Bhaiya. It had a happy ending with the end of anti-democratic rule.

"Emergency was declared on 25th June 1975. When I heard the news on radio, I felt that some important decision is going to be taken. I got to know the same day that many people have been arrested. Arrests in Delhi were probably picking pace. At that time, there were Sangh Shiksha Vargas in Eastern region. Grasping the seriousness of the situation I advised workers from Bengal to return to their areas at the earliest and there was no need to wait in the camp anymore. I reached Guwahati from Bengal and reached the camp, getting down on a station before Guwahati. I gave the same direction to swayamsevaks to close down the camp and return home at the earliest. From there, I went directly to the airport and reached Delhi by air. I met Madhavrao Muley (the then Sarkaryavaah) and found about number of people arrested. I realised that I must reach Lucknow that very day.[6]

People like Shri Lal Krishna Advani, Atal Behari Vajpayee and Madhu Dandavate had been put behind bars in Bengaluru. There was no reason why other members of opposition were moving freely and RSS was banned. Respected Balasaheb Deoras had been sent to Yerawada jail and thousands of swayamsevaks were being arrested around Bharat. It was opportune that we had some inkling beforehand and we were also cautious. Thus, very few senior workers were arrested.[7]

The day I reached Lucknow, there was government notification that RSS has been banned. I felt that we need to take some required items from the office. I picked up a few items and clothes in a bag and went to another place from Lucknow. I discussed the matter with Jay Gopalji and decided that I should change my centre from Lucknow to Kanpur. I was not so well acquainted with Kanpur. Local swayamsevaks felt that the Collector was a knowledgeable and gentlemanly person. The Lucknow office of Sangh was raided the day I had visited it. It was sealed and workers there arrested. So, moving out of Lucknow proved to be a good decision.

Kanpur became centre for Bhaurao, Ashok (Singhalji) and myself. Due to good relations with many families, we got a chance to stay in many such homes. We met people of various types, some totally new. They were also frightened. Some of them told me that they could not sleep at night. Many of them took all these troubles in their stride. I also used to stay with homes that had five or six members. I was fortunate to stay with old swayamsevaks in 15 to 20 homes in those 19 months. I would stay as a relative and sometimes as a Professor. I changed my name. I used to keep some cash, some cheques that carried my name as Gaurav Singh and I had letter heads and letters in this name.

Our first central meeting took place in Mumbai in which Nanaji was present who was the General Secretary of Lok Sangharsh Samiti then. Many plans were worked out and it was decided that none of us should get arrested. Important people will remain underground. We will take forward our plans and make new ones, meeting people, expanding our contacts with more people. Since I had good relations with people in the government, I was given the responsibility of meeting people in government and also keep a tab on what was going on in the field of education.

Unfortunately, Nanaji was arrested. Ravindra Verma became the next General Secretary of Lok Sangharsh Samiti. When we had our first meeting with him in Kanpur, he was of the view that we should begin satyagraha immediately, because leaders were getting arrested and it was difficult for them to stay hidden from police eyes. And it would be difficult to conduct big satyagraha after the leaders were arrested. However, we wanted to see that large number of people should take part, for which we needed more time. We would not be able to do anything noticeable if we did it in a chaotic manner in a rush. We needed to keep a track of who was being arrested in which area. We should have live contacts at all the places. Based on this information we could then decide how many people will go to jail.

I recall that according to Vermaji if sixty thousand people could go to jail in next 3-4 months the struggle would be in a good shape. I requested seven days from him and took a tour of Uttar Pradesh and Bihar to get an idea. I told him that atleast fifty thousand satyagrahis will definitely join from Sangh and allied organisations. We will need two months to prepare properly. Finally, satyagraha took place and we all know that fifty five thousand satyagrahis from Sangh and allied organisations went to jail. On the other side, very few people from experienced parties like Samajwadi, BKD and Congress went to jail. After Sangh, the largest number of satyagrahis were from Akali Dal who sent about twelve to thirteen thousand satyagrahis, followed by people from Jai Baba Bhagwan. Congressmen were very sad. When I met a few of them at Shanti Bhushan's home, Ashok Mehta shared his sense of despair that they from Congress, who are supposed to be experts in satyagraha, could collect only three thousand people.[8]

In the chain of events that took place, one good outcome was that many of our important leaders could not be arrested. Except Yadavrao Joshi and Abaji Thatte, all others were working outside. Outside the jails, plans were not just to offer satyagraha. We did not leave aside any chance to defame the dictatorship of the government wherever there would be crowds. Wherever there were foreign tourists, an ambassador coming for a meeting, some sports event, inside or outside the courts, sometimes in markets, our people could be found distributing pamphlets. We published those news items in those pamphlets which newspapers were finding difficult to publish because of the censorship. Slowly we got ready for underground struggle. We were well prepared in six to eight months. Our activities were taking place all over the country.[9]

This was our first experience in staying and working underground. So, there were many interesting incidents. I can't talk about all of them. But I utilised this period as a chance to meet many important people to understand what was going on. There were many educationists whom I met; like Rajani Kothari, Ratan Shankar Mishra, Ramcharan Malhotra, Ajit Ram Verma, and Dr. Devendra Sharma etc. I also met many ministers, IAS officers. I found that I could gather lot of information by just talking to them and that there was no need to be afraid, the way the atmosphere had been built.

I will narrate two interesting incidents. One gentleman was a senior IAS officer. I went to Jaipur and stayed at his home. I asked him if he was worried. He told me, "Your name has not yet been circulated. If anyone enquires, I will tell them yes, he had come. If they ask me why police were not informed, I will tell them your name was not in the list. And if they ask, where have you gone, I will tell them he never tells where he is going. He comes, meets me and goes away. I don't know his whereabouts. So, I am not worried at all. You can stay as long as you wish." Similarly, Leela Singh Bisht and Shravan Tandon, who was IG at that time, were old friends. It needed a lot of courage to meet them. I used to give my name as Gaurav Singh. I would have very interesting chats with them. Whenever I went to Delhi, I always met them.

Once I asked him, has there been any meeting these days, of IGs of Police or IAS officers? He told me, yes. Indiraji herself took the meeting. DGs from 15-16 states had attended the meeting. She was very upset and fired them, accusing them that they did not know how to work. "I had given you a list of 2,000-3,000 senior workers of RSS. You have not probably arrested even 10-20 of them. You people have arrested 20,000 to 25,000 people in states to settle your personal animosity but you have not been able to arrest RSS people. All this is giving me bad name. Why have you not been able to arrest these people?" He continued, "We were in a bind, how to respond. But a senior IAS officer said, "We arrested people of other political parties whom you named, but RSS people are different. They don't stay in hotels. They stay as relatives in individual homes. They stay as Chacha, Mama, and Mausa (uncle) etc. We have no photographs of them, because they don't get photographed. So, it is difficult to arrest them. If we go to any home for enquiry, they tell us that Mamaji had come; he stayed for two days and is gone now. Therefore, we have been able to arrest so few of them. It is not our failure, but their working style is different." I felt very happy listening to this account because the working methodology that Doctorji had developed wherein senior prachaaraks would keep away from public gaze and stayed at homes had been very useful."[10]

Rajju Bhaiya also responded to some questions raised by Shridhar Damle about Emergency when he stayed with him. Responsibilities had been distributed. Responsibility of underground activities was with Nanaji, that of labour field with Dattopant and maintaining contact with political leaders, government officers and opinion leaders was with Rajju Bhaiya. Shri Balasaheb Deoras, the then Sarsanghchaalak had cautioned him that "It is a war of nerves. It is a long-drawn struggle. It may even last 15 years. One, who has the stamina, will win."[11]

Rajju Bhaiya kept travelling continuously across Bharat and meeting people during the period of Emergency. He did all this fearlessly and with a carefree approach. Past Chancellor of Prayag and Gorakhpur University, Prof. Vishwambhar Dayal Gupta recalls his highly active life. "One would hear a knock at the door at 12 in the night and Rajju Bhaiya would be standing at the door when one opened it. I used to stay in the Lucknow university campus those days. When Rajju Bhaiya came to our house after declaration of Emergency, he was wearing his routine dhoti kurta. There was fear in the air. I advised him to change his dress and he agreed promptly. After this, whenever he came, he would be dressed in trousers and pants.[12] Prof.

Mahendra Singh was teaching in IIT. He says that Rajju Bhaiya stayed for six months in the campus at the home of Prof. P.S. Dan with false name and western attires.[13]

His nature of working, presence of a natural charming smile in any situation is highlighted by Shantanu Raghunath Shende. "Rajju Bhaiya came to Pandit Deendayal Sanatan Dharma Vidyalaya at 11 in the morning wearing trouser, coat and a felt hat with an office bag. I took him to my room on the first floor and told our principal that the education inspector had come visiting the school and he had called him upstairs. He asked, "How can he go to the upper room? He should have come to the office." Then I requested him to accompany me. By the time we went upstairs, Rajju Bhaiya had removed his hat. We had a long chat with him, had lunch together. After the school was over by 4 p.m., 'inspector sir' left the school.[14]

Rajju Bhaiya shares some more experiences about the period of Emergency. "I used to travel a lot during those days. As I visited different places in Uttar Pradesh and Bihar, I got introduced to hundreds of families and I met Raja Dinesh Singh too. I found that he was courageous and not at all worried about meeting me. His personal assistant was an old swayamsevak from Prayag. I had lot of discussions with him about what could be or may not be done. He told me, "All this will keep happening till you do not have hold in politics. You kept organising shakhas, open Shishu Mandirs, established many Sewa projects, but you did not make any place or did not make efforts in political intervention." V.P. Singh was an old student of mine. I thought of meeting him too. He, however, sent a message that he was under watch and meeting him would be dangerous. But I met many others during this time. We met two kinds of people - ones who were courageous and ready for struggle and the others who were scared and were not ready to do anything except worry.

We had lot of new experiences during the 19 months of Emergency. Police and government were very alert for the initial 4-5 months. Om Mehta, V.C. Shukla and Chaudhary

Bansilal were considered among the harshest people. They got many people arrested and tortured. But after 6 months, when there was relaxation, one could travel easily. Once in a while I would also do advance reservation or it would be quite easy to travel sitting in 2-tier and 3-tier. We had fixed one home each in all the places. Wherever we went to major centres, we would hold meetings and fix up the programmes for next 3-4 months."[15]

Senior prachaarak Ranga Hariji, who was active in Kerala during those days, shared some of his experiences about Rajju Bhaiya. Rajju Bhaiya was traveling in Kerala as Gaurav Singh. He used to travel in third class and used to interact freely and joyfully, chit chatting with co-travellers. He had an amazing collection of foreign currency and coins. He would use them to enjoy his time with the co-travellers and also avoid being asked inquisitive questions by them. He was staying in a place called Pazayandakkavu in Thrissur. He had kept long hair, wore pant-shirt with clean shaven face and carried a brief case. He satisfied his love for shopping there and would shop all day long in different markets. Some swayamsevak would drop him off at a place so he wouldn't lose his way. Purpose of his visit was to understand political situation. He would seek information about the situation on the ground, how many candidates may be put up by different parties, who had better chance of winning and which way was the wind blowing. He went to Kalladi to visit the birthplace of Shankaracharya and used that excuse to take a meeting of Jan Sangh workers.[16]

Atmosphere was changing slowly and workers too had begun to understand about how to work in that situation. Rajju Bhaiya reminisces, "We had no experience in staying underground and working in that situation. But we found that any worker of a disciplined and patriotic organisation learns to work in any situation fast. Thus, everyone worked wisely with common people to create an atmosphere against Emergency. Workers would collect news that did not appear or could not be given in newspapers. These would be published in weekly bulletins and distributed. Their distribution used to be done in a very easy manner and hundreds of people would enjoy reading them. We also heard many stories about brave mothers and sisters in this activity."

Here, Rajju Bhaiya talks of an amusing incident. "Once, about 2000 freshly published pamphlets had reached a home. As soon as they were stored in the room, police raided the house for reasons unknown. People at home knew that if the pamphlets were seized, not only all the workers would be arrested, but members of the family too would be harassed. But the respected old mother turned out to be too smart. She told the worker, "Son, keep all the pamphlets under my small sitting bed. I will sit down there as if I am sick. Police will come and search home and return empty handed." When police came, she climbed down from her bed and told them, "Brothers, you can search for whatever you have come. I am not well; I will come down from the bed and sit on this small sitting bed." She pulled up a big blanket with the excuse of cold and kept sitting on that small bed. Police searched entire house but could find nothing.

We conducted small activities to connect with the society. For example, when respected Balasaheb Deoras was in Yerawada jail, he had completed 60 years. It was nothing important for us. And, we have no custom of congratulating Sarsanghchaalak or Sarkaryavaah. But it was felt that there is an atmosphere of fear all over the country. Celebrating 60 years in a grand manner, sending letters to him and praying and wishing him long life would be a good idea. Doing all this on a large scale would impress upon the government that he was still very popular and respected by the society. As per plan greeting cards, letters and telegrams began reaching Yerawada. Amount of such material that reached the jail would not have, probably, been received by anyone except Balasaheb. More than 5000 letters praying for a long life landed in the jail in 3-4 days. This must have made the government realise that despite being in jail, Sarsanghchaalak was still respected highly by the society.[17]

Though I was not present in Yerawada myself, I knew that about 500 sanghchaalaks, karyavaahs and kaaryakartas (workers) were in jail at that time with respected Balasaheb. They were Principals, lawyers and labourers too. Despite such different background all of them lived peacefully with love. There used to be good programmes in the jail, there were no quarrels despite the numbers and diverse backgrounds. Surprisingly, there were only 25-30 socialist party workers but they would have bitter conflicts on some issue or the other. Balasaheb told me that when they saw the calm conduct of Sangh workers and conduct of their own colleagues, they asked Balasaheb, "Why don't you get into arguments? Why is there no difference in opinion between you? Why is it that you don't even fight?" Balasaheb laughed and told them, "Because, you people believe that Sangh is a place only for playing Kabaddi. However, we also inculcate good values. We nurture habit of working together. Therefore, even when our workers show their differences, they do it in a civilian language that doesn't hurt the other person. We know that utensils will make noise when they are kept together. But we are alert that the noise would be minimal and we talk with each other with faith and respect."

There are many amusing incidents we experienced during Emergency. Some university teachers, lecturers and readers were also imprisoned in the jail along with Sangh swayamsevaks. But police also arrested a few people, probably from Sarvoday or some Gandhian movement and kept them with RSS people. Directions were to chargesheet them at the earliest in different places. In a chargesheet, it was written that police saw one person carrying a heavy piece of luggage. In another it was written that one of them climbed a pole and was attempting to start a fire. There was one, Raghuvanshji, who was handicapped due to weak hands and feet and could not even write on a board. Some such charge was filed against him. There was a humorous Professor in jail who commented,

"Government failed to make one charge against you that you tried to carry and run away with an engine and two bogies under your arms." Such was the ham-handed approach of the government.

I realised during this period that habit of meeting each other, exchanging notes and having discussions is very important work. I can share many such incidents that show how small meetings resulted in proper action.

Advocate Narendra Singh had been released after six months in jail. He was a famous lawyer in Kanpur. He had never fought an election. When we met, we decided to fight elections for the Bar council. He refused first, saying he had never fought an election. I explained to him that it will tell us what kind of faith the society has in us. Initially, no one was ready to stand against him. With great hesitation a communist candidate finally agreed to fight against him. He hardly received 50 votes while our Barrister bagged more than 600 votes.

One programme would lead to another programme. When people came to know about it, their confidence rose further. We conducted another programme after this. Advocate Virendra Pratap Chaudhary was arrested in Prayag. We had good enough an idea that because of the sections under which he was charged, he was not going to be free soon. Still, we organised a programme where many advocates were to sign a letter stating that "they know Advocate Virendra Pratap Singh very well. He is a very civilised person with high character. He cannot do any wrong activity and we believe that he should be released soon." We had felt that not more than 100 people would sign such a memorandum as it would be seen as defiance of the government. But we were surprised that when signature campaign began, we could collect 500 to 600 signatures in just four days. His son, Yateendra Singh and his friends including Shanti Bhushan's son had run this campaign and it was conducted very successfully."[18]

To keep morale of the workers high, Rajju Bhaiya would go and meet them frequently even during those difficult and scary times by changing his get-up or using some other tricks. This showed his fearless nature and love for his colleagues. Advocate Virendra Pratap Singh tells us, "I was in Naini jail. My application was being heard in the High Court. My clients would frequently call me to the court for arguments. I would normally sit in the Bar Council room. Despite all the prohibitory orders, I used to get my lunch from my home and family members would come to meet me. It was a strange time when people who would normally claim to be my friends, avoided meeting me. It was in this atmosphere that I was sitting in my cabin under police watch and waiting for the call for the case. At that moment a gentleman in complete dress of a lawyer, wearing lawyer's band barged into my room and told me in a voice loud enough so others could listen, "I had come to Kanpur for a case and I saw you. I had sent you a case some years back and you had got a stay order in that case for me. I am Gaurav. I was surprised, and looking at his lawyer's gown etc. I wondered, who is this man? His personality, his style of talk was totally different. Looking at my troubled and surprised look, perhaps, he told me that his name was Gaurav. This was the name that Rajju Bhaiya was carrying during Emergency. After initial shock, the clouds of doubt disappeared. I shook hands with him formally and began talking in a typical lawyer's style. We sat together and had a long chat. Police squad was doing its duty somewhere outside."

He continues, "I began suffering from severe headache in the jail. I was sent to hospital where they found that it was a case of migraine. Doctors kept me in the hospital for a month. I was taking a walk in the evening in the campus one day. 'Gauravji' arrived at that time. All of us were so overjoyed. He never forgot about swayamsevaks' well-being even in those difficult times and took time to keep a track of their health and other problems."[19]

Rajju Bhaiya recalls a few important episodes of those times. "Though there are unending stories of those time, I remember two very distinct incidents. There was exchange of letters between Balasaheb Deoras and Vinobaji. He also wrote to Indiraji. As the head of the organisation, he had written about a few things very clearly. As an organisation, our language is always polite but despite this there was clear firmness in those letters.[20]

Vinobaji had formed a council of Acharyas (Professor and senior teachers). It had excellent teachers from universities. Vinobaji wanted to utilise their services. The meeting of this Acharya Kul (council) was held in 1976. I knew many of those professors personally and I had met them. I went to Pavnaar Ashram in Wardha. I told them they could say something in the resolutions that would get Vinobaji's stamp of approval. These issues should reach Indiraji. She should know that people do not like that so many leaders are in jail and there is censorship on newspapers. This leads people to wonder whether news is true or not. All the news doesn't reach them. The social service organisations have stopped working as workers from tribal areas have been put behind bars. They should also start functioning. Society should start functioning in a normal way. They passed these recommendations. We were also surprised when this news was published in newspapers. Shriman Narayan Agrawal was going to meet Indiraji with the resolution. I was given the responsibility to find out what was the outcome of that meeting.

Dr. T.N. Singh was a member of the Rajya Sabha and also a Chief Minister for some time. He was not yet arrested despite being in the opposition. I met him. He knew Shriman Narayan Agrawal well. Both were members of Rajya Sabha during the same time. I requested him to find out, what transpired as soon as Agrawalji went to meet Indiraji. He happily agreed to do the job. But he asked me, "Rajendra, do you think if we will come out of this? Or will dictatorship of Indiraji will continue?" I told him with confidence, "Perhaps, you are not meeting many people, nor are you moving around. There is strong opposition all over the country against Indiraji. Officers have begun behaving recklessly. A group of Congress people are quite unhappy with Sanjay Gandhi's style of working. There are many projects to improve the administration, but it is not happening. I feel that sooner or later Indiraji will have to declare elections and I am confident that she will face a terrible defeat." He told me that it was for the first time he had heard a person speaking about these things with such confidence.

Whenever I used to go to Mumbai, I would meet Usha Behan (Ashok Singhalji's younger sister). I would feel not many people know me, so I used to wander very freely. But, one day, I received a shock. Usha behan and I were returning on a bus. We were just 3-4 people. I was talking freely and loudly with Usha behan. Suddenly, a gentleman came from behind and told me, "Your voice is so similar to Professor Rajendra Singh. Do you know where he is and what he is doing?" I told him, "You are right, I know that person and he is fine and doing his job. But I have not met him nor gone to his home for a long time." Such unexpected incidents used to happen many a time.

Indiraji could not gauge that the atmosphere was slowly turning against her. Because, whenever police officer gave her such information, he would be fired very badly that it was not possible. So, slowly, such information stopped reaching her. I met Hazari Prasad Dwivedi who was her teacher at one time who went to meet her. When I met him I asked him, how was the conversation? He told me, "She told me that she is lonely now. Very few people come to meet me and no one opens his heart to me. I told her that this is the fate of any dictator. He is not left with anyone who can give the right advice."

While I remember those days, I recall some more incidents. There were all round efforts to oppress Sangh, its allied organisations and their workers and damage their confidence. There were many efforts. Rana of Udaipur was Vishwa Hindu Parishad's President at that time. He was feeling isolated because all his colleagues had been jailed. There was lot of pressure on him to declare that he had resigned from Vishwa Hindu Parishad. But, fortunately, a senior worker and secretary, Rajabhau Degwekar got a chance to meet him. He told Maharana, "Ranaji, we are being insulted these days. Think over the legacy you come from. You belong to the clan of Maharana Pratap who never compromised with his self-respect and dignity. Therefore, if you write something under pressure then it will be very painful for the entire nation and compromise with your dignity." Maharanaji understood the feelings and said, "I will leave for England immediately. I have a home there and I will be free from any pressure. And I am confident that I will not do anything that can bring down the prestige of people from Vishwa Hindu Parishad or Sangh." After Emergency was lifted, I got many opportunities to meet him. I could observe that if a person is reminded of his great traditions, then the person can perform many great deeds."[21]

We will recall that many leaders like Rajmata Scindia did not defect from her party but faced imprisonment. A few like Madhavrao Scindia bent over and joined Congress. Same was the condition of media, government officers and many intellectuals. But there were many people who stayed firm in those conditions and re-established faith in humanity. Rajju Bhaiya shares an example—

"A surprising incident took place in UP. I had very good relations with the Director, Education. I told him that you have not been able to dismiss 600-700 officers of our Shishu Mandir, nor have you been able to suspend them so they can atleast get suspension allowance. You have put them in jails. Please take some decision about them." He said that he will try to do something about it. He met the Chief Minister and discussed this issue with him and asked him to take a decision. When he met me after 6-7 days, he told me that CM says, "Let things be as they are for now. If we suspend them, they will have to be given suspension allowance and we have no evidence to dismiss them." All the schools had been taken over by the DIO at different places. The director then added, "Though I could not do something as per your idea, I am telling you about a letter that DIO has sent that will gladden your heart. Inspector of education in the area is a Muslim gentleman. In his letter he has noted that he had received an order from the government to take over the school. "Sir, I went to inspect the school. No such school runs in any of my districts. If we take over these schools then the schools that have their own specialties like these will be destroyed. Therefore, I request that the government should not take over these schools. They should not be disturbed so that good education in these schools continues." On reading the letter, I felt that good people recognise good work and if they are courageous, they can talk about them too.

I remember that Chaudhary Charan Singh had been released from the jail. He was not ready to be present in the UP Assembly because his colleagues were in jail and it won't be proper to attend the assembly. I met him and told him that there are so many things that need to be told and are not being published by the newspapers. Still, you know that there are 300-400 members of assembly and you can present your views there. If you present our views forcefully it will give good results. Please do not let the chance you have got to speak in the assembly. Then, I told him many things including the information that 600-700 schools had been taken over by the government, teachers had been dismissed, put behind bars because the students refused to wave flags in the rally of Sanjay Gandhi. I also gave him firsthand information about some good programmes that had taken place. I told him about kind of people arrested, how even people repairing tyres and cycles were put behind bar in Bulandshahar. These things that are not known, can come out in the assembly. Fortunately, he agreed to go to assembly and gave a very powerful speech in which he spoke about all these issues. Though these facts were not published in the newspapers; 300 members in the assembly, that included MLAs and officers, received important information through his speech."[22]

Though Rajju Bhaiya has not talked much about special role he played in the political changes, his colleagues at that time have shared some information about it. One of those is being shared here. Dr. Rajnath Singh 'Surya' writes, "Indiraji had begun releasing people who might become obstacles in formation of one party. Chaudhary Charan Singh was the top name in this strategy. Rajju Bhaiya took an intelligent decision. He called some of journalists like us and told them about the emerging situation. He said, "While most of the leaders are in jail, Prakashvir Shastri is trying to bring Chaudhary Charan Singh closer to Indiraji. We should keep meeting Chaudhary Saheb personally, on and off, and remind him of history of his opposition to Nehru and stories about it and motivate him by appreciating his patriotism strongly. Because of this, he went to Mumbai on invitation of Jai Prakashji despite refusing it once. This meeting had been called to discuss the possibility of creating one party by merging different political parties in the 1977 elections.[23]

Dr. Rajendra Singh, Kashi Prant sanghchaalak, shares some more information. "When elections were declared during Emergency, he played an important role in future changes. He visited jails to meet top leaders to boost confidence. They were in a depressed mood. The mood was, "What is the use of elections? Who will work for us? Who will vote in this atmosphere of terror created by Indira Gandhi? You Sangh people have lost your mind. Please, leave us to our fate." Many such disappointing remarks were being made. But he kept trying. We finally saw that all the parties came together under the flag of Janata Party and dictatorship ended. Untiring efforts of Rajju Bhaiya definitely played a major role in these efforts for unity."[24]

When pressure began to build from the global community, Indiraji talked of amending the constitution and many meetings of the people, who were favorable to the idea, were held in Delhi. It was then decided that people who were outside the jails, should also hold a meeting to discuss constitution amendment. It was also decided that this meeting should be held in a hall, but speeches should be given with courage and resolution too should be passed.

Rajju Bhaiya talks about this courageous programme. "Because, not many people knew me in Delhi, Krishnakantji was put in touch with me to work on this idea. Dattopant Thengdi had good relations with him since long. I met many important people with Krishnakantji. I realised within 10-15 days that our nation had many able and courageous people while some were scared. We could meet Soli Sorabji and Daftaryji who was Attorney General at one time and was a renowned attorney; Kakkadji, who was once the Advocate General of UP, and leaders like Chaudhary Charan Singh and Acharya Kripalani. There was a series of correspondence with Chaglaji, who was in Mumbai, requesting him to come for the programme. We received a very encouraging and courageous letter from him. He noted that he was watching the situation around him and was very worried about the future of Bharat. "But when I see the courage of young advocate colleagues then I feel very happy. My health and financial situation do not allow me to come for the programme. I bless your programme and wish it a great success." Daftaryji too assured that though he could not argue when the case against this amendment came up, he would share important points with young lawyers who would argue in the case.

I attended many sessions wearing the dress of Supreme Court advocate and saw how everybody was working with great grit. Many brave youths I saw then went on to become Presidents of Bharat Vikas Parishad. Apart from them, we found many of the good judges seemed scared. Judges like A.N. Ray and Chandrachud did not prove to be upto mark in the test of integrity. However, the work that Justice Khanna did was incomparable. We printed small personal visiting cards that we kept in Patel complex in the Loksabha campus.

I used to roam on scooter and wore helmet so I could not be recognised. I was careful not to stop at any place for more than 15-20 minutes. Hand over the work and move, this was the trick. There was a feeling in governing circles that the meeting about constitution amendment bill won't be much of a success, so permission was granted. When the programme finally took place, the hall with 200-300 capacity was filled to the brim and powerful speeches by Chaudhary Charan Singh, Acharya Kripalani and Soli Sorabji amazed the people. They were surprised that such meeting can be held in this atmosphere of fear and how people can speak against Emergency so openly. Then, we organised many such programmes where about 500 lawyers and citizens came together. Thus, a big change took place in the country.

Due to all these reasons, Indiraji suddenly announced elections. Possibly there was pressure from the world community. May be Jimmy Carter said that what was going on was not correct. Sheikh Mujibur Rehman was assassinated. She received information from CID that people were in her favour, there was discipline due to Emergency, people were happy and would vote for Congress. This led to the idea of elections. As soon as the elections were declared and there was some openness in the society, atmosphere began changing rapidly.

The elections were declared in January 1977 when Magh Mela (fair) was going on. The most important work to be done was - to bring every opposition party together. If people would have fought against each other, opposition would not have won the elections. I explained this to Chaudhary Charan Singh because many of his people were in jail while most of our people were outside who knew Chaudhary Saheb personally. I suggested that it would lead to a very nice environment. Though only his party and Jan Sangh were strong in UP and Haryana, still it would be better to take everybody together.

Based on these discussions and due to Sangharsh Samiti that was working during Emergency, parties came together in the name of Janata Party. The atmosphere in the nation changed in a big way. First meeting was held in Delhi and it was realised that entire scenario has changed. Atmosphere of fear is over and people are coming out with strong will and courage to defeat Indiraji.

I went to meet Dr. Kothari one day. He was the Chairman of UGC at one time. He asked me, "Brother Rajendra, what do you think? How many seats will Congress win?" I told him, "I do not know about other regions, but I work in UP and Bihar and I can tell you that Congress will not win even one seat." He exclaimed with surprise, "How can you make such a statement? You are a man of science! You can state something with 10 per cent error." But, the atmosphere in the country was truly such that from Bihar to Madhya Pradesh, Bihar, UP, Haryana and Rajasthan, hardly two people could win - one from MP and one from Rajasthan.

Another thought that became crystal clear was that Bharat being a big country, a handful of people cannot rule the nation. The Aatmaa of this nation being healthy, people cannot tolerate wrong doing for long. Hearts and minds of our Bharat definitely stand up against injustice. This is the big lesson from Emergency that even the rulers of coming times may not be able to impose such oppressions in future.

Even today, people remember and take out processions against Emergency. I learnt that we should keep meeting people, talk to people and explain simple things. People get ready for any long-term goal and programmes and forget the information being spread by thousands of TV discussions. I could see that by paying attention to small factors atmosphere of the society changes, environment changes."[25]

This is the story of those 19 months in which for the first time after independence, efforts were made to impose dictatorship and destroy democracy. The struggle against it has added a new chapter in the history of democracy of India. In the words of Rajju Bhaiya, Bharat gave an incomparable example of victory of people's power over state power. Workers of RSS got a chance to meet and exchange ideas with people outside its sphere of work and showed their readiness to struggle. This turned out to be an opportunity for other people, leaders and organisations to understand Sangh and its different dimensions. Thus, a new important chapter was written in the history of Sangh.

For the first time, a non-Congress government was formed in the centre. After this period of struggle, with lifting of ban on RSS, all the Sangh kaaryakartas began preparing for running regular shakhas, carrying on other social programmes in an organised manner. Responsibilities of Rajju Bhaiya increased too. He joined the top team of Sangh leadership. In his words,

"March-April went into issues like new cabinet ministers of Janata Party and other semi-political issues. Because, it was too late to organise yearly training camps or Sangh Shiksha Vargas, it was decided that respected Sarsanghchaalak be felicitated in public programmes in major places so people shed their fear totally and feel confident that there is no ban on Sangh work and the environment is now positive.

Pratinidhi Sabha met in July in Nagpur. Madhavrao Mulye, who was the General Secretary, added two assistants or joint general secretaries to help him due to his ill-health that had plagued him even during the Emergency period. They were Bhaurao and myself. Since, both of them were senior colleagues, I was not worried at all and I did not object to this appointment. However, after touring the country and being in Delhi for a month or two, I felt that there was very favourable atmosphere for our work and it is necessary to work with full force. Since atmosphere was favourable and opposition had come to power for the first time, many suppressed feelings began coming out in the open.

Pratinidhi Sabha met in March 1978 in Nagpur. Madhavrao told the meeting, "Though I have got treatment at various places, I am told by everybody that I cannot be treated properly since I am too busy with my responsibility as Sarkaryavaah. Therefore, I should get treated after getting free from the responsibility." I could gauge that after his retirement, I will have to take up the responsibility because it may not look correct for Bhaurao to take up the responsibility of Sarkaryavaah as he was younger brother of the Sarsanghchaalak, Balasahebji.

Therefore, I agreed to his insistence and accepted the responsibility. What was destined, happened. That very year, respectable Madhavrao breathed his last in 1978 November in Pune and I had to take up the responsibility completely as agreed. It was very helpful that I received full co-operation from Bhaurao and Balasaheb and other senior colleagues. But I carried this responsibility for nine years after this from 1978 to 1987. It was a period of major changes and I gained from many experiences."[26]

We need to recall that during this period, mass conversions in Meenakshipuram in Tamilnadu in 1981 had shaken up the entire nation. Sangh and VHP organised many programmes to address this problem. An all-India programme, named *'Ekaatmataa Yatra'* was organised in 1982-83 to awaken the Hindu society and instill a sense of harmony. These yatras received more than expected success. Entire Hindu society had been awakened with a new energy. It was followed by the Ram Janmabhoomi movement to build a grand temple on the Ram Janmabhoomi. It had visible and unseen effect on the nation and the society. There had not been any such programme from Himalayas to the Indian Ocean in the thousands of years of history of Hindu society that brought people from every section and class of the society together. Rajju Bhaiya was carrying the important responsibility i.e., Sarkaryavaah in this entire period.

References

1. Audio file, 3 B, op cit
2. Ibid
3. Audio file, 4 A, op cit
4. Audio file, 3 B, op cit
5. Audio file, 3 A, op cit
6. Audio file, 7 A, op cit
7. Ibid
8. Ibid
9. Ibid
10. Ibid
11. Shridhar Damle, telephonic conversation, 22nd October, 2103
12. Prof. Vishwambhar Pandey, Vichar Pravaah, op cit, p. 73
13. Prof. Mahendra Singh, Vichar Pravaah, op cit, p. 74
14. Shantanu Raghunath Shende, letter received on 5th October, 2103

15. Audio file, 7 A, op cit
16. Ranga Hari, Memoirs of Kerala swayamsevaks, email dated 31st July, 2103
17. Audio file, 7 B, op cit
18. Ibid
19. Adv Virendra Pratap Singh, Vichar Pravaah, op cit, p. 6
20. Audio file, 7 B, op cit
21. Ibid
22. Ibid
23. Dr. Rajnath Singh 'Surya', Vichar Pravaah, op cit, p. 22
24. Dr. Rajendra Singh, Vichar Pravaah, op cit, p. 48
25. Audio file, 7 B, op cit
26. Audio file, 3 B, op cit

□

9

Rajju Bhaiya in the highest ranks of Sangh leadership

Rajju Bhaiya had been appointed a Sah Sarkaryavaah in July 1977 and was elevated soon to the post of Sarkaryavaah in 1978 as respected Madhavrao retired from the post due to a long period of sickness. He carried this responsibility for nine years, till 1987 for three terms. Then requesting the highest body to promote younger generation and due to his own health, he suggested the name of Shri H.V. Sheshadri as the Sarkaryavaah and began working as his deputy (Sah Sarkaryavaah). There was no false sense of ego about working as a deputy to a kaaryakarta who was his junior. This was an ideal example of giving primacy to the need of the society and Sangh and keeping oneself behind. Respected Balasaheb Deoras decided to give up the responsibility of Sarsanghchaalak in 1994 due to his ill health and he nominated Rajju Bhaiya as Sarsanghchaalak. Rajju Bhaiya carried this responsibility till the year 2000.

The period from 1975 to 2000 was a decisive period in the life of our nation when social and political environment took a decisive turn. Role of Rajju Bhaiya was very critical in this entire period. In the last chapter, reader has understood his important role in the movement for restoration of democracy that resulted in the first non-Congress government being installed in the centre for the first time since 1947. After this important period of current political history of India, Sangh turned to its basic work of creating men and organising the society.

This was also the time when petty political jealousy led many Janata Party leaders to raise the spurious issue of dual membership of people from BJP. It was an attempt to isolate them as these cadre-less party leaders, particularly from Socialist strain, feared that an organised membership drive may see the control of the party going to the erstwhile Jan Sangh members. Jan Sangh component already held the highest number of seats in the new parliament party, around 94-95. This artificially created dispute resulted in old Jan Sangh members being pushed out of Janata Party and birth of a new party – Bharatiya Janata Party.

The Ekaatmataa Yatra in the wake of Meenakshipuram mass conversion to Islam took place when Rajju Bhaiya was the Sarkaryavaah. There were six main yatras and hundreds of local smaller yatras. The processions would have a huge portrait or sculpture of Bharatmata (Mother India) and a big pitcher of sacred Ganga water. Small bottles of 'Ganga Jal' (water from Ganges), used to be distributed where the vehicles stopped over. These yatras received tremendous response from the people. Around 8-10 crore people participated in this yatra. This may be considered the biggest mass contact or outreach attempt by Sangh that proved to be highly successful. Many people consider this programme as the precursor to Ram Mandir movement.

Ram Janmabhoomi movement also moved forward under his guidance. When attempts were being made to find a solution to Ram Janmabhoomi issue, Congress party efforts were led by Shri Narasimha Rao and Sharad Pawar while the temple was led by Rajju Bhaiya and Moropant Pingley from Sangh and Bhairon Singh Shekhawat from BJP. Rajju Bhaiya was in Delhi on the fateful day of December 6. He was waiting to be sent to jail in 1993 after the demolition of Babri structure. But he was not arrested. The talks had reached an important stage during Chandrashekharji's Prime Ministership. One of the reasons for the possible breakthrough was good relations that Rajju Bhaiya had with him. When the critical time to take a decision came, lack of political will led to abandoning the possible solution. This led to demolition of the structure. Balasaheb Deoras had clearly stated RSS position when he said, "Demolition was unfortunate but inevitable."[1]

After considerable passage of time, Bharatiya Janata Party that had progressed with reawakening of Hindu society and inspired by Hindutva, formed the government in 1998. It was the first government led by a party leadership that did not have roots in Congress culture and was not inspired by it in any way. For the first time, a Sangh swayamsevak, Atal Behari Vajpayeeji became the Prime Minister of Bharat.

In Sangh, decisions are not taken by one person. A consensus is arrived at among the senior most leadership. Implementation of that decision is given to a person. At this historically decisive moment, Rajju Bhaiya was in the top echelons of the leadership. Thus, we can understand his contribution in this huge change in the cycle of time.

Rajju Bhaiya was the living example of a leader who exemplified how to keep one's balance in the period of change on the back of a struggle. His calm and cultured conduct, preserving the best of values and ability to stay balanced were inherent qualities of his personality. You have seen in previous pages how he had warm and affectionate relations with people of every social and political ideology. He always met people without ego or sense of pride, with same warmth and affection, whatever be the station in life of that person, and wherever he might be. He got more and more people involved in service to the society.

Respected Ranga Hari recalls his dignified personality and how it impressed a person on the other side. He shares an incident. When Rajju Bhaiya was Sarasanghachalak, he toured Kerala. Because of lots of clashes in Kerala, many swayamsevaks were in jail. Some were undergoing life imprisonment. Rajju Bhaiya went to the central prison of

Kannur to meet them. Fortunately, the jailer was a law-abiding gentleman. He allowed Rajju Bhaiya to meet the swayamsevaks. Rajju Bhaiya had an informal meeting with the swayamsevaks in a long session inside the Central Jail. He reminded them of the lessons in discipline they had received in Sangh shakhas, the lessons of respect for senior and brotherhood. How they needed to preserve those qualities of brotherhood; and keep discussing and exchanging ideas with each other was very important. He told them that it was necessary that they found time for Kirtans and prayer during free time. Sangh was collecting funds for 'Punjab Peedit Sahaayata Samiti' for the victims of terrorism in Punjab at that time. The imprisoned swayamsevaks donated whatever they had earned in the jail from their labour. They also presented him a handicraft they had made. The jailor found this behaviour very strange. There were no hot headed lectures, no slogans and oaths about the struggle or revenge against the atrocities. Not only that, no assurance was given about their well-being. Generally, whenever a leader visited jails, such dramas would take place. Even jailor would be threatened. Here was a leader who was very calm and evolved. He was a stable and civilised leader who was telling his workers to respect the jailor. The jailor bid a goodbye to Rajju Bhaiya, telling him about positive qualities of the swayamsevaks. He said that because of the 30 plus number of swayamsevaks the atmosphere of the jail had changed completely. For three consecutive years the Kannur Central Jail has been awarded the top prize as number one mail among Kerala mail. Because of this prize the Jail Superintendent got extra increment in his salery.[2]

Sangh has taken interest in politics only in rare times and in case of special situations. But it has again kept a distance from politics once the situation changed. There was no confusion in the minds of the swayamsevaks. Vachnesh Tripathi tells about an incident. "Once Rajju Bhaiya told us about the distinction between power and Sangh work while a discussion was going on. He narrated a few words from a poem in Lucknow in Keshav Bhavan.

'जिन मधुकर अंबुज रस चाख्यो, क्यों करील फल खावे,
परमहंस को छाड़ी महातम और नदी में न्हावे।'

The bee that has tasted the juice of lotus, why would he eat bitter fruit,
Why would one bathe in a river, giving up the qualities of a great swan."

Janata Party formed the government in 1977 under Morarji Desai. The election was fought with full organisational power of the RSS, because all swayamsevaks were wishing to get the ban on Sangh lifted. This was the first instance of a direct intervention in politics. So, to bring the swayamsevaks back to RSS work a geet was introduced in 1978 Sangha Shiksha Varg as Varg Geet. Adheesh Kumar quotes the poem written by Rajju Bhaiya—

पथ का अंतिम लक्ष्य नहीं है, सिंहासन चढ़ते जाना,
सब समाज को लिए साथ में आगे है बढ़ते जाना।
इतना आगे, इतना आगे, जिसका कोई छोर नहीं,
जहाँ पूर्णता मर्यादा हो, सीमाओं की डोर नहीं,
गुण की पूजा, न्याय व्यवस्था, अखिल विश्व में है लाना,
पथ का अंतिम लक्ष्य नहीं है सिंहासन चढ़ते जाना।[4]

The ultimate goal of the path is not to ascend the high chair of power.
We have to take along entire society and keep moving ahead.
March ahead, move ahead so much that there is no end to it.
Where being complete is the only limit, no string drawing limits.
We have to herald the worship of good qualities and rule of law in the entire world.
The ultimate goal of the path is not ascending the high chair of power.

Incidentally, I had the great fortune of listening to another song from Rajju Bhaiya in 1974 at the residence of my mentor Bimal Kedia that exhibits his vision. It was written and set to tune by Rajju Bhaiya and it is still very popular in RSS. It shows global vision of Hindu philosophy. Even today when I hear this song, I am reminded of his melodious voice.

'दसों दिशाओं में जाएँ, दल बादल सा छा जाएँ,
उमड़-घुमड़कर हर धरती पर नंदनवन सा लहराएँ।'

Let us move in all ten directions, spread out like rain filled clouds,
Let us provide rain over each land and make it blossom like a beautiful garden.

Rajju Bhaiya always saw to it that protocols are followed and ensure the dignity of a post that a swayamsevak is occupying in public life. Former Chairman of Uttar Pradesh Public Service Commission, Prof. Krishna Behari Pandey shares his experience, "I became Chancellor of Kanpur University. Respected Rajju Bhaiya was very happy when he was told about it. After a few days he was to come to Kanpur to unveil the bust of Barrister Narendrajeet Singh. I planned to invite him to my home and get his blessings. I was to receive him at the station at 4 a.m. But I received a message that I should not go to station. Just before the programme, I was told I will not be attending the scheduled programme. I asked with disappointment whether I will be meeting him or not? I was informed that I will be allowed to meet him at Virendra Jeet Singh's home at 4 p.m. I reached the designated place with my wife and I touched his feet. He blessed me and my wife very affectionately. Then he disclosed, "You are chancellor of a university now. You have to follow the protocol of a Chancellor. I stopped you from coming to the station and also for the programme. I don't want anyone to raise a finger towards my kaaryakarta. Public expression of your faith in me or RSS is not expected."[5]

Omprakash Singh too shared a similar experience. "I became a minister for the first time in 1977 and went to

Varanasi as a minister. I came to know that there was a lecture by Rajju Bhaiya in the morning shakha. I met him there just before the lecture. When Rajju Bhaiya was about to get onto the stage and I moved away to sit with other swayamsevaks, he suddenly called me, escorted me to the stage and arranged a chair for me. I showed my reluctance, but he was not ready to listen." He told me, "You are a minister in the government. Dignity of UP government is attached with your presence in public places. Every one must take this into consideration."[6]

He would give the same respect to all, whether the person was a office bearereor a swayamsevak. Arun Kankani from USA tells us that he got a chance to visit RSS office in Delhi when he came to Bharat. Shankarrao Tatwawadi had given some items to be given to Rajju Bhaiya. He had just become the Sarsanghchaalak and I was very happy with anticipation of meeting him. He discussed Sangh work with me. During that time another worker came to meet him and bent down to touch his feet. Rajju Bhaiya held his hand and asked him to sit beside him and said, "We are colleagues, you need not touch my feet." I had read an article by Shri Guruji, "I am an ordinary swayamsevak." At that moment, I could understand the true meaning of that article. I have read many memoirs of his students who would touch his feet. But he would clarify, "He is my student; therefore, I am allowing him to touch my feet." He would keep in mind his role as a teacher and a normal swayamsevak.[7]

Rajju Bhaiya was a strong supporter of national language. When a swayamsevak got stuck due to his insistence on Hindi, Rajju Bhaiya did everything possible to resolve his problem. Adheesh Kumar gives details. "Agra's student, Munishwar Gupta from Sarojini Naidu College had decided to do his MD after MBBS. He had resolved to write the research thesis in Hindi. Medical Council of India, the official governing body, that controls the medical education and exams allowed studies and research work only in English. So, the University did not accept his thesis. Rajju Bhaiya was Sarkaryavaah at that time.

He was told about this problem when he came there during his tours. He gave his full backing for respect of national language, Hindi and asked Munishwar to meet him in Delhi. Rajju Bhaiya put in his efforts and also got an appointment with the President, Zail Singh, with the student. When he realised that help of Supreme Court may be required to get the law changed, he took Munishwar to meet the honourable justices and prepared for a petition. He took him to the top attorney and senior lawyer Shri Laxmi Mal Singhvi's home. Ultimately, the Hindi listings of medical terminology were accepted. His thesis was accepted finally and Munishwar received his MD."[8]

He had an inspirational quality. 1988-89 was the centenary year of Dr. Hedgewar. A Reception Committee had been formed to celebrate it and Rajju Bhaiya was appointed as its secretary. Rajju Bhaiya had come to Mumbai to inaugurate its Mumbai chapter. Bimal Kedia tells us about his quality of inspiriting with simple affectionate words. "We had a meeting with Rajju Bhaiya before the inauguration. We told him that we have decided to have a target of 1 crore rupees as a fund for Sewa projects. He remarked, "This is fine." However, when he stood up to speak at the inaugural programme, he said with an affectionate smile, "In our Hindu culture, we don't keep targets of one, two or three four etc. Thus, in a very light hearted manner, he raised our target to 1.25 Crore and we accepted it willingly. It may be the magic of his blessings that Mumbai city collected one crore and ten lakhs for the Sewa fund. Thus, Mumbai touched the highest mark in entire Bharat."[9]

Thalasseri district of Kerala saw the series of violence between CPM and RSS. Sangh people suffered heavy damage to life and property. Their resettlement, medical support and legal expenses needed lot of funds and Kerala's organisation of Sangh was struggling with this problem. Rajju Bhaiya had come for the Sangh Shiksha Varg of Palghat district and understood the seriousness. He arranged for a statement from him in Organiser and Panchjanya weeklies for support from all over India. Not only this, he also gave his own contribution of

500 Rupees. He made it clear that this amount came from his own pension and funds, not from Guru Dakshina.[10]

Ram Mandir movement started in 1984. Moropant Pingleyji and Rajju Bhaiya were to guide the movement and Ashok Singhal was to take the responsibility as he was the General Secretary of VHP. Rajju Bhaiya worked continuously to coordinate the working and thinking of different organisations. Two dates were being discussed for the *Kar Sewa* in 1990 but no decision could be taken. Seniors met Rajju Bhaiya. He suggested, "It suits the brave people to do the work in a way that assures victory and this is the movement to awaken the nation. We need not fear violence or counter violence nor the oppression by the government. Take a decision that will take us forward. He used to say, do not perpetrate violence on others, but for a great purpose, be ready for self-sacrifice."[11]

Vinay Katiyar tells us, "When I met him in Delhi during a tough period and talked about it, he told me, you are free to take any decision based on the situation. Do keep me informed about your decision. Keep faith in workers junior to you that they will not take a wrong decision. This was his quality. During the Ram Temple agitation, I was criticised regarding some incidents and I was naturally in pain. I told Rajju Bhaiya about my pain. He asked me to keep patience and said, "Do not worry, I am with you. If there is any problem anywhere, tell people without any hesitation that Rajju Bhaiya has told me to take this decision. My heart felt light after this talk. Readiness to take the load of worries on his shoulders was a specialty of his character."[11]

Rajju Bhaiya would love a person just as a person. No one saw him differentiating between junior or senior, nor looking at a person as a worker from a village or town. Respected Mohan Bhagwat tells us that in response to a question Rajju Bhaiya told him, "Look brother, all the people are fundamentally good and we should deal with every person assuming that he is good. A person's behaviour can be affected momentarily due to anger, jealousy, unhappiness etc. We should work on the basis that basically a person is good and fundamentally each person is trustworthy. He also said that it doesn't serve any purpose by being angry at anybody. He had attained this balance in interacting with people. Therefore, he could take along most of the people.[13]

We sing a song in Sangh, 'शुद्ध सात्त्विक प्रेम अपने कार्य का आधार है' (Pure, positive truthful love is the basis of our work.) When we think of Rajju Bhaiya, we remember this line of the poem, because he was a living image of this sentiment. Whenever he spoke, it was as if stream of love flowed from his voice. Noone had ever seen him angry. He would explain anything with lot of affection.[14]

Ramgopal Sand shares his experience about his affectionate nature. "My daughter suffered from blood cancer in 1994. I called up Rajju Bhaiya with a heavy heart in Jhandewalan office of Sangh. She was being treated in Christian Medical College, Vellore in Tamilnadu. The expense for the treatment came to around 8 lakhs, of which I had to deposit 5 lakh rupees immediately as advance. I was not in a position to arrange for such a big amount. I was surprised beyond belief when I received calls from some very well-known leaders for contributions. Two of them were Chief Ministers of their states. This had been possible only because of softness in his heart towards any pain."[15]

His compassion for anyone in pain and trouble was such that he thought it was his duty to take care of that pain. Swami Chinmayananda remembers an incident. "I was going to Bhagalpur on Vikramshil Express with him. There was a programme for dedicating a Saraswati Shishu Mandir to the society. We both had lower berths opposite each other. Both of us slept at around same time. In the morning, I found that someone is sleeping on his birth and he is sitting in a corner of the bed. When I tried to ask him who that new guest was, he signaled me to keep quiet by keeping his finger on his lips. Later I came to know this was what had happened – When he got up at four in the morning to finish his morning activities, he found that someone was hanging onto the handle of the door from the outside. It was winter time. When he opened the door, he found that a 9–10-year-old child was sitting on the stair outside the door, shrunk with cold and holding onto the handle. He had called him in and made him sleep on his bed silently. He was signaling me to keep quiet so the child's sleep wouldn't be disturbed. Milk had been arranged for him on a small station on way. He woke up the child and gave him hot milk from his thermos flask. When workers came to meet him in Patna, he handed over the child to them directing them to find out his family and arrange for his safe return to home."[16]

Rajju Bhaiya was a completely self-sacrificing person. RSS had begun relief work after terrible earthquake in Uttarkashi. The first cheque received by Uttar Pradesh secretary of RSS, Dr. Nityanand, was from Rajju Bhaiya. The letter accompanying the cheque was an inspiring one. He had also noted in it, "I am sending this contribution from the savings from my teaching days."[17]

He was supervising a Sangh Shiksha Varg in Thrissur. There were about 50 swayamsevaks taking care of the arrangements. He noticed, "The ratio of prabandhak (care takers) and trainees is more than normal." Prant prachaarak told him that they were not paid labours but own swayamsevaks. Some swayamsevaks were barbers, some auto drivers, cleaners and cooks too. He said, "Then it is alright. But this is not so in other places and your expenses are lower too." He was happy that even prachaaraks were doing all types of work.[18]

It was his innate nature to work in difficult situations with courage and with a smile. Swami Chinmayananda, Mahant Avaidyanath and Rajju Bhaiya had been kept under arrest in Jim Corbett park guest house during 1989 Ram Janmabhoomi movement by Mulayam Singh government. Swamiji remembers those times, "He would take his diabetes injection himself with ease while he was chatting with others.

Sometimes, he would make his own tea. Three of us used to go for a walk in the evening with police personnel trailing them. Once he told them in good humour, "Brother, Mahant and I are old, we cannot run away. Chinmayananda cannot leave us behind. Then, why are you following us?" When the security person told him that they were following them to save them from wild animals, he said, "This is the area where tigers live. Don't you know tigers never attack tigers? We three are lions too. We don't need any security."[19]

Sangh was banned in 1993 but it was not as strict as it was during Emergency. Ranga Hari had gone to Nagpur for a meeting and he was housed in a safe place. Next day, Rajju Bhaiya came to pick him up for the meeting driving a car. Regular driver was sitting in the back seat. Rajju Bhaiya laughed and said, "Police will never suspect that a senior office bearer is driving a car himself and taking along the all-India head of intellectual training!"[20] He could be found laughing and in good humour even in toughest situation.

Rajju Bhaiya had extraordinary memory. Swami Chinmayananda gives an example, "R.B. Singh, who had just retired from UP police service, came to meet me. I was getting ready to go to Jhandewalan office of RSS to meet Rajju Bhaiya. Singhji remarked that he had been a student of Rajju Bhaiya at one time and he too wished to meet him. I took him along to Keshav Kunj office. As soon as Rajju Bhaiya saw him, he exclaimed, "Hey, Ran Bahadur, when did you arrive?" Hearing him say this, R.B. Singh began crying. He said, "I am meeting you after twenty years, how did you recognise me?" "Can our memories fade over years? You have been my student; how can I forget you?"[21] – Rajju Bhaiya responded.

A prachaarak in Prayag at that time, Vireshwar Dwivedi too shares another example. "Whenever Rajju Bhaiya went to the railway station, many professors, teachers, police officers, administrative officers would touch his feet out of gratitude and he would call them all by their names with affection and say, "Aren't you a student of xyz batch? Where is your abc friend?" There are thousands of people who were fortunate to have received his affection.[22]

According to Vijay Ganesh Kulkarni, Rajju Bhaiya's first love was education. There was a meeting of Vidya Bharati in 1993 in Agra where Rajju Bhaiya was nominated as the patron in Shri Bhaurao Deoras Trust. We all knew that education was a topic of his deep interest. He said in the meeting, "If I would have been asked to choose an organisation to work, I would have preferred to work for Vidya Bharati." He always used to guide teachers and Professors. He had already donated his own parental house to Shishu Mandir. There was a programme in Rayganj in Bengal state in 1995. There was a Shishu Mandir near the venue. As soon as the meeting was over, he told the Prant prachaarak that he would like to visit Shishu Mandir. A high school came up in Rayganj later due to his inspiration. Till then, there was no CBSE school in that city.[23]

Every worker and colleague have a story about encouragement they received from him. Muzaffar Hussein shared his experience. "A person could learn from him, how to encourage a junior colleague. Rajju Bhaiya came to Aurangabad once. 'Devgiri Samachar', a Hindi newspaper used to be published from there. Fortunately, at that time, I was the consulting editor of this newspaper. Date was 14th September 1992. Rajju Bhaiya called me. Just as I bowed down to seek his blessings, he embraced me. Giving his blessings, he said, "I liked the main page of your newspaper today very much." To me the pictorial illustration was average. Illustrating Bharat's map, we had marked out Devgiri and inserted the word 'naa' in it to make it appear as 'Devanaagiri' He liked the idea of connecting Devgiri with Devanagari like this. He gave me pat on the back with affection.[24]

If there was a need to give a clear advice, he would do so in an unattached manner, even if it was not a popular opinion at that time. Mahant Narayan Giri talks about his experience. "When he was in Ghaziabad in 1989, Rajju Bhaiya had visited Saraswati Shishu Mandir in Nehru Nagar for a meeting. At that time, many people met him and proposed my name for the upcoming Loksabha elections. When they lobbied for it too hard, Rajju Bhaiya called me in a separate room and asked me, "Maharaj, do you wish to fight elections? After a pause, I told him, "Sanyasi does the job of nurturing sanskriti in society. It is their love for me that they have proposed my name to you without informing me." He then said, "Maharaj, you have spoken what I had in my heart. A sanyasi should become the guide of the society only then he can serve the society in the best way and only then can he become its 'Swami' (or guiding authority). Then he gave me many inspirational ideas. He said, "A person can become great very easily, but it is very difficult to remain simple. One can guide the society and motivate society to walk the path of truth only with simplicity. His thoughts that day left a deep mark on me and I pondered over them to imbibe them in my life. I received the inspiration to serve the society and inculcate values in the society."[25]

He never cared about his time and efforts if he had to motivate a worker or take some trouble too. Thakur Prasad Verma writes, "A seminar had been organised on the topic of 'Elements obstructing Indian history' in 1989. I was invited to chair the seminar. Title of my lecture was, 'Ancient Bharat and Western World.' I was in Jhandewalan and Rajju Bhaiya was staying there. I sent a copy of my lecture to him. He asked me about the time and location of the programme and I informed him accordingly. Next day, while we were standing together at the venue, I saw Rajju Bhaiya alighting from a car with his security staff. I was confused about giving him a place in keeping with his personality. So, I requested him to sit on the stage, but he insisted that he had come to hear him so he would sit in the audience. With lot of difficulty, I finally found courage to speak in front of him and finished my lecture somehow. During the tea break, he told me encouragingly, "I had read the speech yesterday night but I wished to hear it from you. This is the best lecture I have heard on this topic." This was the best possible reward for me. I treated it as a landmark in my future journey in life."[26]

Prof. Bishan Kishore tells us that he respected every work done by a swayamsevak. It was his hobby to write poems and set them to tune. "Once, I offered him my poem *'Dhwaj pranaam'* in a camp in Basti. He held it and touched it on his forehead with reverence and kept it in his pocket. What could be a more respectful gesture for an ordinary swayamsevak? When I was being introduced in a camp in Dhammaur, he added many more points about me. I realised how attentive he is and remembers qualities of a swayamsevak."[27]

He gave a lot of importance to songs as a medium to inculcate values in a person. Whether it was the first batch of Sangh Shiksha Varg or any other camp, respected Rajju Bhaiya could be seen exchanging notes with the singer and would be there with his taperecorder during practice sessions. Our lunch used to be mostly in the second batch. Something similar happened during a training camp of about 375 prachaaraks in Deendayal Puram near Varanasi around the Holi festival of 1973. He asked Padmakar Mishra, "So, do you have a new song?" Padmakar Mishra responded, "Yes, but so far I have written only the first and the fourth paragraph." He said, "Ok, go ahead and sing." I sang *'Kitne hi yug se hey janani...Bhagawati Bharatmata.'* Despite my disclaimer, he realised that it was my own effort. He said, "It is good. When will you write the other two paragraphs? Send it to this address in Prayag." While I was preparing for the Sangh Shiksha Varg in my area of work, Dumraon, I received a postcard with a reply card attached. He had written, "You have a forgetful nature, so I am sending this reminder. If you could write the other two paragraphs of the song, please send them." In the address, with my name was added (B.A.), so the postman and neighbours would note that this prachaarak is well read. But I had not yet written the sentences, how could I send them? Just before the Varg, I had to face him again in a meeting in Patna. Without embarrassing me, he told me, "Arrey, just pick up a pen, it will be completed.

Your lines in the poem should mention that it is our tradition to offer sacrifice for the good of the world rather than snatch things from others." In those busy days, I had woven those emotions in the song and reached Samastipur varg as a teacher. He was sitting in the room of camp-in-charge, the senior most officer of a camp. He asked me, "Is it done?" I said, "Ji (yes), and then sang it for him. He noted, "It is good, and suggested a few corrections. Then, he took out a paper from his pocket, tore it into pieces and threw them into dustbin; and said, "I thought, perhaps, you may not find time, so I had written the missing two paragraphs. But now they are not required." He had his own way to inspire and motivate a worker."[28]

Kaunteya Deshpande shares his experience about Rajju Bhaiya, "There was a meeting of top leaders of RSS during Diwali time in 1994 in Keshav Srishti near Mumbai. In that cheerful environment, I was given the responsibility of the residence of Rajju Bhaiya. I had just begun my university education. As a young swayamsevak, I would look consciously at his way of sitting, walking, chatting etc. I could meet him only for a few seconds in those three days of meeting when he was going out or coming in. He would chat with swayamsevaks managing the campus in the evening. Once, I insisted him to listen to my poems. He heard my poems very happily and encouraged me too, though he could not have understood my poems in depth because they were in Marathi. After completing my studies, I went as a prachaarak in two places in Maharashtra in two years. During that time, I could meet Rajju Bhaiya in my area of work or Sangh Shiksha Varg twice or thrice. He was our respected Sarsanghchaalak. But he would call me out in a crowd of swayamsevaks whenever he saw me and ask, "How are you Kaunteya?" I would feel uplifted with happiness and also felt embarrassed. He had such a wonderful memory even at the age of 75 years. I guess a very simple reason for this. This memory was not achieved due to any conscious effort or exercise. This was just a manifestation of his deep sense of oneness with every swayamsevak in Bharat."[29]

Respected H.V. Sheshadri also writes about his sense of oneness with the swayamsevaks and dealing with every one of them with same affection. "I had worked with him for 15 years while he was Sarsanghchaalak, Sarkaryavaah and also Sah Sarkaryavaah. But I never saw any change in his dealing with me. As a colleague he had an excellent way of dealing with his colleagues as friends."[30]

Describing Rajju Bhaiya's personality, Shridhar Damle quotes Samarth Ramdas, "Speech is like the wife of a great person, because the person has an authority and control over her." Rajju Bhaiya too had that kind of authority and control over his speech. He was a soft spoken, dignified and friendly personality. You would always find him in happy mood and he met people with joyful warmth. He had an open smile that went upto his eyes. He was very polite and even after he became Sarsanghchaalak, his conduct did not change at all."[31]

Tarun Vijay remembers that, "He had a nature that always welcomed anything new and good. He was not a ritualist; he was not orthodox. It was not in his nature to tie down or control or to hurt anyone. If he found a person skilled in a work and wishes to progress in that direction, he would support him fully, despite others opposing him. I wrote a series on Kailash-Mansarovar yatra in Panchjanya. He called me and told me, "You are writing well. This should appear in a book form." I talked to 2-3 publishers. They were talking about pricing it at a minimum 800 to 1,200 Rupees. Rajju Bhaiya said, "No, this book should be low cost so it can reach more people. Give an advertisement in Panchjanya and ask people for advance booking." I followed up the advice and did the same. There was opposition of some members within the publication team telling me how can you do it? It is your personal work. Rajju Bhaiya scolded those people. "He is our swayamsevak. If he is doing something good, why are you opposing him?" He went on to publish advertisements for the book free of cost. This book could get published only because of his backing.[32]

Former Chancellor of Prayag and Gorakhpur universities

Prof. Vishwambhar Dayal Gupta remembers that whenever he used to come to Gorakhpur or called on phone, he would say, "Never deviate from the path of karma, whatever may be the situation. Vishwambhar, stick to your stand at any cost." His chats would raise self-confidence and I could keep working even in difficult situations. He helped at every step in my career building. It seemed as if he was born only to help others."[33]

He never cared about his personal problems. He would think of a worker and Sangh work first. Jaiprakash Chaturvedi tells us that in 1983 in June Rajju Bhaiya had a small operation. "He had to go to Rajasthan Sangh Shiksha Varg. He used to get fever as an after effect of surgery. Doctors had advised him to take full rest. But he was not deterred. As per his wish to travel for the varg, I booked his ticket in first class coach so he would suffer less. When I handed over his ticket on the platform, he was very upset. Then and there he changed his ticket to lower class and sent me a letter after reaching Rajasthan, "I get angry only about two things. One, when someone incurs unnecessary expenses and second when someone speaks untruth." He also apologised in the letter for being angry. He was such a great person. I have preserved that letter even today."[34]

Prof. Bishan Kishore talks of another incident. "During a train travel, my wife and I had lower berths and Rajju Bhaiya had upper berth. I suggested that he should exchange the berth with me, but he refused flatly. When I insisted again, he was unhappy and did not accept my request. He never liked to trouble another swayamsevak for himself. He always blessed and offered affection to all swayamsevaks like a father.[35]

In his homage to Rajju Bhaiya, Dr. Mohanji Bhagwat writes, "During travel to Nagpur, Rajju Bhaiya was suffering from very high fever. I could figure it out when I touched him accidentally. He didn't tell us. When asked, he told me that it was there for last 2-3 days. But he told me not to postpone the programme, saying, "I have to sit and speak, there is no physical programme, right? I am walking, I am eating, so I can speak too." He always kept himself behind and kept the objective ahead. Looking at goodness of entire society, taking everybody along and keeping oneself behind the goal – these two fundamental things should be part of every swayamsevak's thinking.[36]

Though he was always busy travelling all over Bharat and in touch with thousands of families and swayamsevaks. He always gave importance to family relations. In fact, he underlined this thought in a question answer session and said, "Sangh is not a social organisation, it is a family organisation. When he spoke of Emergency and remembered those days, he used to repeat how family relations were useful.

Whether it was a host family or a senior worker, he would try to be always in touch with them. A swayamsevak from Kerala named Mohandas remembers, "He had a quality that whenever he stayed with a host family, he would always write letter to the family after returning. Without using the word, 'thank you' he would talk about something that delighted him and appreciate it. Once, he had a programme in Kochi in a school where Ranga Hariji's home was in the lane opposite the school. A swayamsevak introduced Hariji's brother to Rajju Bhaiya. Rajju Bhaiya decided to offer his salutation to Hariji's father by visiting his home. He met Hariji's father, had tea with him and informed him about his son's activities and health. Hariji came to know about his visit to his home much later."[37]

Whichever family he stayed with, would become his family. Building such affectionate relations with people was a special quality of Rajju Bhaiya's personality. Raman Khanna, who hosted Rajju Bhaiya twice, tells us that after his meetings were over, he would sit down with children of the family and chat happily with them. The atmosphere used to be delightful. His food was very simple. Once he was lying down in the verandah of his home. Ramanji felt that he had dozed off. When he opened his eyes, Raman asked if he could sleep well. Rajju Bhaiya told him, "No, I was enjoying the chirping of the birds." He could enjoy every kind of things in life. He never let his life be boring. After his retirement and shifting to Kaushikashram in Pune, he sent a message to Ramanji to come and meet him in Pune.[38]

Rajju Bhaiya stayed with Ladsaria family twice in Mumbai. Ladsaria tells that he would discuss science and global issues at length with his son and daughter and tell stories to children. He would talk with each member of the family keeping in mind that person's inclination and have light chit-chat skills. Nothing like ego or sense of being a big person ever touched his personality and he was very calm and straightforward. One could never imagine that he was such a scholarly person. He was always ready to learn at his age and would discuss and understand something new. He had a cotton bag that had 2-3 sets of dhoti and kurta. But, when he was ready to go out, one felt as if one was in the company of a saint, such was his halo. He had kept a silk kurta for special programmes. He would insist on going to shakha daily, that too in shakha dress in a half pant. A host family had gifted him an umbrella. He gifted it to a family.

Ladsariaji had the chance of glancing at his habit of keeping away from party politics and his non-attachment. Many people used to come to meet him at home. When he was staying at Ladsaria's home, Shankar Singh Waghela episode was at peak. There were many phone calls that he wished to meet Rajju Bhaiya. But he refused to talk to him. He just sent an instruction that he should talk with the party. Many people came to seek BJP tickets. He told them politely that they should meet party leaders and refused to interfere at all.[39]

He never carried more than required clothes in any travel. He was like a simple saint. He received a shawl in Kerala as a gift. Rajju Bhaiya told the person humbly with a smile, "Brother, I have so many shawls that they will be sufficient for next ten years and I may not even live that long. Why don't you give it to someone who really needs it?"[40]

Rajju Bhaiya used to read important dailies and weeklies diligently and regularly. He would read the newspapers and periodicals that promoted Sangh philosophy. Panchjanya weekly was his favourite. He would send notes and guide the team with lot of interest. He believed that these magazines take RSS views to the areas where Sangh swayamsevak cannot reach. Once, his car had a breakdown in the night in Uttar Pradesh. Despite all the efforts car could not be repaired and night descended. No arrangement could be made for food too. The roads leading to villages looked unfamiliar. We kept asking about Sangh workers on way, but we did not succeed. Suddenly, Rajju Bhaiya asked a person about 'Panchjanya'. Hearing the word 'Panchjanya' that person brought another person from the village. Rajju Bhaiya asked him, "Have you heard the name of Rajju Bhaiya?" The person shook his head in agreement. Rajju Bhaiya smiled broadly and said, "Then, I am that person." Hearing this, that pleased swayamsevak bowed down with respect and took him home.[41]

He was always in learning mode not just as a teacher but also as a student. Shreesh Deopujari, who was his personal assistant for many years, shares a very inspiring incident. "His bent of mind was always that of a teacher but also of a student all his life. Even after becoming Sarsanghchaalak when he realised that former Sarsanghchaalak Balasaheb Deoras used to quote Sanskrit shlokas to highlight the essence of what he was saying, and he too felt like learning and doing the same. But he would make some mistakes because he did not know the rules of grammar. When he felt that one of the media to learn Sanskrit can be Sanskrit 'Chandamama' magazine he paid annual subscription and read it with lot of interest. He would always carry Sanskrit edition of Chandamama in his travelling bag. Understanding his interest, I got drafts of congratulatory messages for marriages and condolence messages for bereavements from the All-India secretary of Samskrit Bharati, Shri Chamu Shastri and got them printed as if it is my hand writing. I would add the name of the concerned persons and get it signed by Rajju Bhaiya.

Respected Rajju Bhaiya used to stay for a month in an Ayurvedic clinic in Thrissur in Kerala. In the last year of this three-year treatment cycle, respected Sarkaryavaah Sheshadriji too gave him company. There was time at hand. A Sanskrit speaking course was organised in the clinic in the company of other people who had come for treatment. These included my father, my maternal uncle, people managing the stay, Tehsil sanghchaalak Shri Madhavan Namboodiri and myself. It ran for ten days for two hours each. Samskrit Bharati teacher use to teach every day and important students in the programme were respected Sarsanghchaalak and Sarkaryavaah. After completing 75 years of life and heading a global powerful organisation, he was ready to learn Sanskrit in the mould of a student. It was an extraordinary and a highly inspirational scene.

Janseva Nyas, a trust run by Karnataka swayamsevaks decided to launch 'Ved Vigyan Gurukulam' in 1996. This Gurukul not only teaches Vedas, Sanskrit Grammar, Vedant but also English and computer. When they thought of inauguration of this Gurukul, it was but natural to think of Rajju Bhaiya. Whenever he got a chance, he would always ask about its progress from Gurukul Acharya Ramchandra Bhatt. He would make it a point to be present in any programme related to Sanskrit. Whenever he had an opportunity, he would encourage the workers of Samskrit Bharati who had a vision of bringing in a change in Bharat on the basis of Samskrit speaking classes and raise their morale."[42]

When Balasaheb Deoras handed over the mantle in 1994 to Rajju Bhaiya, he was Saha Sarkaryavaah. Though, the nomination of the succeeding Sarsanghchaalak is done and announced traditionally by the retiring Sarsanghchaalak, people who understand Sangh know that Sarsanghchaalak consults and exchanges notes with many senior workers of Sangh before he makes the announcement after achieving a consensus. The post of Sarsanghchaalak is very crucial in giving direction to the organisation and leading it. Sarkaryavaah has more responsibility of running the day-to-day affairs of RSS, and he is an elected office bearer. His nomination by the seniors in Rajju Bhaiya showed their faith in him. Vijay Kumar describes the scene at the time when announcement of this change was done—

"The date was 11th March, 1994. It was the second day of the Akhil Bharatiya Pratinidhi Sabha. In the second session of the day which was held in a huge hall of Hedgewar Smarak Samiti in Reshim Bagh in Nagpur, Balasaheb made the announcement in front of more than 1,000 delegates who had come from all over Bharat, "Poojaniya Guruji had handed over this responsibility to me in 1973. I have fulfilled the responsibility with your cooperation. But I am not able to undertake tours due to ill-health. So, after consulting all the senior workers, I have taken the decision that Prof. Rajendra Singh, who is well known to all of you, will carry on the responsibility now onwards. I have full faith that all of you will offer the same co-operation that you gave me. I will also do whatever I can as a swayamsevak."

Every eye was moist and everyone was looking at stage without battling an eyelid. Balasaheb Deoras offered a sacred coconut and a bouquet to Rajju Bhaiya. Rajju Bhaiya accepted the responsibility with bowed head and sought blessings from him. In his short speech, he sought blessings and co-operation from all present."[43]

Another of his qualities was readiness to listen to a kaaryakarta affectionately, give him solution and keep his morale up. This was the reason no worker felt hesitant to bare his heart to him. Tarun Vijay writes, "He was our highest authority. But he was so close and affectionate to us that we would cry on his shoulders, fight with him, complain to him, did what we wished to, and would bear with his scolding too. Some incidents would agitate me a lot and I would not feel like working. The kind of news about politics we published, I would feel that rather than working here, just circumambulating this atmosphere was enough. I resigned from Panchjanya four times in this agitated state of mind and emotional turbulence. He refused all the four times and told me, "Do not do such a thing in future. You have come here to work. Everything else is minor. Do not pay attention to others' conduct and actions. Write what you wish to write. Just pay attention to that. This is the quality of a swayamsevak." Once, when I complained, he told me, "All these are stupid emotions. Don't worry about what is happening around you or how you are being dealt with and never give a written complaint." His view was, don't condemn anyone, do not criticise someone personally. Why? Because, someone will be useful to the organisation due to some quality of his."[44]

He never let go his nature of worrying about workers all through his life. It was the reason why his name carried the affectionate address of 'Bhaiya' – elder brother. Former prachaarak, Vijay Kumar had returned to family life and was taking care of his family in Guruvayoor. Unfortunately, he died and his wife and children were leading a poverty ridden tough life. Sangh workers decided to get a home constructed to help his family. Rajju Bhaiya was on a tour of Kerala at that time. swayamsevaks requested him to inaugurate the auspicious work for collecting contribution for this cause. Rajju Bhaiya asked for the receipt book in a very low voice after dinner and silently offered a cheque of 500 rupees. In the next all India meeting, he enquired about construction of the house from Kerala Prant prachaarak and was very satisfied and happy when he was informed that house had already been handed over.[45]

Kashi Prant sanghchaalak writing in the special homage issue of magazine 'Vichar Pravaah' noted that Rajju Bhaiya was highly educated and came from a prestigious wealthy family. Even his student life, life as a teacher and RSS prachaarak was worthy of being proud, still ego never touched his mind and heart. His meetings and lectures were simple to understand and he spoke like a teacher. He could get even the toughest ideas and topics across very easily to the audience. Even after reaching the highest level of leadership as Sarsanghchaalak, he was the same, simple straight and easily available person.

He was opposed to the use of prefix *'param poojya'* (most respected) that is used for the Sarsanghchaalak. He would say, "I am the same Rajju Bhaiya that you all know; I love being called as Rajju Bhaiya."[46]

Sureshrao Ketkar, very senior prachaarak, told us that Rajju Bhaiya was afflicted with many diseases. Travelling so much even at an elderly age and taking care of so many issues, working continuously had taken its toll. He had sleepless nights. Postural hypo-tension, diabetes and Parkinson troubled him. However, no one ever saw him complaining or see that he was fed up with these problems. He would smilingly take injection of insulin himself. He sought complete information about his sicknesses from doctors very objectively. He had complete knowledge about medicines and followed all the do's and don'ts. He would jokingly say many times, "I enjoy the sickness." When he came to know that he had diabetes, he said with an easy smile, "I have got a friend forever now."[47]

No one ever saw him worried or pained by his multiple diseases. A worker from Kerala said that Rajju Bhaiya was taking treatment in Ollur near Thrissur. He was a very obedient patient. Being a scientist, he would take every medicine in correct measure. He would gather information respectfully about the components of a medicine. But he did not wear dhoti in Kerala style, saying he felt more at home in UP style dhoti. He had dictated his autobiography during those days. He helped the Vaidyashala to open a branch in Delhi after he returned.[48]

He had imbibed the lesson of keeping away from publicity from Sangh. Dr. Rajendra Agrawal discloses that on completion of 75 years in 1997, a celebration, called 'Amrit Mahotsav' was arranged as per Hindu traditions. Lokahit Prakashan in Lucknow decided to publish a small book about his multifaceted personality and life. "I was given the responsibility of talking about it with Rajju Bhaiya and have a conversation about it to publish the proposed booklet. But, when he came to know about it, in keeping with traditions of self-abnegation of ancient rishi-munis and avoiding any glorification, he did not allow the proposed publication."[49]

Rajju Bhaiya was a living example of simplicity. Bimal Kedia remembers the 1998 Pratinidhi Sabha of Lucknow. Ram Mandir was the major issue of discussion. But, Rajju Bhaiya gave a lecture for thirty minutes about importance of 'simplicity' (*saadagi* in Hindi). He explained that Sangh work should always be done with simplicity. There should be no show off and grandeur. He presented this subject with many small examples.[50] Explaining a deep and difficult topic in simple language was hallmark of his speeches. He explained that success of one's life comes from serving the society in a simple way.

Vachnesh Tripathi tells us about his way of putting things in a natural simple manner. There was a function to celebrate 60 years of Dr. Murli Manohar Joshi. Nearly all the speakers offered him best wishes. But, when Rajju Bhaiya gave his blessings, he gave it in a very different manner. He said, "I am not giving Joshiji a blessing of living for 100 years because it is possible that my blessings may or may not bear fruits. Therefore, on this auspicious occasion, I pray to omniscient God that every second of Joshiji's life be fruitful and he may serve the society and people as a goal of his life. May his life be busy serving the nation."[51] Everybody received a lesson.

Arun Kankani once asked Rajju Bhaiya a question that had been in his mind for a long time. "Why do young people still join Sangh and take so much of trouble in working for the society?" His prompt reply was, "Purpose. Purpose or goal is a major reason for attracting youth." I was really surprised, because I had thought that affection and sense of brotherhood was major reason for attraction of youth for Sangh. Rajju Bhaiya clarified, "Our working process has many facets that are very important for organisation. But, the primary reason for attraction of youth towards Sangh is our principles."[52]

His quality of explaining a difficult topic in simple easy words has been talked about by many. To keep one's lecture simple and easy despite such a scholarly mind remained his rare quality. Bimal Kedia remembers his 1974 tour of Mumbai. He conducted many informal meetings with young shakha level workers and he answered most of the questions. Then he said, "Now, I will ask you a question and you have to answer." He asked, "What is the biggest task of a swayamsevak?" All the young workers let their imagination run far and wide and gave many interesting answers. Rajju Bhaiya heard them all and then told them, "The biggest task of a swayamsevak is to create more swayamsevaks. Similarly, the main task of a kaaryakarta (worker) is to create more kaaryakartas. It means that you have joined Sangh as a swayamsevak, but many of our brethren in the society do not know about Sangh. Your biggest responsibility is to bring them to shakha and make them swayamsevaks."[53] Similarly, he gave five simple formulae that he called '5-S'. Those are – *Sanch* (team), *Sankhya* (numbers in the shakha), *Sanskar* (inculcating value system), *Sampark* (good contact) and *Sneh* (affection). I have provided a note about this talk in the annexure of this book.

Kaunteya Deshpande says that he used to get spell bound listening to him. "There were no dramatics, nor expressions of high or low emotions. He could still keep young and old focused on his words. Not many speakers have this skill. For example, he would be pressing hard for uprooting caste system and importance of bringing harmony in the society and then suddenly shift to problem of Kashmir. But the listener could not make out this transition in topics. His skill was to present Sangh view that All the parts of Bharat are but branches of the same tree and the root of this tree is Hindustan. Lack of organisation of Hindus in Hindustan is very clearly."[54]

His speciality was that anyone listening to him, would be able to come out of the meeting with some clear points of doing something practically and the reasons for doing it. One would be clear about what work is to be done, when, why and how. Rajju Bhaiya gave some very simple and effective ideas in Savarkar Smaarak meeting of workers sometime in

1980 that could be followed by any person. First, we wear different clothes for different kind of work we do daily, but we should wear our traditional clothes during religious and social programmes. Our dress, our clothes are important markers of our culture and if we use them, we will nurture it. Second, we see that in cities both husband and wife have to work to run the family. It may be necessary in certain conditions. But, can we think about a way where either husband or wife will work for living while the second person keeps busy with serving the society? It is not easy to differentiate between 'greed' and 'necessity'. It is difficult to understand when the necessity turns into greed. Many workers have done this successfully. Others should also think about it. Third, many people spend a lot of money in weddings and other social functions. They feel that to make the celebrations dignified, one has to spend that kind of money. They may be right. There is a very thin line dividing 'dignity' and 'exhibition'. Can our swayamsevaks think that whatever they spend on such functions, they will donate 10 per cent of that expense to a Sewa project of their choice? This could, perhaps, be a good guideline for us. If they feel that 10 per cent is very high then it will come to their attention that spending, they are incurring on that celebration is crossing the thin line of dignity.[55]

In a meeting in Mumbai for senior workers, he gave a very simple idea for staying rooted. He suggested that one must visit one's village atleast once a year. Senior prachaarak and member of central committee, Hastimalji, disclosed that Rajju Bhaiya used to visit his parental village, Banail, atleast once a year.[56]

Ranga Hari tells us that Rajju Bhaiya was very particular about time. He never took more time than the allotted for his lecture or meetings. If any other speaker took away more time, he would tailor his speech to adjust the time for timely closure of the programme. He would complete his speech in such a way that noone could even make out that he left out some points due to shortage of time. Once it so happened that the Chairperson of the annual Vijayadashami festival in Nagpur extended his speech much beyond his allocated time. Rajju Bhaiya, without showing any discomfiture, completed his own speech in a few minutes. He omitted many examples and stories (his specialty) and many special notes surgically to complete the programme in time. However, copies of his complete speech were given to the media. He had excellent mastery over Hindi and English, but he used to employ simple and short sentences in his speech.[57]

Muzaffar Hussain underlines an issue that became important again during Rajju bhaiya's terms. "One question used to be raised time and again in discussions whether it is necessary for Sangh to get into politics. While answering to this question, Balasaheb had said that for the present we have no such plans. But Sangh is not allergic to politics. If need arises, Sangh will not think twice about it. Such a moment arose during Rajju Bhaiya's time. Sangh did not play the role of a political party, but the birth of Bharatiya Janata Party that was inspired by the samskaras given by Sangh. The process had begun in 1980, but it gained velocity during Rajju Bhaiya's term as Sarsanghchaalak. Due to his hard work and valued guidance, BJP finally rose on the political horizon of Bharat. Not only that, it became a very important force in national politics. The firm call for construction of Ram Mandir gave it a new life. BJP leadership accepted the challenge of building of Ram Temple along with building of the nation. Rajju Bhaiya will be remembered in the contemporary history of free Bharat as a visionary for giving political shape to a cultural and social organisation with Kshatriya pride."[58]

Rajju Bhaiya's health had weakened a lot due to years of hard work, continuous travel and other physical sicknesses. Only a healthy person can carry the responsibility of leading such a big all India organisation. With this assertion, he gave up his post on 10th March, 2000. After consulting senior RSS workers, he appointed Shri K.S. Sudarshanji as the fifth Sarsanghchaalak.

One must acknowledge the specialty of Sangh's tradition that after handing over the responsibility to Sudarshanji, he went down from the stage and sat with the other workers, as if he never carried the onerous task of heading Sangh at one time. It also showed his simplicity and grace.

References

1. Shirdhar Damle, telephonic conversation, 22nd October, 2103
2. Ranga Hari, Kerala memoirs, email dated 15th July, 2013
3. Vachnesh Tripathi, Vichar Pravaah, op cit, p. 53
4. Adheesh Kumar, Vichar Pravaah, op cit, p. 14
5. Prof. Krishnannath Pandey, Vichar Pravaah, op cit, p. 83
6. Omkar Singh, Vichar Pravaah, op cit, p. 66
7. Arun Kankani, email, op cit
8. Adheesh Kumar, op cit, p. 13
9. Bimal Kedia, Keshav Srishti Samachar, August 2003 edition
10. Kerala memoirs sent by email, op cit
11. Vinay Katiyar, Vichar Pravaah, op cit, p. 9
12. Ibid
13. Dr. Mohan Bhagwat, Vichar Pravaah, op cit, p. 2, 3
14. Bimal Kedia, written note
15. Ramgopal Sand, Vichar Pravah, op cit, p. 31
16. Swami Chinmayananda, Vichar Pravaah, op cit, p. 18
17. Adheesh Kumar, op cit, p. 15
18. Kerala swayamsevaks' memoirs, op cit
19. Swami Chinmayananda, op cit, p. 18
20. Ranga Hari, Kerala swayamsevaks' memoirs, op cit
21. Swami Chinmayananda, op cit
22. Vijay Ganesh Kulkarni, Vichar Pravaah, op cit, p. 24
23. Edited out
24. Muzaffar Hussein, Tarun Bharat, 20th July, 2003
25. Shri Mahant Narayan Giri, International Secretary, Shri Panch Dasnaam Juna Akhada, through email of Rajendraji, 14th October, 2013
26. Thakur Prasad Veram, Vichar Pravaah, op cit, p. 36
27. Prof. Bishan Kishore, Vichar Pravaah, op cit, p. 37
28. Padmakar Mishra, op cit, email dated 22nd October, 2013
29. Kauntey Deshpande, Keshav Srishti Samachar, August 2003 edition
30. H.V. Sheshadriji, Vichar Pravaah, op cit, p. 7
31. Shridhar Damle, op cit
32. Tarun Vijay, Panchjanya, 27th July, 2003
33. Dr. Vishwambhar Dayal Gupta, Vichar Pravaah, op cit, p. 73
34. Jaiprakash Chaturvedi, Vichar Pravaah, op cit, p. 63

35. Prof. Bishan Kishore, op cit.
36. Dr. Mohan Bhagwat, op cit
37. Mohandas, Kerala swayamsevaks' memoirs, op cit
38. Raman Khanna, personal conversation, September 2013
39. Ladsaria family, personal conversation, September 2013
40. Kerala swayamsevaks' memoirs, op cit
41. Muzaffar Hussein, op cit
42. Shreesh Deopujari, email dated 24th October, 2013
43. Vijay Kumar, Apne Param Poojaniya Sarsanghchaalak, p. 44
44. Tarun Vijay, op cit
45. Kerala swayamsevaks' memoirs, op cit
46. Vichar Pravaah, op cit, p. 48
47. Sureshrao Ketkar, Gomant Shakti, 10th April, 1998
48. Kerala swayamsevaks; memoirs, op cit
49. Dr. Rajendra Agrawal, Vichar Pravaah, op cit, p. 48
50. Keshav Srishti Samachar, op cit
51. Vachnesh Tripathi, op cit
52. Arun Kankani, op cit
53. Bimal Kedia, personal conversation, October 2013
54. Kauntey Deshpande, Keshav Srishti Samachar, op cit
55. Arun Kankani, op cit
56. Kamlesh Pareek, personal conversation, December 2013
57. Kerala swayamsevaks' memoirs, op cit
58. Muzaffar Hussein, op cit

□

10

Overseas travels of Rajju Bhaiya

Rajju Bhaiya undertook many overseas trips as Sarkaryavaah and Sarsanghchaalak. It would surprise the readers that none of the earlier three Sarsanghchaalaks had travelled overseas ever through hundreds of swayamsevaks had gone overseas for their livelihoods since 1946-47 and built many organisations to serve the Hindu society there. They were doing their personal and social work very well. When Rajju Bhaiya conducted his last overseas tour, nearly forty countries had different types of organisations for Hindus run by RSS inspired swayamsevaks who had settled overseas.

Rajju Bhaiya went to Kenya in December **1979** as Sarkaryavaah. In April **1981**, he toured Myanmar and in **1982** he toured United States and Canada. In **1989** he went to Africa, where his second visit to Kenya was the main programme. He went to Europe and England in **1995** after his appointment as the Sarsanghchaalak. In **1997**, he had an opportunity to visit African continent again when he visited Mauritius, South Africa and Kenya. His last overseas trip was in April **1998** to Japan and Hong Kong. His main agenda was to encourage various organisations working for Hindus outside Bharat and guide them. Every trip had something special and there used to be one central issue that he addressed in each of them. Following are some details in brief about his tours.

Rajju Bhaiya was present in the winter camp of Bharatiya Swayamsevak Sangh in 1979 in a place called Kikuyu in Kenya.

People from far off places and countries like Tanzania, Uganda, Nigeria, South Africa, Seychelles and Mauritius had joined the camp too. Accompanying him on this trip were Shri Laxmanrao Bhide, the first prachaarak of Bharatiya Swayamsevak Sangh and Shri Chamanlal who kept in touch with the overseas Indians for years to keep their morale high from the time when there were only letters, rare telephones and no internet. Rajju Bhaiya mentioned in his first lecture that respected Madhavrao Mulye should have got the honour of the first overseas visit by a senior Sangh functionary because it was due to his inspiration that swayamsevaks had taken Sangh philosophy overseas with them wherever they migrated. But he could not leave Bharat due to Guruji's illness and unfortunately, he left this world after Emergency was lifted.

He reminded people in his lectures that without strength, even a great philosophy has no meaning. He shared the experience of Gurudev Rabindranath Thakur in this regard when Japanese students did not turn up for his felicitation. He also talked about story of most of the countries' unwillingness to play Kabaddi though its exhibition match was highly applauded in Germany during 1936 Olympics. He reminded how there is race to copy the western world because it is powerful, influential too. Bharatiya philosophy did not spread with the help of kings or force, but due to people with high character. We always borrow from the society, but we should repay to the society. He stressed that people of Bharatiya origin should keep alive their pride in Dharma and Sanskriti. They should take a pledge to spread our excellent Dharma and Sanskriti. No nation can become great only by virtue of its geography or population. A nation becomes great due to the society that populates that nation.

He inaugurated a Bharatiya Swayamsevak Sangh office building built in the memory Madhavrao Mulye with unveiling of a plaque in his name. Later, he went to Kisumu and Nakuru where he visited two prestigious industries and planted a tree as a memory of his visit in Ruiru Towel Industries apart from addressing people in BSS programmes.[1]

Rajju Bhaiya undertook a trip to Myanmar in April 1981 for a week. He visited all the major cities and towns like Yangon, Mandalay, Myemo, Pai U, Tang U, Jiyawadi, Chautaga etc. There were meetings with the workers of Sanatan Dharma Swayamsevak Sangh in all these places. He met prominent Buddha and Hindu leaders and many families. Open programmes were not possible due to military rule there. He also met some government officials. A photocopy of his remarks in the visitors' book in Sanatan Dharm Seva Sadan in Chautaga appears in the appendix of this book.[2]

Rajju Bhaiya stayed with Shridhar Damle for some days during his 1982 trip to America. At that time his visit to renowned institution Fermi Lab was an important landmark of the trip. This laboratory is famous for cutting edge research in nuclear science. Fermi is as important place for nuclear research as the famed Cern Lab in Switzerland. Initially, Rajju Bhaiya tried to avoid the visit telling him that he was not up-to-date about the topic. But when he finally paid the visit, he had discussions with the scientists there. They were highly impressed with his mastery over the topic and his knowledge about the latest developments in the field. Another of his session was with the students of Purdue University including question-answer session. That too was highly appreciated.[3]

He also visited Canada during that trip. When his former student Bharatendu Shrivastava came to know about the visit of his respected teacher, he requested a senior kaaryakarta, Jagdish Sharda 'Shastriji' to allow him to take Rajju Bhaiya around Toronto. He also requested him that Rajju Bhaiya should stay with him. Shastriji told him that because of his very tight schedule, he would not be able to meet him and if he wished to meet him, he should be present in one of his programmes. He was not a Sangh swayamsevak. When he met Rajju Bhaiya in the programme, he complained to Rajju Bhaiya that he was not given an opportunity to serve him. Rajju Bhaiya called Shastriji aside after the programme and told him that even if a social worker does not come in Sangh, it is important to allow the person to meet the senior workers, otherwise Sangh work cannot pervade the society. A person not coming to Sangh has same rights as those of a swayamsevak. Therefore, we should not have such a sense of right over our leaders that we do not give opportunity to people from other sections of the society to meet them. Shastriji wrote, "I will never forget this lesson in my life. I accepted the lesson and it was very useful in my work in the society."[4] Later Rajju Bhaiya did stay with Bharatendu and went to Niagara Falls with him.

During his tour of England and Europe in 1995, convenor of Hindu Swayamsevak Sangh (HSS), Dr. Shankar Rao Tatwawadi accompanied him. He has shared his memories with me. Respected Rajju Bhaiya was Sarsanghchaalak at that time. Respected Laxmanrao Bhide, Chamanlalji, Jayprakash Agrawal and Sarasanghachalak's personal assistant Shreesh Deopujari were also with him in this tour. His first programme after touching down in London on 12th April was a public programme to celebrate the birthday of Dr. Babasaheb Ambedkar. It was organised by Friends of India International (FISI). National Hindu Students' Forum and Vishwa Hindu Parishad also organised programmes at that time.[5] He addressed a press conference organised by FISI in London on 19th April where he gave frank and honest answers to all the questions raised by journalists.

He addressed the swayamsevaks of HSS in Leicester, Bradford, Leeds and London while he was in England. When they were going by road from London to Leicester, he was very keen to understand the signage on the roads and routes. He kept asking questions about various towns, locations, roads and also rules; making notes about them. When workers took them to different places, he would gather information about various places and routes very enthusiastically and enjoyed every minute of travel. He would first collect information about local situation and problems and only then did he address the people there. British officer Johan Hambleton came to meet him in London. He had good relations with HSS there and knew about their activities from close quarters. He conveyed his appreciation about the qualities of swayamsevaks and their work. He suggested that if the local youth too get the training that youth of HSS get, then crimes could go down in England.[6]

In the programme conducted on 14th April to celebrate 104th birth anniversary of Dr. Babasaheb Ambedkar in the Royal National Hotel, Rajju Bhaiya remembered his highly inspiring but hard life and paid his respectful homage to the great intellectual leader. He reminded the audience about his struggle to get the Dalit brethren a place of dignity and equality in the society. When Dr. Ambedkar realised that it is not possible to change the thinking of Hindu society, he announced in 1935 that he was born as a Hindu but he will not die as a Hindu. After his announcement, many Muslim and Christian leaders tried very hard that he should join their religion. Nizam of Hyderabad went to the extent of offering him crores of rupees if he joined his faith. But he refused to follow any religion that was not rooted in the soil of Bharat. After a lot of studies, he found refuge in Buddha and he accepted Buddha sampradaaya with his followers. He gave an important message that he had accepted Buddha philosophy because it is born in this nation's soil; and assures us of equality and harmony of all the human beings. The followers of this sampradaaya have same sentiments and thoughts like other sampradaayas of Bharat; therefore, it would not allow Dalits to be separated from our sanskriti. He added that we should take a pledge on the occasion that we shall clean Hindu society of its negative aspects and build a wonderful society that creates equality and harmony that is filled with knowledge and self confidence; so that we can spread the message of great rishis of Bharat in the entire world.[7]

In the Hindu Kendra in Ilford in eastern London, he said on 14th April, "It is only Bharatiya philosophy that gives us an experience of completeness. This thought is capable of guiding the entire humanity toward peace and harmony. It is the duty of Hindu activists that they take forward the foundational values of this philosophy. An organisation gets energy from its workers. The guiding principles of an organisation are tested on the basis of the conduct of its members."[8]

While addressing a camp of Hindu Sevika Samiti in Hazelwood he underlined the importance of women being strong in body and mind in the current scenario, so they can protect themselves. He reminded them of the importance of Bharatiya family system where mother occupies the most important position. This fact was also appreciated by Ms. Margaret Thatcher when she had visited HSS shakha in 1990.[9]

He reminded the participants in Vishwa Hindu Parishad (VHP) programme held in London in Bharatiya Vidya Bhavan's premises about the birth of VHP in 1964. He underlined that this became possible because of the sense of personal dedication of great people like respected Guruji, Swami Chinmayananda and Kanyhaiyalal Munshi and heads of other 19 sects. Talking about the scientific nature of Dharma, he said scientists more or less agree that the ultimate truth cannot be exhibited or proven in a laboratory. Now, great scientists of the world have begun taking deep interest in Dharma. They have begun to accept that the principles of the Jain *Syaatwaad* and Buddha theory of impermanence propounded by the Bharatiya philosophers are closer to theory of relativity and quantum theory. Bharatiya way of life is not in conflict with science anywhere. In fact, entire Hindu thought is logical and in tune with the nature and ecology and is scientific. He highlighted the importance of cow and importance of keeping environment clean with Dharmic value system. He reminded peoples of the importance of knowledge of Sanskrit, as all the old scriptures are written in Sanskrit and that the scientific aspects of Hindu Dharma explained in Vedas, Upanishads and Puranas are also presented in Sanskrit. But it is not easy to learn Sanskrit in Bharat because the government is not in favour of Sanskrit. A journalist who interviewed him on BBC radio asked him "People from Sangh look different from other Hindus. Should we consider them militant?" He replied, "We are neither militant, nor are we submissive. Actually, we are not even aggressive. We are assertive. We speak truth and present our views with full confidence and strength. We have to speak strongly so others don't insult us." To another question, he responded, "Hindu philosophy is humanist philosophy." In a programme he appreciated an American report in which Indians are described as hardworking, professionally committed and followers the laws. He hoped that people like Swami Vivekanand and Swami Ramteerth would rise from among these Indians who will work for the welfare of humanity and make their motherland proud.[10] In the same lecture he narrated a story, "When every person was fighting for the nation, one professor was studying in a library. When he was asked why he was not taking part in the war with the army, he countered with a question, "Why is the war going on? Is it only for a piece of land or something more? Is it not for protecting people's culture and traditions?" He explained that he was studying that very tradition and culture. He thus indicated the importance of culture.[11] A booklet about this tour titled, 'Sarsanghchaalak Goes Abroad' was published later.

There was a public programme in Bradford where he spoke on 'Spirit of World Dharma'. He said that Hindus will have a very important role to play in 21st century. They should be ready to fulfill it. World can see peace and harmony when we imbibe the idea of oneness in diversity in our own lives. Therefore, it is necessary that Hindus realise their true self. We should nurture Hindu culture and traditions, the heritage that our forefathers have left for us. We should make our coming generations worthy of it so that they can carry it forward.[12]

In the Leicester programme of HSS, he underlined the importance of mother tongue, necessity of our religious values and qualities of ideal Hindu family. He indicated, how family helps bind members of the family with mutual affection, happiness and strong relations between young and old; and what is its importance. He was surprised that the newspapers in England publish so little about Bharat and Bharatiyas have to read about the news from newspapers published by Bharatiyas or from newspapers coming from Gujarat. Hindu New Year festival was organised in Preston High School where he highlighted the life of Dr. Hedgewar who was born on this day. He stressed that only Hindus can help establish peace and harmony in the world.[13]

He gave direction to the Sewa International in its convocation ceremony in north London that this organisation should support Sewa work in Bharat, but it should pay attention to Sewa work in local areas too.[14]

Addressing the HSS workers in Hedgewar shakha he advised that programmes of the shakhas can be modified and tuned to the local needs and conditions. He cautioned that whenever those changes are brought in, they should be done keeping the fundamentals of the organisation in mind. We should give place to Yoga etc. in our programmes so that western people understand its importance. There are two types of activities in Sangh – one is the regular and the other is moulded as per situation of a given time.[15] Rajju Bhaiya asked, "What are the qualities of a good shakha?" He explained that value of a life is to reproduce another life. Similarly, value of a good shakha should be to reproduce another good shakha. His tour was highly energising and inspiring.[16]

He appreciated the workers who created a centre for serving the Hindu society in Leicester by establishing a Hindu Sahitya Kendra. He congratulated them on stocking equipments, items and books useful for Hindu society for religious Sanskaras, Pooja etc. Books on history, philosophy, religion and for children were visible in their stock. He hoped that Hindu volunteers would be able to spread the word about it and share books with people at large.[17]

He spoke at School of Oriental Studies in central London and analysed the two basic ideologies of the world at that time – Capitalism and Socialistic pattern of society. He explained why they will ultimately fail; because they do not take an integral view of the human being. He highlighted how Hindu philosophy showed the third way. Western view of a human being is partial. One cannot create equilibrium in the society without thinking about Dharma and Moksha.[18]

Rajju Bhaiya visited Rotterdam in Holland to attend the Easter camp of HSS. He also went to visit the ashram of Mahesh Yogi in Den Hag. This ashram is near the border of Germany and Holland. He had a conversation with Mahesh Yogi for nearly one hour and also visited the homes of a few people who were working for Hindu society there. He conveyed the thoughts expressed by respected Shankaracharya of Kanchi Kamakoti while speaking in the Rotterdam camp. Rajju Bhaiya told that the first ideal swayamsevak is Hanumanji. He is a scholar, he has high character, he is highly skilled and he is always ready to serve Bhagwan Shri Ram. Expanding the thought, he said, "Though he is scholar with high character and skills, he has no personal desires. His only urge is to work for Prabhu Ram. In other words, he is fully dedicated to the goal. Swamsevaks learn these qualities from Hanumanji and imbibe them in their personality. Though Ravana had all the resources, but ultimately Ram won the war, because he had the strength of dedicated warriors.[19]

The third trip of Rajju Bhaiya to African continent took place from 11th January to 28th January in 1997. He visited Kenya, South Africa and Mauritius at that time. He was accompanied by Dr. Shankar Rao Tatwawadi, Laxmanrao Bhide, Dr. Yashwant Pathak and his personal assistant Shreesh Deopujari. The main objective of this trip was to take part in the Golden Jubilee celebrations of Bharatiya Swayamsevak Sangh and this trip was undertaken due to their invitation and request for his presence.

His first visit of this trip was on 11th Jan to a Jain Temple there. He highlighted the special features of *'Pratishtha'* and *'Paryushan'* of the Jain community. When the trustees told him that 60 per cent of the students in their colleges were from African community, he appreciated it highly. He reminded them that only Hindu Dharma can establish peace in the world. The religions that consider only their religion as true and all others as false will definitely fail. There was a programme in Mangal Mandir on the same day. This temple has murtis of Mother Durga and Shivji. In his speech he explained that we should milk the nature and not exploit it. He quoted Gandhiji that Mother Earth has enough for our needs but not for our greed. The biggest programme was held on 12th January, the celebration of Golden Jubilee of Bharatiya Swayamsevak Sangh. A grand procession was taken out that had 22 exhibits and 32 Bharatiya organisations took part in it. A 100-member musical band added to the grandeur of the procession. This programme ended in the form of a huge public meeting. About 7,000 citizens were present in the big hall of the temple and its campus. Due to lack of space, a huge TV screen too had been installed. The Indian ambassador was also present in the programme. Rajju Bhaiya explained the difference between Dharma, sampradayas and Sects in his lecture. He reminded people that there is no proper word for Dharma and *Moksha* in English. Quoting the Bharatiya Supreme Court, he explained that Hindutva is a way of life not a way of worship. Hindus have belief in many faiths and respect all of them. He repeated the golden words of Guru Gobind Singhji—

सकल जगत् में खालसा पंथ गाजे,
जगे धर्म हिंदू, सकल भंड भाजे।[20]
Sakal jagat mein Khalsa panth gaaje,
jaage dharam Hindu, sakal bhanda bhaaje.

Meaning, may the pure faith be victorious, may Hindu dharma get awakened. Hindu Dharma does not believe that there is only one path and all others are false.

He reminded the audience that Christianity has been trying to convert people since last 2000 years. Like Jomo Kenyatta said, "When the British came, they had Bible and we had land. They asked us to close our eyes to pray. When we opened our eyes, they had the land and we had Bible in our hands!" Both Islam and Christianity have put in untiring efforts to convert. Last two world wars have been fought primarily between the countries following Christianity while the Islamic nations of Middle East are fighting between themselves. Hindu dharma accepts that 'मुंडे मुंडे मतिर्भिन्ना' (*munde munde matirbhinna*) that each mind has different views. Therefore, everyone has freedom to follow one's own God and faith. Just as entire world is made of different nations and different races and communities, similarly it is unavoidable that different faiths will grow.[21]

We all know that for an aatman to reside in our body and to carry our Dharmic duties we must have a healthy body. शरीरमाद्यं खलु धर्म साधनम् (*shareermaadyam khalu dharma saadhanam*). Similarly, for spiritual ideas to nurture, the society must be strong and healthy. He stressed that Hindus can never be 'fundamentalists'. These two views are contrarian. We have hundreds of scriptures, not one. We do not have one prophet, nor only one type of worship. He thanked the Kenyan society and the government that there is such a liberal atmosphere that all the faiths and sects are able to follow their beliefs.

One of his lectures was organised in the Department of Science in Nairobi University. The topic was – Science and Religion. Professor Ugala mentioned how a scientist had changed his life from a scientist to that of a social worker to serve the society. Most of the teachers and students attending the programmes were from African roots. A summary of Rajju Bhaiya's speech is quoted in the annexure of this book.

Wahid Chaudhary of Kenya TV interviewed Rajju Bhaiya during this visit. He asked many questions about the current status of Sangh work, its philosophy and how to encourage the Hindu society and youth to be part of it. Rajju Bhaiya responded to all the questions in his usual frank and clear style. There was a question about relation between the Bharatiya Swayamsevak Sangh and RSS. Rajju Bhaiya clarified that there was no formal relation between the two. Both the organisations are inspired by same thoughts. When the swayamsevaks who are settled in Kenya come to Bharat, we exchange ideas with each other. This is the only relation.[22]

There was a Q and A session with the young volunteers of HSS in Nairobi. There were many questions about Hindu Dharma, the work in Kenya and how to improve it. For example, there was a question that when we are busy with social work, the ladies of the home get lonely. How to take them along? Rajju Bhaiya suggested that they could be linked to Sewa activities, Sevika Samiti activities and Vishwa Hindu Parishad work. There could be separate programmes for married couples.[23]

A few programmes were arranged by the Sewa division of BSS in conjunction with the Golden Jubilee celebrations. Under this programme physically challenged people were gifted special wheel chairs and Jaipur feet. Literature in Braille was offered to blind brethren. Cash aid was also given to some organisations that included the Jamhoori High School. Sewing Machines were gifted to an organisation named Mara Catholic Women's Group. The Principal of Jamhoori School disclosed that since the day the school was opened in 1990, not one year passed when BSS had not extended a helping hand. Rajju Bhaiya explained the importance of Sewa and expressed his happiness that he could take part in such a wonderful programme. He told the people that serving human beings is same as serving God.[24]

There was a get together over dinner in Jain Bhavan where 350 guests were present. He shared his views about the Third Way, the Hindu way. He submitted in his speech that there are three important events in the history of the world in last 300 years—1. The French revolution. 2. American War of Independence 3. Industrial Revolution. Then, presenting a bird's eye view of the world history, he critiqued the Communist and Capitalist systems. He exposed the shortcomings of these ideologies. One ideology gives importance to only the society and the social systems are the major concern, while in the other, there is no importance to the material needs of the individual and his/her independence and there is no importance to the family and the society. Both lack balance and equilibrium. So, there is need for a third way and only Hindu way of life can show that path. He then presented 'Integral Humanism'. Only this thinking has nurtured the thought of the world being one family – *Vasudhaiv Kutumbakam*. This thought, alone, will bring the desired welfare to the world.[25]

Makar Sankraman festival was celebrated on 19th January. This was the day when BSS completed 50 years of its official foundation in Kenya. He recalled that this was his third trip to Kenya. He had visited Kenya earlier in 1979 and 1989. In his speech he noted that 'we want *'Sankranti'* not '*Kranti.'* He explained that we wish change that will lead to progress, not just change for the sake of change. He said that Hindu society should keep its focus on awakening social equality, friendship and invoking brotherhood. He described the senior workers as the link in the chain that connects the top leadership with the common volunteers and people; and explained that this is a very critical role. A common person cannot meet the leader. His views about a leader are defined by the senior workers' behaviour. For a leader to succeed, he needs such workers. Without them, no campaign or movement can succeed. He gave many historic examples to strengthen his proposition and said that the major responsibility of a worker is to nurture and create more such workers.[26]

He unveiled the special issue of 'Amar Bharati' on this occasion. It is a magazine published in Kenya and also laid the foundation stone of the new building of the BSS office. He then went to Mombasa and addresses a public meeting. Reminding the Hindu society of its special qualities, he narrated a few sentences of the famous poem of Shri Atal Behari Vajpayee from *'Hindu tan man, Hindu jeevan'*—

मैंने छाती का लहू पिला पाले विदेश के सुजित लाल
मुझको मानव में भेद नहीं मेरा अंत:स्थल वर विशाल

जग से ठुकराए लोगों को लो मेरे घर का खुला द्वार
अपना सब कुछ हूँ लुटा चुका पर अक्षय है धनागार
मेरा हीरा पाकर ज्योतित परकीयों का वह राज मुकुट
यदि इन चरणों पर झुक जाए कल वह किरीट तो क्या विस्मय
हिंदू तन-मन हिंदू जीवन रग-रग हिंदू मेरा परिचय।[27]

To give a paraphrased meaning—

I reared the children from other lands with blood from my bosom.

My open heart does not see any difference between human beings.

I opened my doors to the persecuted people from the world.

My enormous treasures have been looted.

Crowns of foreigners glow with my jewels.

If those crowns bow to me tomorrow, do not be surprised.

Hindu body, Hindu mind, each of my nerve is Hindu –
And this is my identity.

Rajju Bhaiya landed in South Africa on 20th January. He reached the capital city of Pretoria from Johannesburg in the morning. He met the Bharatiya ambassador Gopal Krishna Gandhi. He was welcomed warmly in his office. They had a good courteous meeting and had discussions for nearly half an hour. Gopal Gandhi is son of Mahatma Gandhi. He also visited Durban and Johannesburg. On a lighter note, Gopal Gandhi noted that all the three – Rajju Bhaiya, Dr. Tatwawadi and Dr. Yashwant Pathak were from science stream.[28]

The national TV and radio broadcasted his interviews. There was a public programme. The topic of his lecture there was 'Global scenario and Hindu world view'. It was followed by a Q and A session. He went for a meeting with respected Swami Sahajaanand of Swami Narayan Sampradaay over breakfast. From there he went to Verulam. He also visited Iskcon temple and met their seniors. He visited an institution named Aryan Benevolent Home for the elderly people. On the last day of his visit, he met the missionaries of Ram Krishna Mission at their centre.[29]

He travelled to Mauritius from there. He had an interview on the TV show of Mauritius Broadcasting Corporation. He also met the office bearers of Hindi Prachaarini Sabha. His host in Mauritius was Ramnathji who was the Principal of local college. Incidentally, Rajju Bhaiya was there on 26th January and he celebrated the day in the Indian embassy with the Ambassador Shyam Sharan. He officially inaugurated the Vishwa Hindu Parishad branch in Mauritius. He also visited the centres of devotion and local pilgrimage centres, Ganga Lake and the Maurisheshwarnath temple. He met the Sadhus of Ram Krishna Mission and Kailasan Covil. There was a programme with the Hindu Mahajan Sangham. He expressed his views about the challenges of organising Hindus.[30]

A major programme organised there was a public meeting attended by 3,000 young men and women. He met former PM Sir Anirood Jaganauth, Vice President Shri Ravi Gurbaran and then PM Shri Navin Ramgulam personally. He visited Sanatan Sarvoday Ashram on the last day of his visit and met the presiding Swamiji there. His tour ended with a press conference. He returned to Bharat on 29th January, that was his birthday incidentally.[31]

His last visit was a milestone in strengthening the relations between the Hindu and Buddha people of Bharat and Japan. This trip took place in April 1998. He had been invited for the inauguration of 3,333 stepped Chau-Michi temple on 8th April, constructed by the Indo-Japanese Cultural Centre in Kaumoto. It is the symbolic birth day of Bhagwan Buddha there. Among the honourable guests were Shri Ashok Singhal and Dr. B.K. Modi. Rituals of Shinto and Hindu traditions were conducted. There was also a press conference on April 8.[32]

Rajju Bhaiya and his team had arrived at Fukuoka International Airport. A welcome programme had been arranged in the 450-year-old Dai Koji temple. The programme began with a traditional Japanese dance program. A prayer meeting was conducted for the children of the city. Their schools were to begin in a few days. Respected Uchi Da and Rajju Bhaiya touched the wooden staff on the heads of the children in traditional Japanese style and blessed them for their new stage in life. Former minister and member of Japanese parliament, Toshikatsu Matsuoka, had just returned from a tour of Bharat. He welcomed the young students and guests with a brief speech. He said, "We are enjoying the fruits of Buddhist faith without knowing that its roots are in Bharat, just like we drink sweet water without understanding from which depths of the mountains this water has come. He added that actually there is need to synthesise the cultural power of Hindu and Buddha Sampradaya. More than hundred very-very important guests, who were the cream of political, social and economic fields, had come for the programme. They took part in the closing ceremony. The function began with the national anthems of Bharat and Japan, followed by cultural dance programme, speech by special guests. Modi Foundation presented an account of its Sewa projects.

Rajju Bhaiya was highly impressed with the cleanliness and discipline of Japan during his three-day visit. He said that there is a void in intellectual dialogue in the west due to unending economic race. Audience was listening to him calmly with attention. He said that west is becoming aware of this problem therefore Buddha Dharma, Rajneesh etc. are becoming popular there. In the changing global scenario Hindu and Buddha philosophy has lot to offer to the world. Co-operation between Japan and Bharat is not just important for the two; it is also a right step for the world that will lead to peace in the world.[33]

On the way to Japan Rajju Bhaiya stopped over in Hong Kong to meet the swayamsevaks of HSS in Hong Kong. There was a lunch in Bharateeya consulate where some Bharateeyas living in Hong Kong were invited. Dinner was arranged in Hatel Holiday Inn by the Director of Indus Ind Bank Shree Hari Leela. This last tour of Japan was very important. It was the visible fruition of the idea of Sangh of coming together of Hindu and Buddha nations and their culture and working together to find a place in the world as a powerful block.

Bharat is a sacred land for Hindu society spread across the world. Many swayamsevaks set up organisations in the country where they settled and society where they lived. Living away from their country with other societies, they think about their problems in an organised manner. Achieving a respectable place in the society and live with respect by following one's own dharma is the objective. There is a wide acceptance of the organisations run by the Hindu society and swayamsevaks. Rajju Bhaiya could experience this during his visit. He could also sense that the migrant Bharateeyas looked up to the Sangh leadership as their guardians. Respect of those governments for RSS Sarkaryavaah or Sarsanghchaalak could be clearly seen. One could see an acceptance at every level that RSS was the representative of Hindu society and Hindu culture. Thus, tours of Rajju Bhaiya proved to be morale boosting for the Bharatiya society settled abroad.

References

1. Copy of original report received from Purushottam Rao, 18th November, 2103
2. Dr. Ram Nivas, email dated 10th
3. Shridhar Damle, telephonic conversation, 22nd October, 2103
4. Jagdishchandra Sharda Shastri, email dated 6th November, 2103
5. Dr. Shankar Rao Tatwawadi, email dated 24th October, 2013
6. Ibid
7. Sarsanghchaalak Goes Abroad, booklet, p. 63
8. Ibid, p. 7
9. Ibid, p. 13
10. Ibid, p. 21
11. Dr. Shankar Rao Tatwawadi, op cit
12. Sarsanghchaalak Goes Abroad, p. 17-19
13. Ibid, p. 45
14. Ibid, p. 48
15. Ibid, p. 9
16. Ibid, p. 10
17. Dr. Shankar Rao Tatwawadi, op cit
18. Sarsanghchaalak Goes Abroad, p. 36

19. Ibid, p. 38
20. Ibid, p. 11
21. Ibid, p. 12
22. Ibid, p. 18
23. Ibid, p. 18
24. Ibid, p. 18
25. Ibid, p. 28
26. Sarsanghchaalak Rajendra Singh's Tour of Mauritius, S. Africa & Kenya, booklet, p. 30
27. Ibid, p. 45
28. Dr. Shankar Rao Tatwawadi, op cit
29. Africa tour booklet, op cit, p. 47
30. Ibid, p. 50-51
31. Ibid, p. 51
32. Email report by Rohit, Samvad dated 16th April, 1998
33. Samvad dated 16th April and 1st May, 1998

□

11

Life after retirement

The third Sarsanghchaalak had retired after nominating Rajju Bhaiya as his successor. Despite his poor health he carried on his heavy responsibilities for six years, travelling all over the country and also overseas. Finally, feeling too weighed down by his health problems, he handed over his responsibilities to Shri Sudarshanji and retired. Many of his colleagues tried to dissuade him, but he reasoned with them that it was very important for the head of the organisation to be healthy, or it can lead to serious problems in organisational work.

While handing over the charge he said, "I will keep doing all my duties with enthusiasm as an ordinary swayamsevak. And it is my last wish that I can keep contributing to the expansion and growth of my dear Sangh work till my last breath."

Even after voluntary retirement, he used to be present in nearly all the main meetings and major programmes. He had changed the way he travelled. He would go to a major centre and stay there for many days. Senior workers of Sangh and other organisations would meet him individually or collectively. He used to insist upon all of them that they should keep busy with some work as per their own health and domestic situation. It was not necessary that a person must have some responsibility to keep working. Society gets benefit of a senior worker's experience if he stays active. It also keeps his mind and body healthy. After getting free from the responsibility, he wrote to the government to remove the security staff he had been assigned.

Even in the evening of his life, his thirst for knowledge and intellectual sharpness was still as bright. Prof. Navalkant Prinja describes his meeting with Rajju Bhaiya. "When I had come to Delhi as a member of British Civil Nuclear Trade Organisation under the leadership of Lord Peter Mandleson, I could luckily meet Rajju Bhaiya. This is the time when the Indian government and the political class were discussing nuclear agreement. During our meeting Rajju Bhaiya talked about the complex technology and related issues at length. I was highly impressed with his clear vision and his knowledge about the subject as well as his detailing of the scientific realities. Then, our discussion veered towards science and Hindu philosophy, especially Vedanta. I shared my view that India is progressing in modern science, however its scientists are devoid of knowledge of scientific Sanskrit and its scientific literature. On the other side Sanskrit scholars do not have access to modern science. Indian education system looks at these two streams as separate. Will we be able to see the synthesis of these two streams of science and philosophy? He responded, "You are expecting one more Vivekananda. Yes, he will come. But, it is possible that this time he may come from amongst Hindus living overseas." His view was that there is lot of excitement and awareness about Hindu philosophy along with modern science in the west. I was very impressed with this vision and open minded thinking."[1]

As a general plan for balance of his life he chose to stay at Kaushik Ashram in Pune. It has been built for the old and retired prachaaraks. He spent his last years there. Shridhar Phadkeji was in-charge of his arrangements. He has sent his experience from Pune about Rajju Bhaiya's stay there—

"Kaushik Ashram was important, in a way, because the founder secretary of Vishwa Hindu Parishad, Dada Saheb Apte had dedicated his own property to Sangh for this purpose and it was inaugurated by Rajju Bhaiya earlier after its renovation. He used to tell swayamsevaks about it with a smile that he had inaugurated it and he did not know that he would have to stay there someday.

Rajju Bhaiya had begun travelling to Pune from around 1980s, when he was appointed as an all India office bearer. He participated in the 1983 state level camp of Maharashtra for the entire duration of the camp. In fact, he had reached the camp two days earlier to supervise the arrangements. In his speech on the 14th January on the occasion of Makar Sankraman, he had told them, "We want *sankranti* (upward evolution), not *kranti* (revolution)." All the participants of the camp remembered this direction.

Once, a worker gave a very high flown introduction of Rajju Bhaiya. He explained to him affectionately, "Why do you give such over the top introduction? Introduction of a worker (kaaryakarta) should be simple." He used to guide his junior colleagues from time to time like this.

He would enjoy chats, discussions and light humour with the workers there. During lunch, there would be more chatting and less of eating. He used to eat light but would insist on others eating well. His stress on thrift was there till his last days. A barber came to shave him after his operation. Touching his face after the shave, he remarked, "You have shaved me well, but what do you charge?" When the barber responded, Rajju Bhaiya said, "I have been operated on my waist but my hands are free. So, I will shave myself from tomorrow."

There was a kind of competition between the swayamsevaks to look after the arrangement for Rajju Bhaiya. The reason was his affectionate nature and their chance to learn much from him. Very senior officers, political leaders and leaders of the society would often come to meet him. It was a different kind of pleasure to serve them at that time. Leaders ranging from Atalji, Advaniji, Dattopant Thengdi, Moropant Pingley, Acharya Dharmendra, to other great personalities like Babasaheb Purandare, Dr. Mashelkar used to come. Rajju Bhaiya had warm relations with all the people.

He would bring back gifts like clothes etc. from north India. When he had to attend a wedding, he would ask his personal assistant to take out those clothes and shawl etc. and gift them lovingly to the newly wed couples. For a couple it was a gift they would treasure for life.

Rajju Bhaiya lived a very simple life. If you were to watch carefully, you would find signs of stitches in some places and a patch somewhere in his clothes. People would ask him, "Why do you wear such clothes. Let us bring new clothes." He would politely tell them, "What is wrong with this? If it is torn a little, we don't waste the entire cloth. This is our tradition."

Though he was physically weak, he used to enjoy going to crowded festivals in Pune. He loved visiting Ganeshotsav pandals. He visited all the important temples, historic places and sewa projects in Pune. Pune had a special place in his heart. Whenever a relative or friend visited him in Pune, he would give detailed information about Pune and tell them, "Pune is a very important city from the point of view of history, culture and education. There are many highly knowledgeable people who have spent their lives to understand a subject."[2]

Nana Neurgaokar had joined Pune office of RSS in 1998 after retirement as a librarian. He remembers that when Rajju Bhaiya made Kaushik Ashram his home after retirement, he used to read out many books and scriptures to Rajju bhaiya. During his stay there, he read out Shri Gyaneshwari, Shri Daasbodh, and Panipat etc. These reading sessions would be on from 9 p.m. to 11 p.m. He writes, "If I felt that he is tired and is about to sleep, I used to stop reading. But, he would immediately call out, "Keep reading, Nana, I am awake!"

Nana writes, "I had written Gyaneshwari and Daasbodh by hand as my hobby. I showed them to Rajju Bhaiya after completion. He appreciated me very enthusiastically and encouraged me a lot, saying it should be publicly released. I politely refused and told him that I had hand written them as per my personal hobby; there is nothing great about it. He then told me, "You have hand written these, it is a good thing. But, how would people know?" Then, he arranged for a small book release function in that office that was attended by 60-70 people. Everyone was invited for dinner. Many senior prachaaraks and workers were present in this programme too. Rajju Bhaiya felicitated all the senior workers with coconut and shawl."

When Advaniji came to meet him he introduced Nana to him, telling him, "He is our Nanaji. He reads many books to me." He always took care of his colleagues.

Even at that age, his mind was fully alert. His eyesight had become very weak by then, but he could tell about the tablet that was to be taken at a particular time by touching it. He would insist on Sangh prayer at the given time and he would get ready for it, wearing his Sangh half pant.

Respected Kaka Maharaj Dhekne came to invite him for his birthday. Incidentally, Rajju Bhaiya was not well that day. He had fever. Doctor had advised him not to go out. But, he insisted on going for the programme. He had to return back quickly because of ill health, but he did go. We could understand his commitment to work that day.[3]

Rajju Bhaiya's life was living example of doing Sangh work with simplicity. He was very strict about simplicity and followed it strictly. Bimal Kedia gives an example, "He had retired from the post of Sarsanghchaalak due to ill health. I suggested to him that he could stay in Mumbai. I added that Mumbai is connected to all the main cities of Bharat by air so it would be easy for him to travel anywhere." Rajju Bhaiya was very uneasy and stood up, and told me, "Now, I will never think of staying in Mumbai. You people will send me by air and spend so much of money on a useless person like me!" He then moved to Kaushik Ashram in Pune and stayed there till the end of his life.

Despite his poor health he did not expect any special arrangements for himself. When it was offered he would refuse it. Dr. Yogendra Singh recalls, "When I went to AIIMS, Delhi with Rajju Bhaiya, he did not tell anyone in advance. So, no special arrangement could be made. I told him, "Rajju Bhaiya you did not inform in advance, there are long queues there." He responded, "I should also experience how an ordinary citizen gets medical care in our country." I was quite worried and suggested that I would call some doctor whom I know. In fact, a family friend of Rajju Bhaiya was a director there. But, he stopped me strictly and he met the doctor an ordinary patient. He sat on the bench like any ordinary patient for nearly two hours." It is not that he behaved like this after retiring from the high office. It was his inherent nature.[4] Dr. Sitaram Agrawal remembers that during Rajju Bhaiya's stay in Delhi as Sarsanghchaalak, he was fortunate to take care of his health. Like any ordinary patient he fixed an appointment at his nursing home in Delhi in Roop Nagar. He reached there at the exact appointed time and went back after consultation without taking any of his time.[5]

His personal assistant at that time, Amarnathji gives another example. "He was always eager to do something new, to learn about new places. There is an institution in Pune for serving the physically handicapped. Many swayamsevaks too are part of it. On their request, he agreed to visit the place happily. We had to reach there by 9 in the morning. After the breakfast, he began getting ready. I offered him silk kurta. He was hesitant and said, "Arrey brother, give me an old one. Now it is not good to wear a new cloth." I suggested that it should also be used. Rajju Bhaiya looked at me for some moments, then said, "*Ek ne kahi dooje ne maani, Nanak kahein dono gyani*" (One suggests, the other one agrees. Nanak says, both are knowledgeable.) and wore the new kurta. I used to feel blessed due to his co-operative nature. Another of his quality was that he would appreciate someone, but in a way that his ego did not bloat.[6]

In the programme mentioned above, Rajju Bhaiya stayed with the children though he was physically weak. When some children went to meet him in the ward, he laughed and said, "I am also like you – I cannot see, I cannot walk. I can't get up without support. Our lives are so similar." Hearing this, children were very happy while elder people turned emotional. From there we also went to see Shinde's garrison."

He had tremendous strength to bear pain. Once he had to visit a doctor in Pune, but car came late. Since we were late, the doctor told us to come in the evening. By that time, Rajju Bhaiya's Parkinsons problem had exacerbated. We went again in the evening in that unbearable hot summer, and we had to wait for another 45 minutes. But, Rajju Bhaiya reacted very calmly. He said, "It is ok. I had lost the habit of waiting. Atleast, I could redo the exercise." He had extraordinary capacity to hide his pain and emotions and bear with pain with co-operation and equanimity. He would never get irritated when he faced pain, nor would he show it during such moments. Once, when he reached Delhi from Mumbai, a wheel chair could not be arranged. Parkinsons attack was about to set in. But, Rajju Bhaiya paused at two three places on the platform with lot of pain and sat down in the car. Summer was at its peak. Airconditioning of the car had failed. Rajju Bhaiya was soaked in sweat. I felt searing pain looking at him and felt very bad at poor arrangements. But, Rajju Bhaiya kept silent, bearing the pain and did not utter a word."[7]

A year prior to his death, he had met Shri Bhairon Singh Shekhawat. Rajju Bhaiya told him, "I will be going to my native village on 24th September and you are going to accompany me." 'He told me specifically not to bring anyone with me, nor tell the media about his visit. I wished to know the reason. He told me that he is bringing together the entire family – brothers, nephews, grandchildren. It was a just family get together. I had food with the family in the village. I saw that for the first time Rajju Bhaiya photographed himself with the family. I asked Rajju Bhaiya the reason for the get together casually. He said, "When you had come to meet me for the first time, you had told me not to tour too much as I was not well." I said, "Yes, I had told you, indeed." In the same conversation there was a reference to family. So I thought, why not bring together all the family members once. This is why I arranged this." It seems he had a foreboding that he was not going to be around for many days."[8]

Dr. Bodh Narayan Singh recalls his close affection with every person he met. "This is an incident of 14th January, 2001. A category four worker from his erstwhile university came to meet him. Security staff was not allowing him in. Finally, permission was given after asking Rajju Bhaiya. It was an emotional sight, as if a younger brother was meeting his elder brother. Rajju Bhaiya gifted him a dhoti. He turned emotional with this boundless love; such close affection for a junior colleague!"

सुर नर मुनि सब ओढ़े चदरिया, ओढ़ के मैली किन्ही,
दास कबीर जतन से ओढ़े, जस के तस धर दीन्ही।

He quotes Kabir, "All the humans, angels and munis got their 'sheet' which they soiled. Kabir took this sheet so carefully that he could return it as good as new." He believed that Rajju Bhaiya was a living example of Kabir's philosophy. He went to Georgetown RSS office on 13th September, 2001. He met every one but I can't remember if he spoke. While sitting in car on return, he told me, "I have seen enough, I have seen it all. Now is the time to return." He then hummed something in Marathi that I could not understand.[9]

One could get a glimpse of his rishi like consciousness. According to Rakesh Kumar, he travelled to Prayag on 24th September, 2002 telling him that he would like to see old places and meet his colleagues. While discussing about health in the office of the reader in Economics department, Dr. Girish Tripathi, a scientist told Rajju Bhaiya that research is going on successfully on Genome therapy to come up with cure to make people free of all diseases. Hearing this, Rajju Bhaiya recited an Urdu couplet—

पाल ले इक रोग नादाँ जिदगी के वास्ते,
सिर्फ सेहत के सहारे जिंदगी कटती नहीं।[10]

O' ignorant, nurture a disease for life,
one cannot spend life only with good health.

Vijay Ganesh Kulkarni recalls that his love for cause of education was so deep that he stayed with the full time workers in the training workshop for 3 days in Pune though he was not well at all. He did not go on stage, gave no speech. He just watched the proceeding in the hall and heard them. When I went to meet him, he called me by name and remembered that I was a Yoga teacher. He could remember each and every worker; that was Rajju Bhaiya."[11]

His memory was as sharp even till his last days. Prof. Gopal Krishna gives an example of this. "When he came to Prayag in his last years, he asked me smilingly with deep affection, "Have you got over your stuttering?" He remembered about my problem even after so many years!" In previous pages, we have recounted how he had encouraged this same professor to get over his weakness when he helped him to be appointed as a lecturer.[12]

According to Shantanu Shende, prachaarak in Vidya Bharati, "Respected Rajju Bhaiya was in a hospital in Pune for treatment. The organising secretary of Vidya Bharati, Shri Brahmadev Sharma and he went to meet him in the evening. Nurse had come in to give him an injection. He stopped her for ten minutes and chatted with us. Bhaiji first gave information about the Pune meeting. Rajju Bhaiya asked him about Vidya Bharati's progress and then his strong mathematical mind began ticking. He asked, "How many schools do you run? How many students, how many teachers, how many ex-students, how many parents etc? After doing mental calculations, he said, if you total all the numbers, Vidya Bharati has 10 crore people in its contact. He suggested that taking our views and sanskaaras to all is Vidya Bharati's work. His thoughts about every activity were always on."[13]

He inspected Jwala Devi Inter College in September 2002 when he visited Prayag. He also chatted with students for some time, had light humorous moments with them and also some inspiring talks done with affection. He told us, "We should keep fees in our colleges low, so that poor can also study in good institutions. We should keep this objective in our mind when we run schools and colleges."[14]

According to Shiv Kumarji of Vidya Bharati, last lecture of Rajju Bhaiya may have been delivered in Uttar Pradesh on the occasion of Baal Kumbh organised by Vidya Bharati from 20 to 22 February, 2002. "Rajju Bhaiya came for the programme despite serious health issues. Even in that position he moved around, though he could hardly see, and asked about water, kitchen arrangements etc. and also gave a few suggestions. When we asked him to speak, he said he won't be able to speak more than 2-4 words. But, when he began speaking, he spoke smoothly for nearly 15 minutes.[15]

He had a fracture in his foot in April 2003 that was alright with medical treatment. But, after this incident, his standing on his own and taking a walk with an assistant or a walking stick almost stopped. He would listen to Sangh songs, shlokas etc. on his tape recorder and sometimes he would sing along too after completing his morning chore. He also practised Yognidraasan with the help of tape recorder. Someone would read Hindi and English news for him. Taking food at right time, rest, listening to good audio cassettes etc. was part of his daily routine. On 10th July, senior workers came from Kanyakumari meeting and gave him the details of the meeting. He expressed his satisfaction. It didn't look like he will leave this world so quickly.[16]

Rajju Bhaiya's presiding deity was Hanumanji. He had such deep faith that he always kept a small booklet of Sundarkaand and a picture of Hanumanji in it, with him. It had been gifted to him by Prabhudatta Brahmachariji.[17] The then regional prachaarak Dr. Amar Singh had come to meet him in Kaushik Ashram on his return from Kanyakumari meeting. He reminisces that while seeing him off, he said, "Jai Shri Ram." Whenever he returned to Prayag, he would pay obeisance to the sacred land when he got down from train and he used to call out, "Jai Shri Ram." We have been told that his last words too were, "Jai Shri Ram."[18]

He always looked at the nation as his motherland. According to Shridhar Phadke, Rajju Bhaiya had stated, "For me the entire nation is sacred. Therefore, I should be cremated wherever I die." He passed away on 14th July, 2003 at 12.30 in the afternoon with a severe heart attack. He took his last breath sitting on a chair while he was taking his food. As per his wishes, he was cremated in Pune. Apart from thousands of workers, the then PM Shri Atal Behari Vajpayee, Vice President Shri Bhairon Singh Shekhawat, all the top Sangh senior leaders and members of allied organisations and many political leaders were present in his last journey.[19]

In the condolence meeting later, respected Mohanji Bhagwat said, "I had been assigned the duty of being with him during Emergency. I still remember his alternative underground personality. After his tour of Vidarbh region, reaction of common people was, "He is truly Rajendra (king) and also a Singh (lion)!" A situation where anyone could get angry, I never saw him angry. He always bestowed affection to all from forest dwelling tribals to top leaders. His life's theme was 'पैर में चक्कर, मुँह में शक्कर' (wheels in the feet, and sugar in mouth) and he lived his life the same way. One cannot remember any instance when someone had to face problems or pain because of him. Sometimes, the person given the responsibility would reach late to pick him up, and he would find him holding his luggage and waiting with a smile. He would go ahead with the workers as if nothing had happened."[20]

Former Sah Sarkaryavaah Shri Madandas Deviji told the author in September 2013 during a meeting, "He came from a very wealthy and privileged family. He had everything – assets and wealth. But, he never used this wealth to deviate from the Sangh way of working. He worked with complete surrender to Sangh. Such was his dedication that even after retirement he stayed under Sangh arrangement in Kaushik Ashram. He never looked back. He lived his life with complete detachment. Such was his dispassionate nature and sense of detachment that he said, "Wherever my life completes its journey, submit me to fire there." Because, entire nation was his home. Though he was not attached to anything, he never showed it; neither did he expect it from other people. He kept giving to everyone all his life; in family or to the society outside the family. This is equally true that not everyone reciprocated his goodness with goodness. But, this never affected his greatness. He behaved with all in the same way. He never lowered his own standards. He was a living model of forgiveness. He was a treasure house of great qualities, he was an ideal person and he was big and great in every sense. But, he never expected the same standards of qualities from his colleagues or people who came in touch with him. He didn't measure people on his own scale of achievements. He was very liberal for others but very strict with himself, till his last breath.

He was the first Sarsanghchaalak who had not come out of the ranks of top prachaaraks of that time. He was junior in their comparison. He understood that he did not come from the 'Gangotri' or the origin of Sangh work, that is, Nagpur. He was like a stream that merged with it on way. But, he gained respect from every level of workers due to his actions and nature. The current Sarsanghchaalak at that time, Shri Balasaheb Deoras knew that Rajju Bhaiya will never be unjust with anyone. He would be just with everyone and do justice to every issue. He would take along everyone. Therefore, he had told all the workers in 1990 or 1991 meeting of Sangh that they should meet Rajju Bhaiya in case of any problem. Though, he was a Sah Sarkaryavaah or joint general secretary at that time. Balasaheb had reduced his activities due to his health issues by that time. Rajju Bhaiya's place in Sangh was seen as so important that he was getting security that was of the level of Sarsanghchaalak."[21]

According to Shri Ashok Singhal, Rajju Bhaiya lived his entire life with a sense of tapas, as per the foundational shloka of Ishopanishad—

ईशावास्यमिदं सर्वं यत्किंच जगत्यां जगत,
तेन त्यक्तेन भुन्जीथा: मा गृध: कस्यस्विद्धनम्।[22]

Such was the close relation between Ashokji and Rajju Bhaiya that upon hearing of his passing away, he kept silent for the entire day and did not come out of his residence in Prayag.[23]

Nanaji Deshmukh mentioned that he left this world in the same affectionate atmosphere filled with love, the way he entered the Sangh.[24]

In his homage, Shri Atal Behari Vajpayee wrote, "Truly, name of Rajju Bhaiya was positively meaningful. There is affection in Rajju while Bhaiya has respect. His heart brimmed with affection. One never felt hesitant about speaking one's heart out in his presence. We faced many problems when he was at the helm, but those were solved with his guidance. Strength of the organisation increased, its impact enlarged. And, today, we are moving ahead on our future path taking inspiration from him. May God give us strength to imbibe inspiration from his personality and his achievements."[25]

Rajju Bhaiya had abiding faith in social harmony. Swami Chinmayananda mentions that he was not a political person. But, the impact he had as a personality, is something that no other person would have had in contemporary history. He inspired BJP leaders to rise above political untouchability and despite having ideological difference, to come together with other political parties in the interest of the nation. When the proposal to support a government led by Ms. Mayawati came up, many leaders of the party were against it. Many were very upset with slogan 'Tilak, Taraju aur Talwar...' raised by BSP. At that time, Rajju Bhaiya had said, "Many times company changes the sanskaaras. It is possible that after coming close to you, BSP may keep aside its bitter social thoughts. And when we talk of Hindutva, we should give priority to Dalit and most backward people." He was always in favour of taking everyone along.[26]

Shri B.N. Jog has analysed his period at the helm of Sangh as follows:

"If someone made a statement against some statement of the Sarsanghchaalak, workers would get very upset. It may be so even now. But, Rajju Bhaiya's thinking was very different from this. He would say that a swayamsevak, who is working in the field, has a right to ask questions and submit his view which may be different. One did not have to keep respectful distance while talking to him."

"When Rajju Bhaiya became the Sarsanghchaalak in 1994, politics of power had spread into all the facets of social life. Every action, from where will your child get education to making of atom bomb was directed by the state power. There seemed to be no alternative to take state power in one's own hands. It seemed that hold of state power was inevitable. Two senior most leaders of Sangh who thought on these lines were Bhaurao Deoras and Rajju Bhaiya. I had heard their views from very close quarters during Emergency. This issue was discussed many times in my Dadar home. Their views about how thousand year period of slavery and fifty years of partitioned Bharat, this defeated state power wrought atrocities on Hindus would come up in their discussions. It seemed that both had made up their mind that in the upcoming elections BJP must have atleast 100 Loksabha members. We know the history about how Hindus came to be the centre of politics and their partnership in power. The stamp of Sangh and its omniscient presence in society, strong nationalism, and all-inclusive cultural renaissance happened under the leadership of Rajju Bhaiya."[27]

Vijay Ganesh Kulkarni tells that Rajju Bhaiya always used to say, one needs strong inspiration to work in Sangh. Ordinary human being works with an urge to make money, or for bringing up children or gain popularity in society.

Swayamsevak should have enlightened grand inspiration of supreme prosperity for the nation. Getting rid of misery of poor and hardworking people of this nation can be a grand inspiration. To help one understand this idea, he would recite Maharaj Rantidev's words. These were perhaps his favourite golden words.

न त्वहं कामये राज्यं, न स्वर्गं नापुनर्भवं,
कामये दुःखतप्तानां, प्राणिनाम् आर्तिनाशनम्।

(Meaning—I don't desire kingdom, or heaven or rebirth. My only desire is that insufferable pains of all living beings be destroyed.)[28]

Strong urge to serve the motherland was imbibed in each of the atoms in his body. Talking to his nephew during his last days, Rajju Bhaiya had told him, "I have to serve the nation till my last breath. I pray to God that I can go and lay down on the funeral pyre on my own."[29]

When tape recorders had just come in the market in 1950, Yateendra Singh had requested him to record his views in the tape recorder. He had then hummed a few lines of a Sangh song—

'तन समर्पित, मन समर्पित, और यह जीवन समर्पित,
चाहता हूँ देश की धरती तुझे कुछ और भी दूँ।' [30]

(Meaning—I have surrendered my heart, body and life. O' motherland, I wish I can offer something more to you.)

This was the philosophy of his life. His sentiment of surrendering everything was alive till his last moments. He completed his life's journey with this very sentiment.

References

1. Prof. Nawalkant Prinja, email dated 24th October, 2013
2. Shridhar Phadke, note from Pune
3. Nana Neurgaokar, hand written memories dated 5th October, 2103
4. Dr. Yogendra Singh, Panchjanya, 27th July, 2003
5. Personal memories, October 2013
6. Amarnath, Vichar Pravaah, op cit, p. 88
7. Vichar Pravaah, op cit, p. 90
8. Bhairaon Singh Shekhawat, Panchjanya, op cit

9. Dr. Bodh Narayan, Vichar Pravaah, op cit, p. 49
10. Rakesh Kumar, Vichar Pravaah, op cit, p. 42
11. Vijay Ganesh Kulkarni, letter dated 5th October, 2013
12. Prof. Gopal Krishna, Vichar Pravaah, op cit, p. 71
13. Shantanu Shende, letter dated 5th October, 2103
14. Chintamani Singh, Vichar Pravaah, op cit, p. 66
15. Shiv Kumar, Vichar Pravaah, op cit, p. 65
16. Sureshrao Ketkar, Vichar Pravaah, p. 11
17. Swami Chinmayananda, Vichar Pravaah, op cit, p. 18
18. Vichar Pravaah, op cit, p. 36
19. Special issue, Tarun Bharat, Pune, 2009
20. Dr. Mohan Bhagwat, Vichar Pravaah, op cit, p. 62
21. Madandas Deviji, personal conversation on 27th July. He has been Sah Sarkaryavaah
22. Ashok Singhalji, Vichar Pravaah, op cit, p. 4
23. Vichar Pravaah, op cit, p. 61
24. Nanaji Deshmukh, Vichar Pravaah, op cit, p. 8
25. Atal Behari Vajpayee, Panchjanya, op cit
26. Swami Chinmayananda, op cit
27. B.N. Jog, Tarun Bharat, 20th July, 2003
28. Vijay Ganesh Kulkarni. Op cit
29. Vichar Pravaah, op cit, p. 87
30. Yateendra Singh, Vichar Pravaah, op cit, p. 86

□

Major markers in Rajju Bhaiya's life

29th January, 1922	—	Birth
1942	—	Entry in Sangh, completed first year of training
1942-43	—	Teaching in Prayag University
1943	—	Appointed city secretary of RSS
1946	—	Appointed Prayag division secretary
4th February, 1948	—	RSS ban and jail following Gandhi assassination
1948	—	Satyagrah against RSS ban, jailed
1949	—	Appointed prachaarak for part state (42 districts)
1952	—	Appointed UP state secretary
1954	—	Completes second year training, unofficial prachaarak of state till 1957
1958	—	Appointed state prachaarak of UP
1961	—	Return of Bhaurao Deoras, appointed his junior as joint state prachaarak
1962	—	Reappointed as state prachaarak
1966	—	First global conference of VHP, resignation from his teaching job

1966	—	Appointed regional prachaarak of UP and Bihar
1974	—	Appointed regional prachaarak of entire east, including Bengal & Assam
1975	—	Emergency declared, return to his post for UP, Bihar, Critical role in underground struggle in Emergency
1977	—	Appointed Sah Sarkaryavaah (Joint general secretary)
1978	—	Appointed Sarkaryavaah (general secretary)
1979	—	Major contribution during second VHP national conference
1983	—	Ekaatmataa yatra, beginning of Ram Mandir movement
1987	—	Voluntary retirement as Sarkaryavaah and became Sah Sarkaryavaah
1994	—	Nominated as Sarsanghchaalak
2000	—	Gave up his post of Sarsanghchaalak
14th July, 2003	—	Passed away.

□

The RSS song that symbolises Rajju Bhaiya's life

पूज्य माँ की अर्चना का एक छोटा उपकरण हूँ
उच्च है वह शिखर देखो, मैं नहीं वह स्थान लूँगा
और चित्रित भित्ति का है, मैं नहीं शोभा बनूँगा
पूज्य है यह मातृ मंदिर, नींव का मैं एक कण हूँ। (1)

I am a small instrument for worshipping
the revered Mother
Look at the spire of the temple,
I will not take that place
And I will not become one of the
beautiful paintings on its wall
Revered is the temple of my Mother,
I am just a small particle in the foundation.

मुकुट माँ का जगमगाता मैं नहीं सोना बनूँगा
जगमगाते रत्न देखो मैं नहीं हीरा बनूँगा
पूज्य माँ की चरण रज का एक छोटा धूलि कण हूँ। (2)

The crown Mother is wearing shines bright,
I will not be the gold in it
Look at those sparkling jewels,
I will not be the diamond in it
I am but a speck in the soil
at feet of revered Mother.

आरती भी हो रही है, गीत बनकर क्या करूँगा
पुष्प माला चढ़ रही है फूल बनकर क्या करूँगा
मालिका का एक तंतु, गीत का मैं एक स्वर हूँ
पूज्य माँ की अर्चना का एक छोटा उपकरण हूँ। (3)

Aarti is being sung, what will I do being the song
Garland of flowers is being offered to her,
what will I do by being a flower in it
I am but a fibre in the garland string,
I am just a sound in that song
I am a small instrument for worshipping revered Mother
(Bharatmata)

□

Annexure

Annexure List

1. Letter to Shri Lal Bahadur Shastri written by Rajju Bhaiya from Naini prison
2. The '5-*S*' formula of Rajju Bhaiya
3. Summary of the first speech after nomination as Sarsanghchaalak
4. Science and religion
5. Contribution of Indian Science to the world
6. Speech of Rajju Bhaiya on Vijayadashami–1997, Nagpur
7. Rajju Bhaiya's hand written opinion in the visitor's book after the Sanatan Dharma Seva Sadan programme in Chautaga, Myanmar, dated 29th April, 1981
8. Rajju Bhaiya's affection for Keshav Srushti

□

Letter to Shri Lal Bahadur Shastri written by Rajju Bhaiya from Naini prison

Respected Shri Lal Bahadur Shastri,
Home Minister
Uttar Pradesh

Via
Respected Superintendent
Central Prison,
Naini.

Respected Shastriji,

I was thinking of clarifying many issues since many days, but I could not do so till now. I had gone to Lucknow a few days back on parole due to my sickness. I felt serious urge to meet you and I tried too. But you were not there, and it is possible that you may not have agreed to meet me, though I did not expect it from you. Now atmosphere has settled a bit and there is clarity, so it is possible to think about many things calmly. This is the reason I am writing this letter to you. Reason is not just that you are the Home Minister, but also because I have a natural respect for you; secondly you are famous for your balanced intellect. So be it.

Not only you, but entire society now knows clearly that organisation of Sangh had no relation to the inhuman killing of father of the nation. First, no swayamsevak can even imagine committing such a heinous, hateful crime. Secondly, it was beyond the limits of impossible to think of such an idea about the great soul who was the crown of Hindu society, because of whom we had a glowing persona in front of the world.

It is definitely true that people used to criticise Bapu, and also expressed dissatisfaction many times about his policies. But, don't we express difference of opinion on many things about views of our parents? Don't we criticise them? But, nobody ever thinks that one can take such a step against the parents. Is it not true that respected Tandonji was not happy with his Hindustani policy? Didn't Shri Chandrabhan Gupt criticise him on rationing policy? Had not Pandit Jawaharlalji and Patelji expressed their differences many times? But, no; only we were judged so strangely that a false propaganda was launched that we even disrespect Bapu's picture. Not only this, but we keep shoes on it. We did not expect such a low level falsehood. I had, myself, requested Govind Sahayji to prove this false charge – but who listens? When respected Bapu was alive, we would just brush aside these laughable charges and neither did people pay any attention to them. But, we have now heart breaking experience that these falsehoods proved so capable and horrendous in raising anger, suspicion and false instigation. It is as if newspapers have taken a pledge due to these falsehoods against senior leaders not to publish the truth due to this atmosphere. Not only they did not publish anything about us, but due to instigation, they defamed us and published fake news.

"Godse was the state prachaarak of Bihar. He received a gift of 5000/-" – such propaganda was done freely. As a reaction, homes of swayamsevaks were looted and burnt. (And on advice of some reputed leaders) we tolerated all this, knowing that we were innocent. Thousands of swayamsevaks were imprisoned so nobody can even stand up and senseless hateful propaganda was let lose. We tolerated all this peacefully because our own people did this, otherwise we have not been taught to get insulted by outsiders.

If one were to analyse the situation calmly now, one would realise that the state government had decided to declare Sangh illegal on the basis of a few incidents in Saharanpur in December itself. We also waited eagerly to understand the reason behind it. A little before this, arms and ammunition was found in the homes of Muslim League supporters all over Bharat – especially from Jabalpur, Mathura, Prayag etc. during searches. Police cases were filed against individuals. But, despite arrest of hundreds of people (that included one MLA) for hoarding arms secretly, no case was filed against Muslim League as an organisation. If something was found at a few homes of people from Punjab who had escaped from there after losing everything, how was it imagined that there was a definite Sangh plan? Sangh had been banned just before the Khizrat Hayat Khan's ministry was disbanded. At that time all the places were also searched. But, nothing objectionable was found. It is not even that there was any partiality for us from Punjab police that had overwhelming number of Muslims. Did you find any directive from any senior Sangh office bearer? Or did anyone hear such talks from any of them? In that case, we will have to admit that there was lack of knowledge about Sangh or some secret animosity in the government that we could not detect.

We always wished that all the leaders of Congress should see our work directly and tell us where we are making mistakes, what are their objections. But, they refused to come to our programmes despite many invitations. We don't know whether they found us too small or they feared that they will be infected by us like a disease! Bapu himself had taken a meeting of our 400 senior workers in Delhi and advised us on many things. But, leaders who follow his footsteps never gave us any opportunity to show them what Sangh is in reality. Having failed in our efforts, we decided to present our side to the people. But, instead of paying attention to our expanding work, they had meaningless fear of us; instead of advising us if there was any mistake, they invested their entire might in fake propaganda; and that too without any practical experience and based on hearsay. Respected Dr. Rajendra Prasadji had visited Prayag in December. While listening to his objections and solving his queries, we found that his knowledge about Sangh had come from Shri Sadiq Ali! One could not expect truth from him, because he would not have been fortunate to have seen anything himself. So, Sangh became an institution of landlords and capitalists. Then, many utterances about Sangh like – it spreads communalism, that it is orthodox; fascist began to be used openly. This is how things are these days. Are not Socialists, falsely decorating Congress with such accusations? Don't they make excuses to call Congress communal due to its Hindi policy, its tight control as fascist and calling it an organisation of capitalists due to Birla and Tata being in it? We could not find that except for the king of Jaunpur, Shri Yadavendra Dutt, which other big moneybags, capitalists, kings were members of Sangh. Yes, Sangh was not open to a particular group of people but they were definitely not refused entry.

We could see a strange, totally baseless image about Sangh in the leaders that we had taken pledge to destroy Muslims in Bharat. So much of confusion and ignorance! Sangh never had such a policy that it should mistreat other people. It was true that looking at various failed experiments in this century; we had decided to remove differences within divided Hindus first. It is not hidden from anybody that Hindu society is full of narrow mindedness, selfishness, casteism and parochialism. Sangh's effort was to build unity, patriotism, selflessness, sacrifice and discipline and strengthen them to defend Hindu civilisation and Hindu culture. Despite achieving swaraajya, looking at our peoples' hunger for selfish goals today, won't any true patriot's heart bleed? Our storehouse was the same from where you had brought out your workers. And, looking at the decline and corruption, we felt that till they are taught with more depth about selflessness, patriotism, fearlessness and self-reliance, it is possible that the final outcome won't be any different. Because, if there is no change in the consciousness, and one is coloured only from outside, selfishness washes it out easily when the time of reckoning comes. Our independent nation requires such stable citizens. This was our attempt through our daily programmes to impart values; and we were successful too. Today, where there is lack of devotion and lack of sense of duty on one side, there are thousands of youth on the other side coming together in our camps with boundless affection, trust and sense of duty. Respected Bapu and Dr. Ambedkar had to say that this is actually the practical work, after they visited camps in Vardha and experienced pure love between Harijans and people from other castes there. Sangh is not even orthodox that lives in the past. What is good in the old traditions only that is good for Sangh. We only love our culture, society and the nation. We wish to take it to the pinnacle of development, and for this, anything that is useful, is acceptable to us. We have animosity with none, but we do not wish to stop our development to please others. It is our firm conviction that the nation and the society cannot be built by sacrificing sanskriti (value systems).

Based on our bitter experience of last few years, we do not believe, we doubt. We shall remain doubtful, any thinking person will remain doubtful. From the day the Hyderabad question arose, finding their agent, their spies and increasing number of their supporters in jail, have not government's own suspicions prove correct? At this moment it is not logical to trust them just because they are shouting a lot. Our love for our nation is lesser to none and we cannot remain silent if it is under attack. On such a day of challenge to our nation, if you find any one standing shoulder to shoulder with you, in fact a step ahead, I can say with full confidence, it will be the swayamsevak built by Sangh. When Sardar Patel had called swayamsevaks of Sangh as selfless patriots, it was not excessive praise. You are our own; we shall make our opponents our own when time comes. In his Mumbai address, Respected Guruji has clearly said, quoting the memorable words of King Yudhishthir, *'Vayam panchaadhikam shatam.'* We do not consider Jaichand and Man Singh as our ideals that will let the nation suffer for their own pride or humiliation, or their personal benefits. Our ideals are Rana Pratap and Shivaji. Then, why is this fear for your own – this is a puzzle.

The way, out of ignorance, this great flow of creation of renaissance has been stopped, won't it pain our hearts? Sangh work has stopped. But, selfless, patriotic and disciplined thousands of youth have been created who have got involved in building of this nation, who will keep on the work for growth of their qualities without a break and nurture them in the country, not letting it suffer. You don't have anger, hate or opposition to this work. Yes, it has happened due to lack of knowledge about it, this is the only huge grief. Nation and society are very high above the organisation and individuals, and they should not be damaged due to confusion. We desire to help them rise, and in this effort we shall never lag behind, this is definite. I may be able to meet and converse personally in future with you – this is my wish.

Six months have passed somehow. The baseless fear that the government had, if we remain outside the jails, would have settled down. The past days went by well without any major problem, and if there was sorrow, it was that time was wasted and health of so many people suffered unnecessarily. If this had happened to solve any real problem of the nation, we would have accepted pains with pleasure even hundred times more than we suffered now.

With apologies for misuse of your precious time,

With humility,

Rajendra Singh
S-Class, Prisoner
Naini Central Jail,
(7th July, 1948)

Courtesy–Panchjanya

(Published in Panchjanya weekly in Shravan, Shukla 15, Thursday, Shaka 2005 in the column – Lokwani)

लोकवाणी

[श्री राजेन्द्रसिंह प्रयाग विश्वविद्यालयके एक अध्यापक और यहांके एक सुपरिचित व्यक्ति हैं। आप संघके एक प्रमुख कार्यकर्ता रह चुके हैं। फरवरीमें सुरक्षा-कानूनके अंतर्गत नैनी केन्द्रीय कारागार में रखे गए थे। बीचमें बीमारीके कारण पेरोलपर छूटे थे और लखनऊ जाकर मा० लाल बहादुर शास्त्रीसे मिलनेका प्रयत्न भी किया था पर नहीं मिल सके। पेरोलसे लौटकर नैनी कारागारसे आपने मा० शास्त्रीजीको निम्न पत्र लिखा था। रिहा होनेपर पत्र हमारे पास प्रकाशनार्थ भेजा है। —सं०]

स्पष्टीकरण

माननीय श्री लालबहादुर शास्त्री,
गृहमंत्री, युक्तप्रान्त

द्वारा—
श्री सुपरिन्टेन्डेन्ट,
केन्द्रीय कारागार, नैनी

माननीय शास्त्री जी,

लोकवाणी

शिविरोंमें एकत्रित लाखों स्वयंसेवकोंमें असीम स्नेह, विश्वास और कर्तव्यपरायणता थी। पूज्य बापू और डा० अम्बेडकरको "संघ"के अपने एक शिविर (वर्धा शिविर) को देख और वहाँके हरिजन तथा अन्य वर्गोंमें भेद-भाव—शून्य पवित्र प्रेमको अनुभव कर कहना पड़ा था कि प्रत्यक्ष कार्य वास्तवमें यही है। संघ पुरातनवादी भी नहीं। 'संघ' में पुरातन वही है जो अमर है॥ प्रेम हमें केवल अपनी संस्कृति, समाज और राष्ट्रसे है। उसे हम विश्वके परम-शिखरपर पहुँचाना चाहते हैं, उसके लिए जो भी लाभदायक हो वह हमें मान्य है। हमें किसीसे भी वैर नहीं, परन्तु हम केवल दूसरोंको प्रसन्न करनेके लिए अपना विकास रोकना नहीं चाहते। हमारी यह निश्चित धारणा है कि राष्ट्र और समाज संस्कृतिको बलिवेदीपर चढ़ाकर नहीं बना करते हैं। आज उनपर पिछले कुछ वर्षोंके कटु अनुभवसे हमें विश्वास नहीं आता वरन्, हम शंका करते हैं। हम सशंक रहेंगे, कोई भी विचारवान व्यक्ति सशंक रहेगा। क्या हैदराबादके प्रश्नके प्रारम्भ होनेके बादसे उसके एजेन्ट, उसके गुप्तचर उसकी सहायता करनेवालोंकी बढ़ती हुई संख्या इस देशमें देखकर स्वयं सरकारकी आशंका सिद्ध नहीं होती? अगर इस समय उनके जोरसे चिल्लाने के ही कारण उनपर अधिक विश्वास करना युक्तिसंगत नहीं। अपने राष्ट्रके प्रति हमारा किसीसे भी कम प्रेम नहीं और उसपर आपत्ति आनेपर हम कभी भी पीछे पैर नहीं रख सकते। उस आपत्ति के दिन यदि आपके साथ कंधेसे कंधा जोड़ कर ही नहीं वरन् एक पग आगे यदि कोई मिलेगा तो मैं विश्वासपूर्वक कह सकता हूँ कि 'संघ' द्वारा निर्मित एक पूर्ण स्वयंसेवक ही। सरदार पटेलने अपने लखनऊके भाषणमें जब 'संघ' के स्वयंसेवकोंको एक निस्वार्थ देश-भक्त कहा था, तो कोई अत्युक्ति न थी। आप तो अपने ही हैं, समय आनेपर अपने विरोधियोंको भी अपना बना लेंगे। पूज्य गुरुजी ने अपने वक्तव्य के अन्तमें दिए हुए भारतके सर्वमान्य युधिष्ठिरके उन सदैव स्मरणीय शब्दोंमें स्पष्ट कहा है—"वयं पञ्चाधिकं शतम्।" हम लोगोंके कोई अपमान और मानसिक आदर्श नहीं कि व्यक्तिगत हानि या आपके लिए या मान-अपमानके लिए देशकी हानि होने दें। हमारे तो वाल्मीकि और शिवाजी आदर्श हैं, फिर इससे अपनोंसे भय कैसा—यही पहेली है।

जिस प्रकार अशान्ततापर भय बेहद निर्माणका यह महान् प्रयास असफल कर दिया गया, उससे किसके अन्तःकरणमें वेदना न होगी? संघ का कार्य बन्द हो गया, परन्तु निस्वार्थ देशप्रेमी, असीम-साहसी और अनुशासनबद्ध लाखों उत्साही नवयुवक देशमें निर्माण हो चुके हैं, जो अपने गुणोंसे अपने आसपास राष्ट्रके अन्दर इन गुणोंके उत्कर्षका कार्य सदैव अक्षुण्ण रीतिसे करते रहेंगे। आपके प्रति हृदय कापके लिए क्रोध नहीं, घृणा नहीं, विरोध नहीं; हाँ, यह अनभिज्ञता के कारण हुआ एक बड़ा महान् दुख है। राष्ट्र और समाज, संस्था और व्यक्तिसे बहुत ऊपर है और उन्हें इनकी उन्नतिसे कभी भी क्षति न पहुँचनी चाहिए। उसे हम उन्नत कर सकें—इस उद्योग में हम किसीसे भी पिछड़ेंगे नहीं, यह निश्चित है। भविष्यमें आपसे मिलने का और प्रत्यक्ष वार्तालाप करनेका सौभाग्य मिले—यही अभिलाषा है।

अब प्रायः छः महीने कट ही गए हैं। हमारे बाहर रहनेके कारणसे जो सरकारको निर्मूल ही आत्यन्तिक भय था, अब शांत हो चुका होगा। यह दिन कुशल से ही बिना किसी विशेष कष्ट बीत गए और दुःख यदि कोई रहा तो यही कि इतने लोगोंका समय और स्वास्थ्य अकारण ही नष्ट हुआ। यदि राष्ट्रकी सभी आपत्तियोंके निराकरणमें हमें इससे सौ गुना भी कष्ट मिलता तो सहर्ष स्वीकार होता।

आपके बहुमूल्य समयका इतना दुरुपयोग करनेके लिये क्षमा प्रार्थना सहित—

नैनी विनीतः
केन्द्रीय कारागार राजेन्द्रसिंह
७—७—४८ एम-एस०, लखनऊ

जनराज्य या पुलिसराज्य ?

[उन्नाव जिलेके कुछ सुरक्षा-बन्दी जेलसे छूटे हैं किन्तु उन्हें अपने सामान वापस नहीं मिले हैं। बहुत सी परेशानियाँ सहनेपर उन्होंने निम्न पत्र मा० प्रधान मन्त्री और गृहमन्त्री के पास भेजा है।—सं०]

सेवा में,

माननीय गृहमंत्री जी,
युक्त प्रांत

द्वारा—
श्री डिप्टी कमिश्नर
जिला उन्नाव

महोदय,

सविनय निवेदन है कि हम लोग एक फरवरी '४८ को राष्ट्रीय स्वयंसेवक-संघ के सम्बन्ध में सुरक्षा-बन्दी किये गये और हमारे घरपर सरकारी ताला डाल दिया गया। इस बीच में, हमारी अनुपस्थिति में पुलिस अधिकारियों द्वारा सील तोड़कर स्वेच्छापूर्वक सामान की सूची बनाई गई और उसकी एक भी कापी हम लोगोंको नहीं दी गई, जिससे हम जान सकते कि हमारा सामान पूरा है या नहीं। सामान जिस प्रकार रक्खा गया उससे प्रतीत होता है कि मानों कूड़ा देखकर फेंका गया हो।

जब संघपर लगाये गये आरोप झूठे तथा मिथ्या सिद्ध हुये और वातावरण शांत हुआ तो हम लोग ४ मासके उपरान्त निर्दोष मानकर छोड़ दिये गये, फिर भी हमलोगों से अनुचित जमानतें मांगी गईं। इसके पश्चात् हम लोगों ने डिप्टी कमिश्नर उन्नाव के पास अपना प्रार्थना-पत्र दिया कि हमारे निजी तथा दैनिक प्रयोग में आनेवाले सामान लौटा दिये जावें। पर अधिकारियों द्वारा १½ मास तक यह कहकर टाला जाता रहा कि अभी तक कोई आज्ञा नहीं आई है। फिर बहुत प्रयत्न करनेके पश्चात् केवल कपड़े दिये गये, ट्रंक रोक लिया गया; नाज दिया गया पर भोजन बनाने के बर्तन रोक लिये गये; तेल देकर लालटेन रख लिया गया; दाढ़ी बनानेका सामान तक नहीं दिया गया। इस प्रकार केवल कपड़े तथा अनाजके अतिरिक्त सभी सामान रोक लिये गये। हम लोगों ने कई प्रार्थनापत्र दिये पर एकका भी उत्तर प्राप्त नहीं हुआ। अपनी कठिनाइयाँ डि० क० महोदयके सामने ही निवेदन करनेके लिये हम लोग १५-२० बार उनके घर गए, पर कभी भी हमको यह अवसर न मिला।

जब उनसे घर मिलने की कोई आशा न रही तो हम लोग फिर अपना प्रार्थना-पत्र दिनांक ४अगस्त ४८को कचहरीमें ही ले गये, किन्तु उस समय जो घटना घटी उससे हम समझ गये कि आज भी ब्रिटिश नौकरशाही कुर्सीपर बैठकर तानाशाही चला रही थी। हम आपके सन्मुख वह घटना रखते जिसे पढ़कर आपको भी आश्चर्य होगा कि इस स्वतंत्र भारतमें जो चारों ओर जनस्वातंत्र्य और जनाधिकारका ढोल पीटा जाता है उसी ढोलके पोलमें ही नौकरशाही और तानाशाहीका अब भी खेल खेला जा रहा है। हम लोगोंको न्यायालयमें देखते ही डि० क० महोदयकी आँखें लाल हो गईं और वे गरजकर बोले—"तुम लोगोंने यह अच्छा बहाना ढूँढ़ लिया है कि बार-बार application देते रहो और उसकी आड़में संघकी activities revive करनेकी कोशिश करते रहो। नित्य प्रति मेरे पास इसकी reports आ रही हैं। मैं तो अभी तुम लोगोंके लिये externment order निकालने जा रहा हूँ।" मैं आपसे कहा देता हूँ कि आजसे कभी भी आप मेरे बंगले या यहाँ (कचेहरी) न आइयेगा। जो सामान देना था लौटा दिया गया, अब कुछ भी न मिलेगा। आप यहाँसे चले जाइये।" उनके क्रोधका कारण हम न समझ सके और चुपचाप चले आए। जब डि० क० महोदयका इस प्रकारका व्यवहार है तो क्या हम आशा कर सकते हैं कि उनके द्वारा हम लोगोंके लिये उचित न्याय हो सकेगा? अस्तु

हम लोग आपसे विनय निवेदन करते हैं कि वह सामान जो न तो लौटाया गया है और न जिसके लिये जब्त करनेकी आज्ञा ही हुई है तथा जो निजी है जैसे बर्तन, घड़ी, साबुन, तेल आदि—हमें लौटाया जाय।

जिस सामानके लिये जब्त होनेकी आज्ञा प्रकाशित हुई है (जैसे साइकिल, रेकर्ड, रुपये, चित्र आदि,) वह भी हम लोगोंका व्यक्तिगत है और उनसे संघका किसी भी भाँति सम्बन्ध नहीं है। क्योंकि ये सामान पुलिस अधिकारसे लिये गये वह घर भी संघका 'ऑफिस' नहीं है बल्कि हम लोगोंके रहनेका स्थान है। अतः ये सामान भी लौटानेकी आज्ञा प्रदान की जाय।

जहाँ तक हम लोगोंपर संघका कार्य पुनः प्रारम्भ करनेका आरोप लगाया जाता है, हम प्रामाणिकतापूर्वक कह सकते हैं कि यह आरोप निराधार और मिथ्या है। हम दावेके साथ कह सकते हैं कि यदि इसमें कुछ भी सत्यता है तो कोई भी इसे सिद्ध करके दिखा दे। जब किसी गाँवमें हम कुटुम्बी लोग बरात अथवा भोज आदिके निमंत्रणमें गए तो वहाँ के स्थानीय कांग्रेसी अपनी देशभक्ति दिखानेके लिये यह झूठी रिपोर्ट भेजते हैं कि हम वहाँ संघकार्यके लिये गये थे। अधिकारियों द्वारा भी यह सूचना वेदवाक्य मानकर बिना उसकी सत्यताकी छान-बीन किये स्वयंसेवकोंको तरह तरहसे तंग किया जाता है जिससे गाँवोंमें आतंक छा जाय।

यदि भविष्यमें इसी प्रकार चलता रहा तो निश्चित ही यह तथाकथित जनतंत्र राज्य शीघ्र ही पुलिस-राज्यमें परिणत हो जायगा, जो गान्धीवादको देन है और जो जनता-जनार्दनके कोप भड़क उठनेपर कभी भी भस्मीभूत हो सकता है। आपसे हमें पूर्ण आशा है कि इस जिलेके जो पुलिस अधिकारियों तथा अफसरशाहियों की मनमानी चल रही है उसे रोकनेके लिये आप उचित कदम उठावेंगे।

हम लोग आपसे प्रार्थना तथा अनुरोध करते हैं कि इसका उत्तर हमें अवश्य दिया जाय।

द्वारा— भवदीय
पं० श्यामनारायण राजा इन्दुरकर
एडवोकेट सुरेन्द्रनाथ भारती
लखीमपुर खीरी श्रीकृष्ण मिश्र

The '5-S' formula of Rajju Bhaiya

Many RSS swayamsevaks have heard about 5-S formula of Rajju Bhaiya for an impactful shakha of RSS. Many people have talked about it in their recollections. Therefore, I am giving it here in summarised points. Rajju Bhaiya had explained these points during a two day workshop of Mumbai workers.

S 1	–	Sankhya	–	Numbers
S 2	–	Sanch	–	Team
S 3	–	Sanskar	–	Imbibing values
S 4	–	Sampark	–	Vast contact
S 5	–	Sneha	–	Affection

First 'S'—Sankhya or numbers – average attendance in morning and night shakhas should be atleast in two digits – that is 10 or more. The attendance in evening shakha should be such that they have separate teams. Minimum attendance for baal (young boys) should be above 25. There should be sustained effort to increase the numbers.

Second 'S'—Sanch or team of workers at shakha level. There should be gat system (smaller team). Groups for physical activity. Team of shakha should comprise of shakha karyavaah (secretary), mukhya shikshak (main teacher), gan shikshak (group teacher), gat naayak (team leader), and deputy team leader. This team should hold meeting regularly and think about every aspect of the shakha. Gatnaayak (team leader) is the first step of creating a kaaryakarta (worker), therefore system of 'gat' is necessary.

Third 'S'—Sanskaar that is conduct programmes that instill values. We have to awaken the sanskaar of discipline, selflessness and patriotism. Therefore proper thinking and planning needs to be done when we plan drills, games, exercises, Sangh songs, good thoughts (subhashit) golden words (amrit vachan) etc. There should be variety in the programmes. One can plan for competitive programmes too.

Fourth 'S'—Sampark that is contacts. More the energy to contact people, more will be the progress in that shakha. Contacting swayamsevaks in homes before the shakha and after the shakha. This contact should be till the kitchen of the house. We should be in touch with every home in the area around shakha. They could be contacted for any programme or movement, but it should be in our nature to contact them regularly.

Fifth 'S'—Sneh or affection. Pure, sattvik affection is the very foundation of our work. He is my swayamsevak, he is my own – such should be the feeling that all the members of our society are our own. Occasional programmes like picnics, social festivals, family get togethers, having snacks together and sewa around shakha nurture this feeling of affection. This affection is what gives strength to a shakha.

Workers at shakha level should pay attention to these five points and should watch out where we are in terms of these 5-S. We will find that shakhas can create impact even today and they can create workers too.

Courtesy – Bimal Kedia

□

Summary of the first speech after nomination as Sarsanghchaalak

Our working is like that of a family. Our work moves with free flowing mutual discussions. Today Sangh work has become a multi-dimensional work. This is a natural process for Sangh. We call it 'progressive unfoldment'. Doctorji had clear idea about how it will take a huge shape. While talking to respected Balasaheb, we get a clear idea that Doctorji had all these ideas in his mind. But, in his time our nation was not free. Biggest goal was to free this nation. Independence was the primary goal. This is why Doctorji gave Sangh a political thrust.

We were confused after independence, we lost our direction. What is our sanskriti (culture), what is our dharma, what are our ideals in life, we began forgetting all this. Actually, we began our journey of making this a nation that existed for thousands of years. Watching this, respected Guruji gave this work a cultural thrust. He brought before everyone the supreme heritage and sanskriti (values) with conviction and firmness. It does not mean that Doctorji did not have these ideas about our great ideals of our culture. Because, these are the basis of Hindu Rashtra. It was necessary to have this thought from the beginning.

Balasaheb expanded Sangh work in different directions. Projects in tribal field, student field and sewa etc. received huge boost and our activities expanded in a big way. This process is similar to the natural process of a seed turning into a huge tree.

Idea of Hindu Rashtra is ancient. Idea of 'rashtra' has been given in very simple words in Vedas. 'This land is our mother and we are her children' – this is a Vedic statement. The foundation of our nation is this motherland. During the times of Doctorji and Guruji, this ideal of motherland took a beautiful shape based on thoughts of great personalities like Maharshi Aurobindo, Bankimchandra and Swami Vivekanandaji. Only by awakening the spirit of complete surrender to this motherland, will the spirit of action, devotion to duty and sacrifice will be invoked.

Our prayer begins with *'Namaste sadaa vatsale matribhoome'* – worshiping our motherland. Sangh tried to arouse the emotions that we shall serve this motherland. Unfortunately, this emotion that 'This is our nation' could not be invoked by people working in different fields. This is the reason we see sense of inaction around us. Noone does one's work and duty with enthusiasm. This is the result of breaking the sense of affection in our society. This is our land for thousands of years. We cannot live elsewhere without it — anywhere else. There is no other place where we can live. We have no second place in the world. Till we are able to create this kind of positive emotion in our people, till then the sentiment of working hard and for sacrifice for the motherland, martyrdom cannot be evoked.

Our experience is that emotion of dedication is built in the people who have been nurtured with sanskaaras in Sangh shakha. If they become teachers, they do good work. Saraswati Shishu Mandir is appreciated because of this devotion of teachers. Doctors go to tribal areas despite great difficulties and lack of facilities. In their hearts they believe that 'this society is our society.'

Doctorji said the same thing in simple words, "This is Hindu Rashtra. This nation is built on the foundation of Hindutva. A nation is not created on the basis of land alone. When this land was large, it was a Hindu nation at that time. Now, land has shrunk, still this is Hindu nation. Sanskriti (culture) is the crucial foundation." Doctorji could show this idea's fruition in swayamsevaks.

Second point that Doctorji used to make is, "This is my nation, this is my society, I should do something for it." Doctorji made a small demand initially. "Take out one hour for the country." Slowly, beginning with one hour, swayamsevak begins giving more time. He becomes prachaarak for some years and devotes his life sometimes. One develops a nature to give time to Sangh and do something. This is the reason for good expansion of shakhas. With this, Sangh has also gained trust in the society. Some of our swayamsevaks have put in 50-60 years in Sangh. These swayamsevaks can do some small or big work.

There are elements who are active in tearing away our weaker sections from the society. Missionaries and others are seen very active in breaking Hindu society. Rajendra Prasadji and Gandhiji had opposed conversions very strongly. But, conversion has been allowed very openly. Our Hindu society has diversity. Some people are trying to turn this diversity into class struggle. They are playing the politics of breaking the society. Therefore we have a challenge of meeting and mixing up with that section of the society. They should feel that they are also an important part of this society.

When impact of our work increases, there are definitely some changes. There was an agitation to rename Marathwada University in the name of Dr. Babasaheb Ambedkar. Some people opposed it. But, our people made efforts for this change in name. Public opinion was built by Vishwa Hindu Parishad, BJP, Vidyarthi Parishad and Samarasataa Manch. There were no fights, no bitterness or animosity because of this and we kept up efforts for name-change in peaceful manner.

Due to the atmosphere today, every swayamsevak feels that time has come to expand Sangh work with speed. Accepting the challenge thrown up by this period, we should increase our activism, meet new people and make their views favourable. If we work like this, I trust that we shall see that idea of the golden Bharat that Doctorji had envisioned. Even if you are not fortunate to see this achievement – *"yaachi dehi yaachi dola."* – with this very body and eyes, people who are younger than us, will surely be able to see this fulfilment.

Courtesy – Keshav Srishti, January 2004

□

Science and Religion

This period has been witness to the conflict between science and religion. Many things written in religious books do not prove to be true in the light of modern research. It was written in Bible that Sun moves around Earth, which seems to be true to common people. But, when Copernicus and Galileo discovered that Earth moves around Sun, there were atrocities on them and they were prosecuted in the courts of the Church. Therefore, many people feel that there is fundamental clash between science and religion. But, this is not correct.

Let us look at Hindu dharma. This has not been proclaimed by any prophet or rishi or scholar. Spiritual approach of Hindu dharm is the discovery of the ultimate truth, and science, too, is trying to reach the truth. There is no authority among scientists to whom we cannot question about this. In the same way, any question can be raised about the spiritual path of Hindus, and someone has to prove it. Vedas, Upanishads tell us many things about the birth of the universe and there have been many discussions to establish the truth. In this spiritual atmosphere, there is space for even a *'naastik'* like Charvak and he is also called a rishi. Shankaracharya has gone on to say that if even 100 books tell you that fire is cool, still do not believe them because this is against our actual experience.

Path of uncovering the truth in science is practical. People who research, they divide an object in smaller parts so that it can be understood. Scientists have been able to reach the atom and sub-atomic particles, where they felt they can understand the nature of matter. But, after reaching that stage they discovered the Heisenberg's principle of uncertainty that says that you cannot decide the place and velocity of a sub-atomic particle because even the act of looking at it with that micronic light agitates it. Matter and energy are same and they can be transformed from one to the other – this has been proven by Einstein's mathematics. Therefore, it may be possible for science to reach the ultimate truth.

Bharatiya philosophers did not use any complex instruments but they tried to experience the truth. They reached the conclusion thousands of years back that everything in nature is 'Brahma' that we cannot see nor can we describe. So, integral spiritual view of Hindus that helps us experience the oneness of the universe takes us towards the search of modern science.

Science has made our life easy. But, science has also created arms whose ultimate result is destruction. Einstein says, "Without spirituality, science is blind and religion is handicapped without science." We need contribution from both to solve the problems faced by the modern world. In our ancient literature, science has been called *'avidya'* and spiritual knowledge has been called *'vidya'.* Ishopanishad has presented the need for both in beautiful words—

विद्यां चाविद्यां च यस्तद्वेदोभ्य सह।
अविद्यया मृत्युं तीर्त्वामृतमश्नुते।।

(One can be victorious over death with science, that is avidya; and vidya, that is spiritual knowledge gives ultimate bliss.) This is the call of the times. After this lecture, Rajju Bhaiya explained how *'syaatwaad'* is similar to 'theory of relativity'.

—Lecture in Kenya University, 13th January, 1997

□

Contribution of Indian Science to the World

'Science and knowledge in ancient India' is my favourite subject. When I used to teach, I used to talk about it with my students even at that time.

We have remembered the great personalities born in our ancient land, sung with pride about them. However, it is surprising that none of them wrote about themselves nor have they told about their specialties. But, this was their specialty. Today, if someone publishes even a small book, he will write his name in bold letters on the first page of the book. If someone writes a poem, he will put his name there. But, who wrote the *richaas* and *mantras* that appear in the Vedas? Who has written these Upanishads? Who discovered them? This was not the system in our ancient society. Therefore our literature and our science are not linked to individuals. But, even today their names are being remembered in different ways. We recite their names in our *praatah smaran* and *Ekaatmataa Stotra*. Scientists too are, in a way, rishis, who have discovered the truth. They have presented the true principles in their shlokas. Jagdish Chandra Basu is a scientist of modern period who has discovered that plants are very sensitive in the botanical world. Names of Basu, Ramanujam and Venkatraman appear in this list. Ancient great names are also in it. You also may wish to know, who was Bhaaskaracharya, who was Aryabhata, who was Varaahamihir? This is why we recite these shlokas every day and remember these great people.

A feeling has developed in the western scholars about

Bharat that there were no big names in literature writing in Bharat. Why? Ramayana has not disappeared, nor has Mahabharata. Thus, the names of Valmiki and Vyasa are known to all. Kalidasa's name too is known because we now have his famous books like Meghadoot and Shaakuntalam and also many poems. Bhavbhooti is a known name too. Therefore, western scholars now say that Bharat is great in terms of literature. There are Upanishads and Puranas and there is much more literature that is now available and no other country can be compared with Bharat in this regard. The paintings in Ajanta Elora caves have still not faded or disappeared. They are made from some oils and natural substances with colours from vegetables that the colours have not faded in hundreds of years. They still look good. They are indelible evidence of our chemistry and chemical engineering. Bharatiyas were high level artists. These creations are about 2,500 year old. This was the time when Buddha appeared on earth. Therefore, all the paintings are related to his life and very lively.

People believe that Bharat is the inventor of seven notes in music. There are stories abound about *raagas* and *raaginis*, that a good singer could bring rains with *Megh Malhaar*, while someone could light up lamps by singing *Deepak Raag*. These stories are now old. One cannot definitely say or prove if these things could happen or not, based on legends or folklore. There has been famous singer Omkar Nath Thakur in modern times who spread the word about our music world over. And we remember two more names – Vishnu Digambar Paluskar and Bhaatkhande. Omkar Nath Thakur was a disciple of Digambar Paluskarji. He was a music teacher in Kashi University. He was a great scholar of music. Therefore, I have experienced bliss of his music. He told me once that he reached Italy while touring Europe. Mussolini was ruling Italy at that time. It is an incident of around 1936-37. Second world war had commenced. He desired to meet Mussolini. When he met Mussolini, he asked Thakurji, "What is the specialty of Indian music?" He replied,

"Bharat has made great discoveries in ragas and I sing those raga and they have specific results. I know which raga I should sing in the morning and which in evening. Mussolini told him, "All these are useless talks, can you do something that I can experience? I have not been able to sleep for 5-7 days. I have not slept for days. If your ragas have such quality and fame, then you sing them. We will see if they can put me to sleep." Omkar Nath Thakurji has, himself, narrated this incident to me and told, "I told him it is difficult to tell. This raga is created for Indian minds. Then, I began singing with my taanpura as accompaniment, and he began snoring within 20 minutes. I left silently. When he realised the power of Bharatiya ragas, he too accepted their greatness." It feels good to know about new evidences and share them.

Zero was invented in Bharat. Biggest contribution of Bharat in mathematics is zero. Mathematics, today, cannot work without zero. 1-2-3-4-5-6-7-8-9 and putting a zero after it makes it ten, adding two zeroes makes it 100, and so on. This is the glory of zero. You will be surprised that there was no major work in Europe till 16th century. Because, they had not adopted decimal system yet. They had adopted Italian Roman script. In Roman script there is line 'II' for the inner numerals. V for 5, X for 10, and L for fifty etc. This method of numbering is used even now in Homeopathy. But, there are limitations to this system. Therefore, there used to be discussions that division and multiplication is very difficult. This is taught at higher levels of education in university. We can only do addition and subtraction. '0' had been invented, where the position of zero at a particular place decides its value. All this was taken from us by Arabia. From Arabia these went to Europe and it came to be known as 'International form of Arabic numerals'. It is so surprising that Arabians still call it *'Hindsaa'* that is, received from Hind, that is Bharat. In Europe it is called Arabic numeral. These numerals have not been discovered by Arabians. We had very high level mathematics in Vedas. Today, we need people who can re-discover them and explain them to us. The Shankaracharya of Puri, Swami Ramkrishna Teerth was a great mathematician. I am fortunate to have listened to many of his lectures. He wrote a book called 'Vedic Mathematics'. He also used to give lectures on this subject and he could give answers like a computer, very quickly based on Vedic calculations.

Aryabhata has given the dimensions of Pie, its radius, diameter and Pie ratio in 14th Century, what is now called 'Pie ratio'. You will be surprised that Aryabhata gave the value of Pie Ratio as 3.14159256. He has given answer to this power of decimal. How he must have done it? Would he have drawn a diameter and measured it? But, you cannot easily measure upto so many decimal points. This is a puzzle that still troubles scientists, how he would have calculated upto this value. If we read books on mathematics written by great authorities, we find that they have not clarified how he must have got this answer. There are many such things that people don't understand because they do not know how they were proven and value calculated.

I am a student of Physics and I remember that in Shanti Parva of Mahabharata, there is a small mention of light in Sanskrit. Since I don't know Sanskrit, I could remember only half of the shloka. This has the basic idea, so I left out the balance shloka. At that time measure of roads used to be in '*yojan*'. One yojan used to be equal to four *kosas*, and two miles made a kosa. Thus, one yojan is equal to eight miles. It is written about 'Light' 5,000 years back in Shanti Parva – 'योजनानां सहस्त्रेद्री द्विशत द्वियोजनम' – that is two thousand and two hundred two yojan and further it says that if you multiple 2,202 yojan 8 times then it comes to around 17,000 miles. It further says, that light, that brightness, that light travels this distance in half a '*nimish*'. We salute that light. 'Nimish' is the moment that a person flaps his eye lids. Nimish is sixth part of one second. So, those people calculated that light travels that distance in $1/12^{th}$ of a second. To find the speed of light, if we multiply

17,000 with 12 then we find that speed of light is 2,04,000 – that is approximately two lakh miles per second. This is the accepted speed even today. It is slightly little or more, that is 1,85,000 miles per second. How would our ancient rishis found this? This is present in Shanti Parva of Mahabharata that we salute that light, that energy. How much research and thinking must have gone into it to establish this principle!

The Cosmology that we call today, that is how the universe came into existence, how did it evolve, there is an entire treasure of Sankhya shastra present. We can pick up a *sootra* (formula) from it. Kapil rishi has described this in Sankhya shastra. It says, entire matter was at one place in the beginning. Then it felt like multiplying itself. It began expanding toward Brahma. If we think about the modern theory of Cosmology, it is quite similar to Kapil's theory. It seems that this subject is so ancient for Bharatvarsh.

Reading principles of Bible, it is quite surprising that Christian scholars calculated Earth's age as 6,000 years. We can't even think of such an idea today. Mr. Calvin, after lot of mathematical calculations came to conclusion that life of Earth is ten crores or 100 million years. Then came the radioactive methodology. Based on Radio-activity, someone said, 10 crore years may be wrong, it should be around 1 crore. Someone said may be, 50 crore years. An average Indian knows the Indian method of *panchaang* or calendar. We are in Kaliyuga (age) now. Tretaa yuga is 1,000 years of Brahma and Satyuga is 4,000 years of Brahma. A new yuga cannot arrive immediately after the first yuga. There is a 'sandhi kaal' or turnaround period. The sandhi kaal of Satyuga on both sides is 400 years, and sandhi kaal on two sides of Kaliyuga is 100 years each. If we do all this calculation, the we come to a 'mahaa yuga' or putting all these yugas together, it is 12,000 years of Brahma. It is believed that one year of human beings is equal to one day of Brahmaji. Thus, one Brahma's year is equal to 360 human years. Adding the sandhi kaal, Kaliyuga is 1,200 years of Brahma. So, to calculate the age of Kaliyuga, we shall have to multiply 1,200 years with 360 years. This brings us to the conclusion that Kaliyuga is 4,32,000 human years.

As a yuga changes, there are great changes in Earth. We know that nine planets circumambulate Sun, all at their own velocities. When all these planets come in a line during their movements, then it is said that there is some serious movement in universe and earth. Deluge or part deluge. By this calculation, our people have calculated the age of Kaliyuga as 4 lakh 32 thousand years. By same calculation age of Earth comes to 200 crore or 2,000 million human years. There has been a new research recently. According to this Cosmology study scientists have given the age of Earth as 400 crore years. Otherwise, till 10-5 years back, as per scientific researches, age of Earth has been understood to be 200 crore years. One of our Bharatiya scientist is at high ranks in these discoveries. His name is Subramanyam Chandrashekhar who is nephew of C.V. Raman. He had also said that age of Earth is 200 crore years. All this should bring to our attention, how our forefathers had calculated time.

It is not that we worked only on astronomy and left out mathematics. We recall Bhaaskaracharya. He was there in 11-12th century. One of his main text is Leelavati. Some of our senior teachers may have seen Leelavati. It has short stories and short shlokas, through which he has created questions in mathematics, like riddles. This text was used as a text book for nearly 700 years in Bharat, Russia and Arabia. The astonishing thing is that Bhaaskaracharya had studied the surface of sphere in 11-12th century as 4 PiR and volume = 4/3rd PiR^3 as the surface of the sphere. All these are discovered by Bhaaskaracharya. Western scholars claim that these cannot be calculated till someone knows differential calculus and integral calculus. It is well known that Newton shared the knowledge of these two subjects of differential calculus and integral calculus in 17th century. This means that either Bhaaskaracharya knew these branches of calculus or he used some other methodology to arrive at these results.

Bhaaskaracharya definitely had this knowledge that is why he was the first to establish these formulae of mathematics.

In the same way, Pythagoras theorem that is also known by his name; was famous as Bodhaayan sutra atleast two hundred years before Pythagoras. How are squares of two arms of a triangle are equal to the square of hypotenuse arm, is told in Bodhaayan sutra (formula). This Bodhaayan sutra was used widely to build the *yagya vedis* which used to be built in different forms and shapes. These have been used in our texts two hundred years before Pythagoras. This proves that *Rekhagannit* that is called geometry, Beejgannit that is called algebra and binomial theorems were definitely known to Bhaaskaracharya. He has used them correctly too. So, this was mathematics on the foundation of which science is established. I have just presented a few glimpses of the great discoveries that these great scholars did to show how elevated was our mathematics.

Now we move to medical science. We can call them biological science or medical science. Harvey in England discovered how blood circulates, how it moves in the body in 16th century. The texts written by Sushrut and Charak have described all these actions fully. Sushrut is considered the first surgeon of the world. Sushrut Samhita, recovered recently, was written by him 2,500 years back. We can read the description of different types of knives, scissors, tongs etc. used in surgery. We note that Sushrut had done operations in that period. He did surgeries that had not been done even till 500-700, 100-1,500 CE in Europe. You are aware that our eyes get afflicted with cataract. Cataract is not something new. It must have been in ancient period too and therefore how to cut and remove it surgically, these experiments were done during those times. These techniques are now called gouging in which defective lens is cut and pushed aside so a person can see again. A lens that becomes opaque, could be removed during that time. Stones too used to be formed. His texts describe in detail, how to cut them inside the bladder and take them out.

Most astonishing is the subject of plastic surgery that is quite new in modern medical science. Lot of studies were done about how to put on new skin on hands, feet, cut nose or burning. Possibly, there were great fighters who fought with swords and attacked each other. When they advanced and attacked each other, probably, sword may not be reaching the entire body, so some parts of body may be cut off, like ear or arms or nose. They must have thought about how to repair them. And our surgeons have described the entire process of surgery. How to remove skin from one part of the body and place it in the other part. If one has to place skin in hand, need to take skin from hand only so skin can live. This is how this science kept developing, just as there is a process of increasing knowledge today.

We remember Sushrut and Charak. Charak describes many medicines. These medicines are used not only in Bharat but also outside – Sarpagandhaa in some places and Ashwagandhaa in some. He used Sarpagandhaa to help overcome lack of sleep. At that time they may not have talked of blood pressure or *rakta chaap*. But, they used it for calming the mind and heart. Punarnava was used. Dozens of medicines that are being imported in Bharat have been manufactured using medicinal knowledge of Bharat.

How would our people have found this medical science? These ideas used to come out during Kumbh melas of fairs. All the scholars, rishi, munis used to come to sage Bhardwaj's ashram during Kumbh Mela and stay there for 2-3 months. They would discuss who had done some research, what medicines were made and what were their properties. This is how the medicinal science would, probably, have developed. There used to be discussions and open conversation. In ancient times, it was not their nature to hide their knowledge. Otherwise Charak Samhita or Sushrut Samhita would never have been written.

We thus find that in the knowledge field we call medical science, we made huge progress in chemical and nuclear science. It has been discussed in Bharat in our nuclear science how the universe or cosmology came into being. Just as name of Kapil is linked to Sankhya philosophy, similarly name of Kanaad is linked to Vaisheshik philosophy. We remember in our Bharat Bhakti Stotram or praatah smaran "Vaigyanikaasch Kapilah, Kanaadah." We find name of Kanaad rishi in this who wrote Vaisheshik shastra. He knew that there was a science behind it. My Chachaji (paternal uncle) was considered an authority in Sanskrit. He passed away recently. He used to tell me many times, "You should collaborate with me. I know Sanskrit and I am writing about Vaisheshik shastra these days. We can sit together and see how it can match with modern science." But, I could not find time. I had recently gone to a science seminar. There was a scholar and head of department of Physics. He has done Ph.D. in Physics and also a Ph.D. in Sanskrit. He has studied Vaisheshik Shastra and brought out many scientific facts. I was with him and observed some of them. There is so much of wonderful mathematics and physics in this Vaisheshik Shastra. Very few persons would have read this text.

Vaisheshik Shastra has given name to '*Prithvi*' to Earth. The process of measurements would be similar to what there is today. Like, we measure one meter and put a pencil mark. We know that measure has been linked to Earth. Diameter of Earth was then linked to one meter, and then it was also linked to its length. People who have studied Vaisheshik Shastra, they are aware that the unit of measures used in it. So many details are available there. Kanaad rishi made enormous contribution to this knowledge. Therefore, scholars of Sanskrit and Scholars of Vaisheshik Shastra can come together and do something constructive. There is need of similar studies in other knowledge systems and texts in Chemistry, Physics, Mathematics, Medical sciences etc.

Some people tell us, ok, we have understood about Science. You have given some names of scientists. Mathematics is the base of all other knowledge systems, you have discussed that too. You discussed Medical sciences, but technology was not present in Bharat. It is surprising to hear this. Bharatvarsh was much ahead in technology. For example, scientists in the world have only recently been able to produce stainless steel. Stainless steel is a product of this century. You are aware that there is steel column in Delhi that is there since a 1,000 years. There is no rust on it. What kind of metallurgy would have been there at that time? What kind of knowledge of metallurgy would have been available at that time? How would people be making this kind of steel in old times?

Dharampalji has done excellent study on the kind of technology Bharat had about 100-200 years back. He tells us that we don't need to give any proof on this. British ruled this country for 200 years. Their collectors and officers used to write letters to the company directors. Dharampalji has written a book based on those documents. I am told this book is not available now. Name of his book is "Science and Technology in 18th Century." On reading this book, one finds out how steel was being manufactured in Bharatvarsh. Steel is considered very important and necessary in today's life. England has many huge machines that include furnaces. This was a small scale industry in our country, what we call cottage industry. 3-4 people used to create a special kind of structure with some bricks, bring their own machines, bring some kind of special coal and steel minerals and then manufacture steel. They used to add extracts of certain leaves and some other chemicals. This resulted in high quality steel. At that time we used to get steel for fifty rupees per quintal. Steel was being sold in England at that time at 200 rupees per quintal that is 2000 rupees per ton.

Biggest advantage of this cottage industry was that the manufacturers could take it to a place eight to ten miles away, or wherever it was required and set it up. Steel produced in this cottage industry used to be of such a high quality that it could be used for variety of objects. You would have heard that Bharat was famous for its steel. When Porus (Puru) and

Alexander (Sikandar) met and finally they signed a treaty, Alexander sought a gift from Puru. He told him give us iron and steel of Bharatvarsh. Not only this, but it is written in Indian and books overseas that when there were battles, the fighters would challenge each other and call out, "Beware, my sword is made of Indian steel, this will separate your head from your body!" If this is not technology, what should we call technology?

We have made progress in other areas of technology too. We all know that today we make high quality cotton textiles with automated computerized machinery. If the cotton yarn is of 80-80 count, then fine cotton called *'malmal'* is considered as ordinary. If it is 80-100 count, it is good. But, we cannot think of yarn of above 200 count be manufactured by these computerized machines. The malmal called the Dhaka malmal of Bharatvarsh, in that one pound of cotton would produce two lakh yards of yarn. And the yarn created from this used to be so fine that when Mughal princess appeared in the durbar wearing seven layers of that fabric, every one called out, "She has not worn any clothes! She is naked!" This malmal used to have very high demand in the world and it was sold heavily in Europe. You will probably be surprised to know that England tried to stop this malmal from entering England and levied special tax on it. But, ladies buy what they like at any cost. And imports did not stop. Finally, a law was made that people will have to pay fine if they moved around in 200 count malmal. Women were ready to pay even a penalty. Finally, a law was passed that wearing it would be punishable offence. Then, British tried to stop the manufacture of this quality of fabric. We have heard that they cut of the thumbs of highly skilled workers so that they cannot make such high quality fabric. Manufacturing such high quality fabric and steel shows the superior technology of Bharatvarsh.

It is totally wrong to think that there was no science, no technology in Bharatvarsh. There is need to study this subject. There are enough proofs, on the basis of which we can say that

Bharatvarsh was much advanced in ancient times in science and technology.

I was making efforts since some times to study such texts and scriptures. Just as Bhardwaj has written about the science of aircraft making in Bhardwaj Samhita, he had also written many such texts. There is Agastya Samhita. I tried to find Agastya Samhita in 10-20 libraries in Delhi, but I could not get Agastya and Bhardwaj Samhitas. I have been able to source Vimaan Shastra (Science of making aircraft), it will take time to study it. But, there are so many things that we have available today. We should make efforts to see where to get these books. People, who know Sanskrit should acquire them, study them and understand them correctly. They can present the facts that are beyond any doubts, about these great scientists and technocrats.

What kind of Binomial theorems we had? How did they reach the value of pie? How would they have calculated the area and volumes. It is important to see how we can create hobby and interest in research about these topics in our students.

Finally, I must say that it is a matter of pleasure that our great intellectuals, our rishis after lot of thinking, said, "One cannot see what is reality, what is truth. One can only experience it after one achieves the feeling of oneness with it. What is the universe that very same is our body – *'yat pinde, tat brahmaande'*. Aatma and Paramaatma are related. But is it truly so? Then, we have to admit – 'neti-neti' – it is not that. This is how we describe it. New dimensions have been added to modern science now. Quantum mechanics has come in. Theory of relativity has arrived. Principle of Uncertainty has come.

It seems we have not been able to find the truth. The process of invention itself turns into reality. This is the principle of uncertainty that by the time observer observes, in that short time, the reality of the observed would have changed. One will have discovered light. When that particle of light will return after hitting a point and tell us what it is, by that time the status would have changed. Then, how do we find the reality? Probably, the truth is ultimately the truth we had reached in ancient times. The truth is same in all of us, there is no duality or difference in it and it cannot be found with experiments. People in the west have reached that point by only material sciences. How did great minds of Bharat discover this? We can find an answer to it in Jain literature, in Buddha literature. This is why Dr. Kothari has written a book and gave a short lecture–"Relativity and Syaatwaad." He has also said that there can be two things correct at the same time. In relativity, two trains are running simultaneously. Something seems true from one train. Some other thing looks true from the other train. There is distance and velocity between the two. Therefore, it seems that one train is moving ahead, while the other train which is running faster from there it seems that the first train is going back. So, there is lot of similarity between relativity and syaatwaad. And, there is similarity between Quantum Theory and Buddha philosophy. There is lot of similarity between it and Buddha thought. Therefore, it seems today that all the thinkers, especially those who think very deeply, are reaching the point where our rishis had reached thousands of years back.

We can hold our heads high with pride and we can inculcate pride in our students. We are children of those forefathers who were great inventors and discoverers. Being children of those people we can again raise Bharatvarsh to great heights.

—Courtesy, Pathik Sandesh, Jalandhar,
Vichar Pravaah, page 92-100

□

Annexure-6

Speech of Rajju Bhaiya on Vijayadashami–1997, Nagpur

Today is the sacred Vijayadashami day. This day reminds us every year of events that took place thousands of year back, when a resourceless Ram, living in forests defeated a highly prosperous and powerful rakshasa Raavana who believed that he could never be defeated. Raavana had become the lord of all the three *lokas*, the entire universe. He was destroying what was good in our sanskriti and it did not look possible that someone could defeat him. Then, forest dweller Ram defeated that supreme warrior with the help of forest dwelling communities (*Vanvasis* – now called tribals) went all the way to his own Lanka and defeated him. Raavana had acquired some extraordinary powers. His Lanka was made of gold. Battle was not of equals, as Tulsidasji noted in one sentence – 'Raavan Rathee, Virath Raghuveera – that is, Raavana was astride a chariot, Ram was without a chariot. Vijayadashami reminds us every year that if a human being struggles for higher principles without worrying about resources he has, then he achieves victory.

In this century, the best example of following Ram and throwing all his might into establishing a project of nation building is, possibly, the founder of Sangh, Dr. Hedgewar. It is not necessary to remind people of Nagpur that when Doctorji laid the foundation of Sangh work without any resources, many people had ridiculed him. But that great person had unwavering faith in his working methodology. This is why he could inspire thousands of youth to sacrifice their all for this work. As a result this work spread gradually all over the country. Looking at the dedicated work of those youth, their sense of devotion and patriotism local people in all the areas kept joining them. Today, there is no district or tehsil where there is no Sangh shakha. Swayamsevaks created from this process of shakha have raised many projects for serving the society, because of which they have received the trust and affection of the people. After working for many years with revolutionaries and as Congress leader, Doctorji had gained this experience that good dedicated people can hardly be created from political work. For this purpose, inspired by the high ideals of ancient Bharat, one needs qualities of cooperation and discipline. Today, while one can see thousands of quality dedicated people in Sangh, we see dearth of such people in other organisations.

Gandhiji awakened the society for achieving independence. With this, he also wanted that process of true change and evolution in all the organs of social life should also begin. For this purpose, he trained his followers. He motivated them for foundational work like Shri Vinoba Bhaveji for 'rural development', Shri Thakkar Bappa for 'vanavasi upliftment' and Shri Kaka Kalelkar for 'national language development'. He wished to see the society free of harmful habits. This is why he was very active for prohibition on alcohol drinking. He wanted to protect cows because they are the basis of farming and therefore he supported ban on cow slaughter. He had strong desire that the education of Bharat should be rooted in its soil. Though he had studied in England, he was not influenced by the dazzle of Europe and British mentality. And, he wished to see education of Bharat in Bharatiya language.

Though followers of Gandhiji took over governance and they were in power since last 50 years, but they made Gandhiji meaningless. There was no effort to implement his wishes mentioned above. Mahatmaji was an epitome of simplicity. He lived his life in a hut. Those who claim to be his followers are not happy with their government provided bungalows. They wish to spend lakhs of rupees of the people for their comforts You and I know what kind of ideals other political leaders have set. They go overseas for their medical treatment. They take along their children on their official foreign tours. Reign of 500 princes and maharajas is over, but more have taken birth in thousands in the form of ministers.

Members of parliament described what has not happened in last 50 years, with lot of pain in the special session of Parliament. But, they could not decide what they will do collectively in future. In this atmosphere, citizens of this country should take onus to remove the weaknesses in building this nation.

Economy

In old times, 'daana' or donation had great importance. Rich people did not spend much for their own use. They used their wealth to serve the society by building schools, charitable hospitals, planting trees on the road, digging wells, drinking fountains and dharamshalas etc. It is possible to create different arrangements with donations received from prosperous sections even today. This is not a poor country. Every home, even in a small way like mangal sutra of daughter in law, has some gold. Only management of capital is not proper. We find 'dead capital' in one place and lack of capital in another. Therefore, we will have to encourage spirit of donation. These funds would be used for creating new facilities. When Subhash babu asked for funds from Bharatiyas present in Bangkok, all the women contributed their jewelleries. Today if a leader, who can invoke trust, appeals for economic self-reliance for the nation, thousands of tonnes of gold can come from households. But, who will give away one's wealth to a government ruled by corrupt people?

Development of our country will not happen on the basis of foreign capital or on the basis of foreign technical knowhow. We should be vary of people who show us such dreams. In whichever arena we have moved ahead, for example, space technology, missiles, software, no one has supported us. In fact, they have created obstacles. Our scientists accepted the challenge and they stand before us with a sense of victory.

There is no dearth of capital in big industrial houses. That capital will have to be used in research. Our country has talent. We can see the bright intellect bear fruit in foreign lands. World is astounded with their achievements. But, this intellect is fleeing as there are not sufficient facilities in Bharat for research. We will have to stop them and motivate them to work in our country for science and technology.

Some people can come together and pool their capital to establish industry to produce some products. Therefore, we will need to generate the spirit of 'co-operation.' Cooperative industries could only develop in Maharashtra and Gujarat. Why not in other states? The laws for co-operatives have been made so complex that there is less work and more fighting. This means that our government is not in favour of co-operative industry.

Our industrialists should decide firmly that they will not allow foreign goods succeed in our Indian market; they will give tough competition both in price and quality. People of our country will surely stand with them in this challenge. We have to banish attraction for foreign goods. This is in our own interest. Wherever in the world, multinational foreign companies have been able to establish their foothold; they have interfered in the economy and politics of those countries. Our great rishis have taught us that urge for limitless consumption is the reason for our unhappiness. We will have to remember the words of those great sants, rishis and great persons like Krishna. Our young generation is chasing consumption. But, we cannot forget thousands of years of sanskaaras that flow in our blood streams. If we awaken the youth, then they will surely kick away their urge for personal gratification to achieve bigger objectives. But, we need such people to give them this message. Only those people can speak whose lives reflect these ideals.

Language

Talents of our country are lying scattered in lakhs of villages. We will have to give them opportunities to grow. We have made education very complex with use of English. Till science does not reach the student in a village, how will scientific talent and thinking expand? If a rural student is taught science in a completely unfamiliar language, what will he absorb? Today, half the energy of Indian students is spent in learning English. If medium of instruction is in mother tongue or in the link language of the country, only then will we be able to develop talents. But, unfortunately, we do not understand this issue. A white Sadhu of Iskcon in Vrindavan came to meet me and insisted that you should remove English as it is hurting this nation.

Ram Janmabhoomi Movement

Vishwa Hindu Parishad launched Ram Janmabhoomi movement to awaken the spirit of *'Swa'* – self – in the society of this nation. This large scale movement was necessary to shake up the slave mentality built due to one thousand years of slavery. As we gain victory step by step, we shall stand up as the awakened guards of the nation by giving up the mental slavery.

Many eyebrows were raised when the commitment to build the temple on the Ram Janmabhoomi was announced again when Shri Kalyan Singh took his oath of office as the Chief Minister. It was as if communal harmony has suffered again. Actual situation is totally different from this view. Was there communal harmony before the Ram Janmabhoomi agitation was launched? There used to be stone throwing every year during Ganapati visarjan in so many places in Maharashtra before Shiv Sena-BJP alliance came to power in Maharashtra. The same kind of attacks used to be repeated in Ahmedabad on the day of traditional Rath Yatra. In Kerala a Hindu could not move in a Muslim dominated locality lifting his lungi till knees. Incidents of conversion like Meenakshipuram used to take place routinely. One can give such examples from every state. It proves that the mentality that existed prior to Partition still exists in Bharat. If you sing about unity in such a situation, it would have no impact on people.

Appeasement of minorities a policy had been adopted even before independence. A clear example of this was the 'Lucknow Pact.' Muslim leaders had understood well that they can gain maximum advantage by keeping their separate identity. Then, how would they be taken in by this talk of unity? Muslim editor of a periodical in Kerala had asked a question in an interview, what other facilities are you willing to give to Muslims?" This is the latest example of their mentality. Muslims could not join national mainstream due to this appeasement policy.

With Ram Janmabhoomi movement, we are trying to build a case that there is no minority in this country, and no majority. We are all good children of Bharatmata. Being organs of the same nation, our idols and ideals are same. Shri Ram holds the first place in the series of great national icons. This has also been clearly accepted in the Constitution of Bharat. Therefore, those who believe in the Constitution should also accept Ram as the national icon. It is natural to have a grand temple at the place of his birth, whom the society has accepted as national hero. If we present these views in one voice with insistence, again and again, only then there will be possibility of change in our mentality. Experiments of so-called seculars have failed since long. Now we will have to find a solution to this problem in a different way. This is the second facet of Ram Janmabhoomi movement.

The courts have become active again after 5 years. Therefore, Ayodhya issue is again being highlighted in the media. Pseudo-seculars cannot understand that Ram Janmabhoomi movement is a movement to awaken the sense of self – swa – of the nation, because they have accepted British thinking. Hence, they will advise us to copy foreigners to change the situation in Bharat. They can't relate to Ram

Rajya. Their centres of inspiration are World Bank and International Monetary Fund. They will surely oppose Ram Janmabhoomi movement. There is no surprise here. Raja Jaisingh, as the commander of foreign ruler Aurangzeb had fought with Shivaji who was busy awakening the 'swa' – sense of self, and persuaded him to go to Agra. That same mentality is still creating obstacles for Bharat with its antics. But, our society has different mindset than these pseudo-secularists. When Sangh and VHP were banned after Babri structure fell, swayamsevaks went door to door and collected 10 crore signatures in favour of Ram Janmabhoomi movement. In this signature campaign, only 2 per cent people who did not wish to share their views were pseudo-seculars. These collected signatures were handed over to the President. This clearly showed the mentality of the people. Ram Janmabhoomi movement of awakening self-esteem will be taken to the last person in the nation and it will achieve victory. People who pledge to construct the temple are dedicated to national unity and they wish to make this nation strong again.

National Security

Citizens of Bharat are not convinced that the nation is secure. There have been wars with Pakistan and China. Low intensity war is going on in Kashmir even now. Bangladesh has given proof of its animosity by pushing lakhs of illegal immigrants from Bangladesh. Due to weak and confused policies of the governments they have not been able to throw them out while Arabian and Emirate countries, despite being Muslim countries, have expelled Bangladeshis who entered them illegally. These Bangladeshi Muslims, spread in many areas of the country, are working as agents of ISI. They have modern arms and explosives, that we can see being used in Mumbai, Madras and Assam. There are disturbances in Eastern region from Bodo, Naga and Kukis and Naxals in Bihar and Andhra. What can be more telling and laughable example of incapable administration and police that they have not been able to arrest the famous sandal thief Veerappan despite spending crores? Development of missiles like Agni and Prithvi that can raise our attacking capability, is stopped at any time. Our leaders have spoken aloud against the CTBT but we have not increased our nuclear capabilities. When Pakistan is openly telling the world about its nuclear capability, then shouldn't we develop atom bomb and missiles that can carry them to thousands of kilometres? It is not enough to fly Sukhoi aircrafts as an exhibit. Funds are being with open hands, but we become thrifty when allocating budget for defence. Defence minister seems to dole out with a loud mouth. He has only one answer, "Our services are ready to give a befitting reply."

News of Ulfa extremists being given funds by Assam tea companies is making headlines. Forget private companies, even government officers are giving protection money to extremists to save their lives. I have gone to Imphal four years back. I saw that youth of 20-25 years are extracting money from every shopkeeper in broad daylight. The trader whom I knew told me that they are collecting their monthly fee. When I asked him why he doesn't inform the police, his answer was, their advice is to pay up quietly. Even police pays them money! Traders, industrialists, producers are paying up since years to run their business peacefully and every government knows about it. Gujral doctrine has further exposed this weakness. To talk about in this atmosphere about national internal and external security is like cheating the society.

Encouragement to Quality

While even small countries of the world are winning medals in Olympics and countries like Korea, Cuba and Bulgaria have made a place for themselves in games, India is seen nowhere. In the recently held athletics competition in Delhi, Bharat could not create any records. Even in the period of when we were not free, Shri Rabindranath Thakur and C.V. Raman received Nobel Prize. But, we have not received this prize in last fifty year. Why can't we search and nurture talent despite our size and population? Any nation can raise its head with pride because of its talented people. For last thirty years, we have only discussed about poverty, weak and handicapped. Plans are made to help them, because discussing them and helping them gives them votes. But, if special efforts are not made to search these 2-3 per cent talented people, giving them special training and facilities then how will our players, scientists and technocrats show their talent? If no thought is given to caste, language, faith and party only then talented people can be selected. Whenever I hear about the President is from Dalit community, Chief Justice is from minority, I feel deep anguish. Will choosing and appointing people on the top posts too be decided by caste, language and faith etc.? At that level only qualification should be eligibility, honesty and a life that is worth following. Only then can country grow. Weak, helpless, backward must be helped. This is our responsibility. But, if we wish to see Bharat shine in the world, we shall have to search talented people and train them and nurture their patriotism. If Indians who have gone abroad have shown their capabilities then why this can't be done in Bharat?

Closing Remarks

Bharat is an ancient nation. In every aspect of life – arts, science, bravery, prosperity, spirituality it has been on the top. Then why are we in this poor condition? Founder of Sangh, Dr. Hedgwarji had pondered deeply over it and he came to the conclusion that the national society has forgotten itself. We will have to remind it of its power and remove those faults born in this flow of time.

We are well aware of the life of Hanumanji. Along with being a god of strength, he also has supreme intellect. He is carrying a curse due to which he could not remember his powers. When monkeys in search of Sita mata were boasting about their strength near the sea, Hanuman was quiet. Then, Jaambavant asked, "why are you, Hanuman, quiet." When Jaambavant reminded him, Hanumanji's memory was awakened. Sangh is doing the job of Jaambavant in reminding the national society of its strength. At the same time, removing weaknesses afflicted during period of slavery, differences, selfishness and lack of character etc, it is busy in efforts to create selfless servants of the nation who hold high character and imbibed with patriotism. This is precisely what Sangh is doing since last 72 years. Sangh has been able to win affection and trust of the society despite obstacles being created by our own people. Swayamsevak brothers are running around 1200 schools where around 16 lakh children get educated. Teachers there are also from this country, but due to awakening of self-esteem and patriotism these schools have become much better than other schools. Hundreds of swayamsevak doctors very happily go to forest areas to serve the weak of the society. There is appreciation and respect for their work there. Ekal Vidyalay has made one lakh literate children in nearly 100 such schools. It has been possible due to the trust and financial help of the society.

Doctorji experienced that an organised society can respond to any attack from the outside. Society can progress in different dimensions of life. This is why Sangh has been working hard to bring together entire society. Swayamsevaks understand that the society will become strong only by removing internal weaknesses. Therefore, swayamsevaks are dedicated to serving deprived, backward and dalit poor brothers. Through this we come closer, we feel mutual affection and we can envision the inherent oneness. It is our misfortune that some Hindu leaders are bent upon disturbing harmony in the society due to petty political interests. The latest incident of insulting the murtis is another recent example. It is the duty of the entire society to make these hateful activities of leaders unsuccessful.

Politics cannot create emotions of serving the society and colleagues who trust each other. We saw very painful example of this when a Chief Minister could not find even one MLA trustworthy among 135 MLAs when he left his chair. And, he chose his wife to be the CM. We cannot have a golden future of our country with political give and take and opportunism. For it to happen, it is necessary to have lakhs of selfless, patriotic, disciplined workers who will work for the interest of the nation. These workers will be inspired with our ancient life and filled with '*Sva*' or self-esteem. Preparing such citizens is the biggest service to the nation. But, to achieve this, lakhs of people will have to curtail their personal comforts and nurture the dream of making Bharat the Vishwa guru. Swami Vivekananda, Subhash and Aurobindo saw this dream and showed us their outstanding work. It is the measure of success of our lives to give shape to those incomplete dreams. If our brothers take this pledge and get down to work, then we will see that this sense of despair has changed into bright consciousness and hope. May God give us this capability, this is our prayer.

—Documentation Centre, Nagpur, RSS

□

Annexure-7

Rajju Bhaiya's hand written opinion in the visitor's book after the Sanatan Dharma Seva Sadan programme in Chautaga, Myanmar, dated 29th April, 1981

आज चौतगा सनातन सेवा सदन देखने का अवसर मिला है।
यहाँ संस्कृत पढ़ने की उत्तम व्यवस्था है जहाँ दूर दूर से
आकर विद्यार्थी शिक्षा प्राप्त कर सकते हैं। छात्रावास की
भी व्यवस्था है। भारतीय विद्या भवन से संस्कृत परीक्षा
कराई जाती है। यह जानकर भी प्रसन्नता हुई कि
बौद्ध भिक्षु भी संस्कृत ज्ञान के लिए यहाँ आते रहते हैं।
यह संस्कृत शिक्षा का एक उत्कृष्ट केन्द्र बने और यहां
से संस्कृति का भी प्रसार हो यही इच्छा मन में

राजेन्द्र सिंह

२९. ४. ८१.

भू. पू. प्राध्यापक
प्रयाग विश्वविद्यालय

Annexure-8

Rajju Bhaiya's affection for Keshav Srushti

The first edition of this book was written for Keshav Srushti, a green 200 acre campus 34 km from Mumbai airport in Thane district. This is a tribute by the Keshav Srushti trust to respected Rajju Bhaiya.

It was sometime in 1982. With rapid expansion of Mumbai metropolis, it was getting more and more difficult to find a place for RSS camps. RSS kaaryakartas (workers) of the metropolis pondered over the possibility of purchasing 5-6 acres of land near Mumbai so they could have a permanent campus to host the camps and the yearly trouble for hunting for a location can end. A senior worker Shri Aba Mayekar took the responsibility of the search. Fortunately, he met Dr. Sharad Chandra Ajinkya. He showed his readiness to give his land to Sangh for the purpose. The only difficulty was that his piece of land was not just 5 acres, but nearly 200 acres! It was not possible to raise resources for this huge piece of land, hence he returned without committing anything. Dr. Ajinkya came to meet the then Sarsanghchaalak respected Balasaheb Deoras in Navyug office of Sangh in Mumbai and dedicated his 200 acres to Sangh in his presence. We can call it the blessings for this God given work of RSS that he sent his blessings through large hearted angel like Dr. Ajinkya and sent him to Sangh. A trust was created to take care of this land, named Keshav Srushti, after the founder of RSS, Dr. Keshav Baliram Hedgewar.

When the concerned members of the trust went to gather complete information about the land, they faced a new problem. It came to light that many people had taken illegal possession of the land in a massive way, because no one had paid any attention to it for a long time. There were no survey maps. Not only this, there was also an illicit liquor den. The laws of the state were such that it was not easy to clear the illegal encroachments. Many cases were filed in the courts and people were also persuaded gently with affection. It took nearly 10-11 years when finally a major chunk of land came into possession of the trust. By 1993, the land was in a good shape to do something in a proper way.

It was some call of destiny that the Central Working Committee meeting was slated to be arranged in the time of Diwali in Keshav Srushti. Respected Professor Rajendra Singh aka Rajju Bhaiya was appointed the Sarsanghchaalak of RSS at this time. This was a matter of great fortune for us. By this time, plans had been finalised to build a residential school in Keshav Srushti and bhoomi poojan had been done for the purpose. All the trust members and RSS workers thought that it would be a great idea to lay the foundation stone of the school during the proposed meeting. Nothing could be better than this. We began correspondence with respected H.V. Sheshadri, who was the Sarkaryavaah at that time. But, he told us clearly that there can be no other programme during the meeting as it would disturb the meeting schedule, this was the rule. But, we had some faith that we would be able to persuade Sheshadriji somehow. We got a foundation stone made quietly with respected Sarsanghchaalak Rajendra Singhji on it. However, when we met 8 days prior to the meeting and touched upon our request, he refused us point blank.

Two days prior to this big meeting, respected Sheshadriji asked us for a written note on staying arrangements and other arrangements to attach them with the meeting agenda. We added a line in the programme time table – 'foundation stone laying ceremony after Diwali at the hands of Rajju Bhaiya.' We attached a letter with these papers, noting, "Though you have not given your assent to the programme, still we believe that you will surely bless us." When we went to meet him with this document, Sheshadriji read our letter and laughed a lot, "So you are adamant, you will not budge!" He also added that Rajju bhaiya will be available only for one hour and no other office bearer will attend the programme. The foundation stone laying signage was ready with us anyhow. We completed other arrangements with full energy.

Thus, two days after Diwali, on the sacred day of New Year, foundation stone laying ceremony was conducted with enthusiasm and happiness. A grand programme with good attendance was managed even in a short time. Not only Rajju Bhaiya, but all the members of the national working committee too came up the hill to attend it. This grand stone laying ceremony proved to be also the foundation of the grand vision not just the school but also for Keshav Srushti. It proved to be a milestone for us.

Rajju Bhaiya congratulated and felicitated the seniors who had searched out this land and took control of it and those who did the back breaking work and brought this project to this stage. He stayed in Keshav Srushti for four days. We conducted a small Laxmi Poojan ritual with him. He inspected the entire campus, walking around it. This place is part of a village near Mumbai, called 'Uttan'. After viewing the entire campus, he said, "This is not Uttan, this is Uttam. And, together, we have to make it uttam (excellent)."

We had also declared on the day of foundation laying ceremony that Ram Ratna Vidyalay will be opened in June 1996. Though, Rajju Bhaiya visited this campus again six years after this programme for Vishwa Sangh Shibir in 2000, he would always ask about the progress of the school. It was a coincidence that just four months before June 1996, Rajju Bhaiya came to Mumbai and Bimal Kediaji went to meet him in Dadar office. As always, apart from other queries, Rajju Bhaiya asked him if the school would begin operations in June 1996. It was also a coincidence that the managing committee of the school had met just a day prior to this. Keeping in mind the progress of the project so far, it was decided that it would be opened a year later. So, Bimalji told him about the actual status – that school would open in 1997.

Hearing this, he was upset. He asked him to sit near him on the sofa he was sitting on. Then, asked him in a low voice, "How much money has been spent so far? I told him, two crores. He then asked, "Wont there be a loss due to interest on this 2 crore?" I told him with confidence, "Rajju Bhaiya, we have not taken loan from any bank. These funds have been collected from donations." He became more serious on hearing this. Then, he said, "Is there no value to the moneys received from the society? Does only money from bank has a value? We don't need to pay a price for money received from the society, but we have to give account of all this in the heavens. Money received from the society must be used for the purpose for which it has been collected from it. And we must complete the project in time for which we have collected funds. As swayamsevaks, we have been taught to spend society's money with care." This soft scolding from him taught us a lesson for our lives, we always remember now; that it is our own self-owned social responsibility that whatever we are doing, that should not only be done with proper use of money but we must also complete it in time. We called a meeting after this and decided that the school must open in June 1996, whatever be the cost. And we did it successfully.

Rajju Bhaiya visited Keshav Srushti second time in year 2000 for the Vishwa Sangh Shibir. He had voluntarily given up his post by that time. He was suffering from ill health. But, he would be present in every programme in time and would stay for the entire duration. He also gave intellectual discourses and conducted discussion sessions. He moved around the entire campus on a car and appreciated the progress. A forest area has been created in the memory of the former Sarsanghchaalak respected Balasaheb Deoras, named 'Madhu Van'. Rajju Bhaiya planted a tree here that is growing well, and has become mark of his memory for times to come.

Keshav Srushti has become a prestigious centre for education, sanskaar, sewa, protection of ecology. We have schools, training of social workers, modern centre for nurturing desi cows, manufacturing herbal medicines, agriculture education and Vaanprasth Ashram etc. that inspire the society. We have begun to understand the importance of ecology and importance of alternative sources of energy for the future of human lives.

This book is our homage to the memory of respected Rajju Bhaiya in his sacred memory. We are sure that it will inspire all the swayamsevaks, workers and other voluntary organisations and service oriented citizens.

—Keshav Srushti Trust, Mumbai

□□□